Theodore Francis Powys was born in Derbyshire in 1875; his father was an Anglican priest, his mother a direct descendant of the poet William Cowper. With his two brothers, John Cowper and Llewellyn, Powys is part of a triumvirate without parallel in English literature.

In 1885, the family moved to Montacute, Somerset, but Powys spent most of his early years in East Anglia, where he was educated, and where he tried farming, but with no success. In 1902 he went to Studland on the Dorset coast to devote himself to his writing.

In 1907 Powys's first book, *An Interpretation of Genesis*, was privately published; many novels and short stories followed but all were rejected until, on the recommendation of Sylvia Townsend Warner and David Garnett, Chatto & Windus accepted his work and published *Black Bryony* in 1923. *Mr Weston's Good Wine*, Powys's masterpiece, was published four years later, in 1927.

In *Soliloquies of a Hermit* (1926) Powys describes himself as a 'priest without a God'; though he had rejected the Anglicanism of his youth and his work was often considered shockingly unconventional – if not blasphemous – he was, like both his brothers, a profoundly religious man. He was married in 1905 to Violet Dodds, an uneducated country-girl, and they had three children. He published eight novels and eight collections of short stories; having lived most of his life as a recluse in Dorset, T. F. Powys died in 1953.

MR WESTON'S
GOOD WINE

T. F. Powys

New Introduction by
Ronald Blythe

THE HOGARTH PRESS
LONDON

Published in 1984 by
The Hogarth Press
40 William IV Street, London WC2N 4DF

First published in Great Britain by Chatto & Windus 1927
Hogarth edition offset from Chatto 1940 edition
Copyright Francis Powys and Theodora Gay Potocka
Introduction copyright © Ronald Blythe 1984

British Library Cataloguing in Publication Data

Powys, T.F.
Mr Weston's good wine
I. Title
823'.912 [F]   PR 6031.086.7

ISBN 0-7012-1909-2

Printed in Great Britain by
Redwood Burn Ltd
Trowbridge

INTRODUCTION

Theodore Francis Powys was fifty-two when this, his greatest novel, was published in 1927. He was already thinking of himself as a writer while still in his teens and working a small farm at Sweffling, Suffolk. Having been educated at an Aldeburgh school run by family friends, it probably seemed quite a reasonable thing for his parents to do to place this large, strong, seventeen-year-old in such a situation, to give him independence and to see what he would make of it. There were also considerable family associations in the area, for although Theodore's father, the Reverend Charles Powys, was obsessed by what he believed was his descent from Welsh princes, his mother was equally proud of her Norfolk descent from the poet William Cowper. Theodore had often spent holidays at his grandfather's Norfolk rectory, and what with the close companionship of his headmaster's son Louis Wilkinson, a young man who was to play an influential role in the lives of a number of the Powys children, there was a period during his early years when Theodore must have felt himself less West Country than East Anglian. But his brothers John and Llewellyn were never even partially deceived and with that passionate sibling intuition regarding each other's states of mind and emotional need which was to hold them close to the end, they came to regard Theodore in Suffolk as Theodore in exile.

In any case there could not have been a worse time, economically speaking, to be thrown into farming, than this 'coming down time' of the long agricultural depression. Village life was running into poverty and ruin, and a new kind of harshness was beginning to appear in rural society. Added to which, this son of the rectory, brought up in a secure, unquestioning Anglican orthodoxy, was discovering that he was the kind of person who would question everything. Question but not dismiss, not rout or not replace – which is by far the least comforting of all reactions to what one is told one must believe. It was easier for John Cowper Powys, who replaced the Trinity with the thousand divine essences of the universe, and for Llewellyn Powys, who became an atheist and free of all gods. Theodore's difficulty was to retain a mounting admiration for Jesus which was in proportion to his mounting dislike of God. What to do with God became the Powyses' main dilemma, as a moral and imaginative force, that is. John broke him down into sacred facets which caused every hill, stream, rock and plant to illuminate existence, Llewellyn eroticised him (which all three brothers did to a large extent) but Theodore catechised him, and never more brilliantly than in *Mr Weston's Good Wine*. The title comes from the scene in Jane Austen's *Emma* where the young rector Mr Elton, returning with Emma in her carriage when she knew 'he had been drinking too much of Mr Weston's good wine, and felt sure that he would want to be talking nonsense', has the nerve to make love to her. What is it that God gives his creatures? Theodore Powys asks. Is it dutch courage or a blurred vision, or an opiate? Or that bliss which pours from the fruit of the true vine? Men, particularly clergymen of course, having explained God for centuries, he now very respectfully but firmly asks God to explain himself, which he does as well as he can, and certainly without talking nonsense. It is an audacious theme for a novel and perfectly sustained to the last page.

All three Powyses remained profoundly religious men who had, each in his own way, got themselves unchurched. This was in no sense part of the usual post-Darwinian dilemma and loss of faith but the result of their dramatic understanding of the mystical nature of what we call reality. The effect of the rejection of their conventionally imbibed Anglicanism was for all of the brothers one of expansion and release, for Theodore the heretic most of all. They recognised that they had had made a collective advance into an exciting creed-less dimension and for the rest of their lives they shared the discoveries made there, including the sexual ones. Yet it remained a sacred dimension and the quandary for the modern reader is how to perceive and comprehend this triple-stranded Powys sacredness. Calling Theodore's novels and short stories 'black comedy', Llewellyn's essays and autobiographies 'erotic' and John's novels Celtic fantasies simply won't do. Powysdom continues to be a rare literary height because it offers some of the eternal views in an inimitable language. Writing of the brothers the poet Peter Redgrove made the point that 'the occult or magical life, the life lived according to "a reality behind the veil", the Romantic or symbolic life, gets an exceedingly bad press in the serious journals of our age. It is the positivistic spirit that has prevailed, which claims that the surface reality apparent to our conscious senses is all that matters, and that there are no "unconscious" senses at all, through which the unseen influences the seen. It has been difficult for scholars to accept that the magical view of life of so great a writer as W. B. Yeats was not just an aberration but his very core; and it is likely that the paganism of the brothers Powys has not helped them towards the wide acceptance which is their right.' This is true. It is fatuous to dismiss the core of a writer's imagination as a weakness or as something which can no longer be taken seriously, when it is clearly the centre of his art and originality. At the heart of all three Powys brothers lay what might be described as a Natural mysticism, that sensuous searching and probing of this life, this earth.

Theodore was the third of the Reverend Charles Powys's eleven children by his wife Mary Cowper Johnson and part of a triumvirate which has no parallel in English literature. Although so individual and so different, John, Theodore and Llewellyn project a unity, a blood vision which continues to synchronise whatever they are writing. They remain curiously undated too, even when, as with *Mr Weston's Good Wine*, nothing is spared to evoke an historic moment in 1923. They were near-contemporaries of Arnold Bennett, H. G. Wells, Virginia Woolf, E. M. Forster and John Galsworthy, but their names do not suggest a similar period connection. It is because by imposing a kind of religious timelessness on their stories and essays, they appear to have severed them from the chronological position in which one would expect to find them. 'The Powys Brothers' do not sound Edwardian, or Twenties or decadal in any way, they simply sound very old and very new, like a mountain morning. It is still a disturbing business to become involved with them, and with Theodore especially.

He was born in Shirley, Derbyshire on 20 December 1875, where his father was the vicar. Ten years later the family moved to Montacute, Somerset, and into that myth-filled countryside which was to have such a lasting and profound effect on it. Theodore left school when he was fifteen, soon grew a large moustache which, wrote his friend Louis Wilkinson, made him look 'astonishingly like Nietzsche. I remember him as a heavily built young man with grey melancholy eyes. His manners were courteous to the point of what seemed to me an ironic deference. Always he was a countryman . . .' Wilkinson added that he also saw in Theodore a mixture of fantasy and cruelty, benevolence and poetic sensitiveness, plus a 'goblin humour'. Already he had begun upon that long dialogue between himself and God which he was to bring to such a brilliant conclusion in *Mr Weston's Good Wine*. He wasn't happy and would rarely ever be. In 1902 he went to write in a cottage at Studland on the Dorset coast. Shortly afterwards he met his future wife, a practical, good-hearted and uneducated village girl named Violet Dodds, telling his brothers, 'I don't want anything intellectual. I want little animals' roguery. I don't like ladies.' It was Violet's famous talkativeness and her entrée to a great range of colourful rural experience which brought him into imaginative contact with a whole new world of rural drama. In 1907 his first book, *An Interpretation of Genesis,* was privately published, after which he turned to fiction, and a long stream of novels and short stories, all of which were rejected. But in 1926 he published an essay called *Soliloquies of a Hermit* in which he sees himself as a 'priest' and a kind of secular mystic, someone who is always on the alert to 'catch God in His own thought', and this too shows him moving towards the darkly witty God-or-man argument of *Mr Weston's Good Wine*. About this time he summed himself up in a caustic thumbnail portrait. 'Mr Thomas is married, and he digs in his garden . . . [He is] what we call in the polite world, "a crank" . . . Mr Thomas used . . . to brood in odd corners and try to hatch a little God out of his eggs – a little God that would save his type, the outcast monk type . . .' These years of toil and neglect were brought to a halt when a friend introduced him to a writer some eighteen years his junior, and who as yet had had nothing accepted. Her name was Sylvia Townsend Warner. It was she who immediately understood his uniqueness and excellence, and who got the influential David Garnett to bring his work to the attention of Chatto and Windus. The celebrated country stories then began to appear in rapid succession; first *Black Bryony* and then on via *Mockery Gap* and *Mr Tasker's Gods* to his masterpiece.

In his remarkable collective biography *The Brothers Powys*, Richard Perceval Graves quotes Sylvia Townsend Warner on the way in which Theodore worked. His 'books grew like stalactites and stalagmites. He deposited them, secretively and methodically – a process taking place in a cave. After breakfasting, rather late, and leisurely, he went off to the parlour, sat down before a large solid table, read for half an hour (usually in the Bible) and then set to work. He wrote uninterruptedly for three hours or so, put his work back in the table drawer, and began again, where he left off, on the following morning . . . When I happened to pass the window, I saw the same grave, dispassionate countenance, pen moving over the paper, dipping at regular intervals into the inkpot.'

T. F. Powys's maternal ancestor, William Cowper, could have provided the initial idea for *Mr Weston's Good Wine* when he began a hymn with 'God moves in a mysterious way his wonders to perform' and ending it with, 'God is his own interpreter, and he will make it plain'. The Deity in the guise of a travelling salesman selects an average English village in order to inform himself of the current state of the world. *Has* he made it plain? – that is the recurring question. Life, death, good and evil, time and timelessness? The reader is invited to come to judgment. God, alias Mr Weston, ages past started something which he now needs to take stock of. Not wishing to create too much interest in a country parish, he drives to it in a

Ford van labelled 'Mr Weston's Good Wine' but as this is 1923, it creates interest enough. Especially as Mr Weston's assistant is a staggeringly good-looking young man who is clearly the same person as that painted on the sign of the Angel Inn. The date is 20-21 November, a significant one, for it is the week before Advent, and Mr Weston could be thoughtfully getting his visit over before there is another arrival. The Sunday of the week of Mr Weston's visit would have been called 'Stir up Sunday' by the inhabitants of Folly Down, from the first line of the collect, 'Stir up, we beseech thee, O Lord, the wills of thy faithful people,' and stir them up Mr Weston certainly does, but also himself in the process.

What he witnesses, understandingly, forgivingly, and guiltily, is a marred creation, and what he offers is not the possibility of perfection but a palliative. To be human is to be flawed, badly or slightly, but imperfect all the same. His wine cannot, or perhaps must not (or 'what's a heaven for?') mend these flaws but it can make them privately tolerable and publicly less damaging. What Mr Weston offers, in fact, and here lies the essence of the T. F. Powys heresy, is not the wine of salvation but the wine of comfort. Strict to his quirky Christianity, the writer drew comfort from the weekday liturgy in Mappowder Church but refused its chalice on his deathbed.

The novel opens in the market-town of Maidenbridge which serves as the prelude for the main drama of life which, of course, always takes place in a village. Mr Weston's course is to consult his assistant on everybody who walks down the street or emerges from a doorway. The atmosphere is one of ennui and an exquisite provincial dullness wittily observed. What T. F. Powys achieves here is a view of the town as the rustic eye sees it, a community caught up in a broader but not necessarily more dramatic rhythm than that of the countryside. After it has been tantalisingly set in motion for a few brief pages the whole place disappears until the last sentences of the novel when Mr Weston, deputising for the author, says, 'We have forgotten Miss Nancy Gipps.' She is the first of those 'affectionate and forgiving' women who populate Powys's erotic imagination and who he can hardly bear to fall into the clutches of the mainly brute males who either ignore them or pursue them like quarry. Miss Gipps loves Mr Board the Mayor of Maidenbridge, who could scarcely be less worthy of her. The first girl whom Mr Weston and Michael actually encounter is the one they run over on the way to Folly Down, a mere child who, of course, is at once restored to health. But Michael muses on her future –

'A human girl-child is a creature set in a dish for time to feed upon. She wears garters, frocks, and petticoats, and later, frills and pink ribbons. She walks out on the seventh day of the week and sighs for a pair of holiday trousers. They meet and embrace, and amuse themselves as best they may for a few short years, and then they fall sick and go down to the dead.'

'And what harm is there in that?' asked Mr Weston, guiding the car carefully round a corner.

Before Mr Weston drives down into the hamlet which is to be the representative of all the countless groupings which Christian men have formed on the earth, he stops the car to stretch his legs 'and walk upon this pleasant hill'. Blake's question is answered. Those feet have walked upon England's mountains green. The triumph of *Mr Weston's Good Wine* is achieved by the utmost delicacy of its references, a kind of definite feather touch. This is where it entertains yet is simultaneously profound. Mr Weston-God, who had 'risen, as so many important people do, from nothing', and who 'had once written a prose poem divided into many books', and who can say, 'How often I have to remind you, Michael, that in our trade report the women come last. Ours is the only business, you know, that they do not dominate,' is both Creator and his critique in one. While he puts Folly Down to rights, its people – his creation – are able to tell him a thing or two.

T. F. Powys's English village is far removed from what we have been told by others in fact and fiction. It is his own village-bred sights and deeds and dreams reduced to the common pattern of country life and made to animate an insular community. The characters are all the things he fears or desires. Some are gargoyles, some medieval saints. Class is barely relevant and is kicked around like a piece of meaningless finery. A fiercely protected gullibility reigns. To challenge the general acceptance of what has to be believed would be like cutting short the ramblings and point of some self-satisfying old tale. Everybody knows his or her place, but it is the place in a game. Nobody stops playing when someone gets hurt. T. F. Powys's most brilliant comic invention is Folly Down's gargantuan ignorance, its meticulously maintained state of unknowing. To possess a vision which went beyond the parochial view of life would be a terrible handicap in Folly Down. Was this the reason why Mr Grobe the rector did not send his daughter Tamar (the height of the author's girl-fantasies) away to school? Or was it simply sloth? Tamar's ignorance of the facts of life did at least allow her to marry an angel unawares, so perhaps her father did right.

Before this apotheosis beneath the oak tree, Michael, now in his role of Recording Angel, presents the local inhabitants, one at a time, to Mr Weston, who lovingly assesses which of them needs the wine of comfort, strength and hope, or the wine of oblivion, who needs a not too clear view of reality and who needs the cup to speed him beneath the waters of Lethe. Except for the rector, who doesn't believe in God and who has a benign notion of his fellow men, Folly Down is roughly divided between those who put all the ills of the world down to the Almighty and those who put them down to human lust, or 'wold Grunter', as they call their gravedigger-sexton. Mr Grunter is the village scapegoat or sin-eater, a role he silently accepts; although quite innocent himself of the debaucheries attributed to him, he carries in his person both the guilt and the gallantry. In a small place, you can't go around blaming everybody for every wronged girl, so you blame only one – 'old Grunter', or human failings personified. The villagers are made to reveal their entire characters through their sexuality alone and, contrary to what the Christian religion insists, Powys's God finds this natural enough. What is hateful to him is male cruelty in the pursuit of sex and the blunting of tenderness in some older women. Mrs Vosper, who procures girls for the layabout sons of the squire, is a heartless, voyeuristic bawd who, it has to be said, also procure's keyhole excitements for the author himself. But they are artistically deliberate excitements and all part of a black comedy in which Powys's creative eroticism has to find literary expression. His unmarried girls drift about the lanes in peril and innocence, his married women are house-bound drudges with sharp tongues in their heads. Jenny Bunce, the landlord's daughter and maid at the Rectory, who is the epitome of all good and lovely village girls, is, by the grace of Mr Weston's wine, brought most joyously to the arms of an untypical man, the rather girlish himself Luke Bird (alias St Francis) who, after losing his job in the brewery by preaching teetotalism, now spends his time bringing bulls and sparrows to Christ.

Having interviewed everybody, taken a look into the church (the first time he has ever been in one), and seen the two extremes of human conduct, plus that large middling section of it which does nothing very good and little that is awful, Mr Weston shakes his head, which, of course, is as white as wool, and asks himself, 'where did I go wrong?' In creating the world and the need for each generation of its living creatures to replenish themselves? In not seeing that all men were given a far greater share of God's finer feelings? Saddened, self-critical, Mr Weston's conclusion is that Man since the Fall having become on the whole incorrigible, his love for him is best expressed in healing, or diverting him from the excesses of his waywardness and instincts, or in drugging him when things become unendurable . And so, in faultless allegorical language, Mr Weston does his Folly Down round while time stands still. A perfect balance is struck between the novel's wit and satire, and its profundity. There is nothing comparable to it. Now over half a century old, it joins the classic tales of the English countryside, as well as being one of the most penetrating statements on the role of the Christian God in the post-Constantinian era.

Ronald Blythe, Wormingford 1983

MR. WESTON'S GOOD WINE

I

TOM BURT WISHES
TO STEAL

A FORD car, of a type that is commonly used in
England to deliver goods in rural districts, stood,
at half-past three in the afternoon, before the Rod
and Lion Hotel at Maidenbridge upon the 20th
November 1923.

The town was settled, as was its wont at this time
of the year, into its usual autumn sleep that wasn't
in the least likely to be disturbed by the arrival in its
midst of so common a thing as a tradesman's automobile. But the car was not altogether unnoticed.
It was being regarded by the eyes of three small
children, because, just at that moment, there was
nothing more interesting for them to see.

Town children, as is well known, will watch anything, however ordinary and commonplace it be, and
that for a very good reason, for a town child has always
a lively hope in its heart that some extraordinary
and uncommon beast—an ape, a dog-faced woman,
or an armless man — may appear from a hidden
corner when least expected, and provide the watchers
with the sudden and brisk joy of a hasty flight.

The children remained by the car, having a
curious wish, that they themselves couldn't account
for, to discover what sort of goods were kept inside.

It was a covered car—and by no means a new one —and appeared, from the mire upon its wheels, to have already travelled some distance that day. The driver, whose right hand rested upon the wheel, seemed to be awaiting the arrival of a companion— who was also, perhaps, his partner in business—for he turned now and again to glance expectantly at the inn doorway.

As it is a very rare thing to meet or to see any one that would be worth our while to look at twice in so dull a place as a small provincial town, we must consider ourselves fortunate—more fortunate than we deserve when we think of our sins—at having this opportunity to be introduced to some one who, we may venture to say, was interesting.

The driver's face—for we, as well as the town children, may be allowed to be a little inquisitive here—was, above all, good-natured and loving, though a trifle rugged and worn. His eyes were thoughtful, their colour grey, but at times their thoughtful expression changed to a twinkle of merriment. His nose, we are sorry to confess, wasn't the best part of him, for it showed a certain redness—an unmistakable sign that he had more than once drunk his glass and enjoyed it. He seemed a man somewhat below an ordinary man's size, and was sitting, as little men who are moderately stout often do, with his knees wide apart and his plump thighs smiling.

Although the gentleman had looked at the hotel doorway, he hadn't looked there impatiently, and he now turned to look at the street, moving a little that he might rest more contentedly, as though he was

2

quite prepared to remain exactly as he was in the Ford car in Maidenbridge High Street for ever.

He looked indeed, seated thus, to be an honest trader, a worthy citizen, a happy and thriving one too, with the best power—the power of kindness—in his face, that showed clear enough that this gentleman certainly and honestly believed that the goods he sold were of the right quality and well worth the money charged for them.

The driver of the Ford car had given little heed to the children—indeed, he hardly noticed them—and was now looking straight ahead of him and down the street, at the end of which a woman was walking and coming his way. She was walking slowly, and her figure showed pleasantly, even from the distance she was away, as a pretty woman's. She moved with a light ease and a winning grace that certainly, in these days of loud manners, was a pleasant thing to see. Between the lady and the Ford car the street was empty, and this the lady herself thought to be a little unusual at the hour of the day, when, as a rule, there would be some shoppers about, or else at least a nursemaid, or a cross old gentleman tapping the pavement with his walking-stick.

As there was nothing between the lady and the Ford car, it was the most natural thing in the world that she should look at, or at least notice, the car and its driver. She quickened her pace a little, for she did not care to be thought a loiterer, supposing, as indeed was most true, that the gentleman in the car was looking at her as well as she at him.

The children, whose town manners and behaviour —learnt in Mill Lane and practised whenever occa-

3

sion offered—were not always as respectful as one could wish them to be towards a simple tradesman, had remained with wide-open eyes beside the car, in the hope, perhaps, that the driver would leave his seat and enter the inn, so that they might get the chance to peep into the car without being noticed— though, even to them, the driver appeared to be a cheerful kind of man who wasn't likely to be angry with little children for peeping.

The rude children had wished to laugh at him, but, as he had no beard to point at and was dressed in good clothes, they saw no chance of merriment in that quarter, for they could not laugh at an old gentle-man merely because he was well-fleshed. But still they looked ; for the driver of the car, for some strange reason, attracted their gaze. And they had not to look long either before a chance act of his brought them to laughter.

It now happened that, for some reason or other— perhaps to put it on more comfortably—the driver took off his hat, a brown felt.

His hair was white like wool.

The children mocked him. The gentleman accepted their unseemly mirth good-humouredly, and even as good as encouraged it by holding his hat in his hand for a few moments before he placed it on his head again.

When the rude children were grown a little tired of their mirth, that did not appear in the least to annoy the object of it, one of them happened to dis-cover that the sides of the car, as is often the case, were used for advertising the goods that the car, no doubt, carried. The children—two little girls

4

and one boy—had come directly from their reading lesson at their school, a large ugly building down a side street that led to the cemetery.   And so, wishing no doubt to show off her newly acquired knowledge to her companions, the elder of the two girls spelt each word upon the side of the car, and, having done so, she read the words aloud :

' Mr. Weston's Good Wine.'

The boy, although he could not read so quickly, was ready enough to listen, and as soon as he heard what the advertisement was, he at once became inquisitive to see, so that he might tell those at home, how many bottles—if they were bottles—Mr. Weston, for that indeed was the driver's name, carried in his covered car.   And if he were lucky—and fortune, it is said, sometimes favours the brave—the child thought he might be able to steal one.

Tom Burt, who was already honoured by a little local fame as a cunning thief, ventured, putting his finger to his lips to keep the girls still, on tiptoe to the front of the car, very softly and silently, hoping and even expecting that the driver of the car would be looking a little to the right hand, at the lady who was now coming nearer.

Tom Burt's knowledge of the habits and ways of men did not betray him.   Mr. Weston was watching her.   Tom saw his chance ; he climbed silently up into the car, hoping that he might open the curtain that guarded the contents, look in, take something, descend as quietly, and stand innocently beside the little girls.

Tom did as he wished to do.   He opened the curtain behind Mr. Weston and peeped.   But the immediate result of his inquisitiveness was very startling. Tom fell from the car into the road, and then, picking himself up as best he might, he ran as fast as he could to his home, shouting all the way with fear and horror.

Whatever it was that Tom had seen, it was most evident that he wished to get away from it, and his companions, seeing him flee so fast, caught his fear and ran away too.

II

MISS GIPPS BELIEVES SHE WILL BE MARRIED

Miss Nancy Gipps, walking up the High Street on her way to the apartment-house where she lodged, and coming from Miss Willcox's school where she taught the young ladies, was curiously conscious when she approached him that she felt a strange interest and almost an affection for the driver of the Ford car, though she saw him for the first time in her life.

Miss Gipps was a lady whose manners were loving ones. She was one of the pure in heart, and she had never, since she had first met him—at the Town Hall at a lecture upon botany, where he made a short speech about the growing of hops—given up the hope that one day she might marry Mr. Board, the Mayor of the town.

Even at the lecture, when she saw Mr. Board stagger upon the platform, clutch at the lecturer and fall to the ground, she felt that he was a man to be pitied.

Mr. Board was very rich. He was a partner in the town brewery, and he had no wife to help him to give away his money to the poor rather than employ it, as he was now doing, in drinking himself to death.

Miss Gipps hoped that she might be the means of preventing this sad end, for she had an idea that it is in the power of any good woman to make a man happy without the drink.

And, in order to do so, when she married him, she meant to purchase the largest cracker, stuffed with toys, that his money could buy, so that he could pull it with her, give the toys away, and forget his glass.

Miss Gipps had noticed the children as well as the Ford car and its occupant, and she feared—knowing the habits of the young—that the children did not wait there for any good, but intended either to rob or to make a mock of the driver.

Miss Gipps couldn't take her eyes off him—and gracious, loving eyes they were—for she felt him to be a man made in the same mould as Mr. Board—a man to be pitied and loved.

No lady had ever wished for a husband more than Miss Gipps, who, although she had lost the kittenish merriment of a young girl, possessed all the matured and loving ways of a really kind woman.

Miss Gipps was dark ; she was affectionate and forgiving, and her hair curled.   About one thing she felt quite sure ; she was certain that she could make any man who wasn't too young for the process—a sinner though he might be—round off his life in quiet harmony and die lovingly.   But, alas ! Miss Gipps possessed no money, and no gentleman had taken her hand asking to be comforted.   However, she didn't despair, and she always believed that Mr. Board was exactly the man she wanted.

After the lecture at the Town Hall, Miss Gipps had discovered him trying, with a grim and determined look, to put on her cloak.   She found his overcoat and helped him on with it, for which kindness he certainly thanked her, though he need not have called her Lily, for that was not her name.

But, even following this little incident to its natural conclusion, Miss Gipps was able more than ever to nurse in her heart the hope that, with a husband who could so easily mistake her—Miss Nancy Gipps—for the barmaid at the Rod and Lion, she might, having all his money in her charge, make all the poor in the town happy by sending to each household a generous supply of the best loaded crackers for Christmas.

Miss Gipps's faith—and as soon as she saw the driver of the Ford car she believed—now caused her to be more sure than ever that what she longed for, and asked for in her prayers, would come to pass.

It often happens that a common and ordinary appearance, be it but a business conveyance or a lonely wheelbarrow, may have a very strange effect upon the human mind, and Miss Gipps discovered, as she stepped with her nicely blacked shoes upon the pavement, that she was trembling.

She had almost stopped, being surprised at her feelings, and then she gave a little gasp, for another man, a tall one, was standing beside the car and evidently intending to get in.

' Oh, these dear men,' sighed Miss Gipps, ' they do appear suddenly. But how foolish of me to be frightened, for I might have known that it couldn't have been Mr. Board, because he never comes unexpectedly.'

Even with Mr. Weston's companion now arrived, it was at Mr. Weston that Miss Gipps still looked.

She noticed that He wore a rather heavy overcoat,

of a greenish material, that was unbuttoned and opened. She couldn't keep her eyes off him as she came nearer, and a curious fancy arose in her heart that all her life—even from the early days when her mother would pray beside her cot—some one as fat, as happy, and as kindly had been looking at and loving her.

She sighed for Mr. Board.

And all the time that she had been walking up that street, that she knew as well as the rather nasty little passage, with three steps to go down, at her lodging-house, Mr. Weston's look had been saying to her : ' If you only buy what I can sell to you, Miss Nancy Gipps, you will be everlastingly happy.'

But however much Miss Gipps wished to wait in front of the car now that she was so near to it, yet she felt it to be necessary, when she came to it, to go by.

Miss Gipps did go by, but she looked at the side of the car as she passed, and read—having a quicker eye for words than the rude children— ' Mr. Weston's Good Wine.'

Miss Gipps sighed.

' Could ever Mr. Board,' she wondered, ' look at her and think of her as if she were as good as Mr. Weston's good wine ? '

' I believe he will,' said Miss Gipps.

Miss Gipps walked lightly on. She felt differently ; she was a happy woman. The very reading of the word ' wine ' had renewed her hopes—they had been sobered a little when she was called Lily— in a wonderful manner. She believed that in a few weeks, in time to give away thousands of Christmas crackers, she would be Mrs. Board.

Miss Gipps, from her youth upward, had been fond of crackers. These toys gave, she felt, all that should be given to make any one happy. Everything about a cracker, she knew, could give pleasure. The wrappings, the coloured paper, the dunce's cap, the painted whistle, the child's jewelled ring, could always bring such joy to the young, and carry past thoughts and remembrances to the old, as well as present pleasure. No cowslip, that Miss Gipps knew of, ever culled in May, could feed the heart with such abundant feelings as a cracker—as cheap a one as you wish—when pulled at Christmas. One can cry or laugh then ; but, of course, one laughs.

Miss Gipps had all her life—beginning with her own younger sisters—taught children to do their lessons, and very soon, she hoped, she would only be telling them to be happy and to play. She would give the plain town of Maidenbridge a high holiday. There would be Christmas trees, hung with red crackers, in every poor man's house.

As she neared her home, Miss Gipps saw a new vision of life, happy and joyous, all love and no shame, with malice and meanness and envy departed for ever.

And she saw herself the happy wife of Mr. Board.

III

MR. BURT SHAKES A BOUGH

Mr. Weston, whose own advertisement has most properly introduced him to us, did notice thieving Tom and his hurried departure, for he shook his head then a little sternly, as any elderly gentleman who himself is the father of rather a large family would ; and he smiled a little too at having had the fortunate chance of teaching a rude boy a lesson in behaviour.

Whatever the lesson was, Tom Burt was extremely scared by it, and later that very afternoon a strange story was told in the town that a menagerie had passed through, and that one of the wild beasts, seen in a closed van in the High Street, was a horrid lion. . . .

The Ford car had been in the street for some time before the children had spied it and before Miss Gipps walked by.

Mr. Weston, whose fatherly feelings we have already noticed, had permitted his fellow-traveller, who was a junior partner in the firm of Messrs. Weston and Company, to take a little refreshment— being the younger man of the two he was more apt to be hungry—in the dining-room of the Rod and Lion Hotel.

Evidently Mr. Weston, when left alone in charge of the car, had used the time, until he was interrupted by the impertinence of the children, for quiet meditation.

The atmosphere of the town was suitable to thought. In the air, this November afternoon, there was a dull and heavy feeling abroad, for the joyous expectation of Christmas hadn't so far, unless with Miss Gipps, penetrated the weary autumn days. Nothing was happening of any importance in the town, and very little trade was being done, for, though a few farmers had visited the bank, the day was neither a market nor a fair day.

The winds of heaven were still and quiet too, for the autumn storms had finished their battering and had blown themselves out, and the clouds that had once travelled so swiftly round the world were now stopped dead and were hanging, a stupid, grey mass, over the town.

At the beginning of November the winter had startled the town with a brisk frost that killed the dahlias. This frost was followed, exactly as the Mayor, Mr. Board, predicted, by wild winds, westerly gales, and torrents of rain that washed the brewery chimney on the windward side.

The winds with their wild gusts intended to do some mischief, and succeeded, for they blew against a wall two elderly ladies who wished to go by train to Weyminster to attend a sale where, it was said, a pair of nice new shoes might be bought for five shillings, and broke a leg of one of them.

In the roof, too, of St. Mark's Church a heavy block of oak, that had been placed there by the wise advice of a London architect to support a large beam, became dislodged, and fell in front of Mr. Board as he was walking up the aisle to receive the sacrament. He fell over it, to the great amusement of a pious old lady who knelt near and who wore a bonnet.

All this wind and rain had in its turn been followed by dark and dull weather, that made the High Church rector of St. Mark's wish more earnestly than ever to go over to Rome—in reality as well as in doctrine.

So gloomy and sad was this sunless weather become, and so depressing to all in the town, that Mr. Milsom, a tailor in the High Street, would every morning go to his shop window, and looking out between two pairs of nicely ironed trousers, curse for half an hour by the town clock the fool who ever thought of inventing so hideous a thing as a town street with a church at one end and a prison at the other.

' And where the hell are the girls ? ' Mr. Milsom would conclude by saying ; and then he would retire in a very sulky mood to eat his breakfast.

Maidenbridge appeared now to be fast asleep, except for the striking of the clock in the tower of St. Mark's Church—nay, almost dead ; and Lily, sitting in lonely state behind the elegant bar table in the genteel saloon at the Rod and Lion, could only wish peevishly, as she darned a silk stocking, that young men were a little more plentiful and the old ones more thirsty. She was grown tired of the stocking, and stepping daintily to the window, she looked out, but only saw a very common-looking car. With her eyes still upon it, she couldn't help wishing that either the bank manager or Mr. Board, the Mayor, might enter and amuse her with pleasant talk such as she loved.

There were still some leaves in the walks of the town that hung mournfully from the trees and were noticed by one man—Mr. Burt, the town gardener, the father of Tom—with much annoyance. For Mr. Burt had, after the storms, swept up the leaves that were fallen, and he could see no reason why these others should remain hanging in the trees, except that, having malice in their hearts, they meant to make more work for him later on. He saw the leaves of these chestnut trees as mere summer decorations, and felt that they ought, if they had the least sense of decency, to fall all at once and be carried away in the corporation wheelbarrows, with high sides affixed.

Mr. Burt had known these trees for so long that he had grown to think of them as entirely artificial, and being so, they should, of course, function to order, as did the town gardens' clock that faced all ways and behaved the same in all weathers. The leaves mocked the gardener by falling now, one at a time, instead of in showers as when the winds blew.

Mr. Burt was standing in the walks, with his broom in his hand and his wheelbarrow near. He looked up at the trees and cursed them.

' It was most likely,' he thought, ' entirely owing to their stupid and ignorant habits that his wages were lowered.'

Mr. Burt approached one of the trees and angrily shook a bough that had a few leaves upon it. He hoped that this tree, at least, would permit him to finish with it. But not a leaf fell.

' They be only waiting till I be busy in they gardens, the dirty cowards !' said Mr. Burt gloomily.

15

IV

THE TOWN GETS MORE LIVELY

THE man who appeared a little suddenly beside Mr. Weston's car and so alarmed Miss Gipps that she made a sudden exclamation, was, as we have said before, a partner in Mr. Weston's concern.

This gentleman had risen to high distinction in the firm, having once, by his strength and courage, quelled a mutiny that arose amongst the workers in Mr. Weston's bottling department—a mutiny that, had it been successful, would have entirely ruined the wine merchant's vast business, whose ramifications were everywhere.

The newcomer had arrived suddenly, but it is easy to step across a street, and still easier to step across a pavement from the door of an inn, without being noticed. We will note his behaviour ; that is more important to us than the suddenness of his arrival, for it is from a man's behaviour when he does not know that he is being watched that his character, as well as his situation and rank in the world, may be discovered.

The gentleman behaved to Mr. Weston with a respect that did honour to them both, for it was the loving respect that is never given unless the object is entirely deserving of it. This respect was utterly natural and unassumed, and was by no means dictated by the immense magnitude and long standing of the firm of which Mr. Weston was the senior director, but came rather from the love of one good heart to another—a more lofty and an older one.

The young gentleman bowed low.

No one noticed this simple act of politeness except Miss Gipps, who passed at the moment and considered the bow quite right and proper, and liked the young man the better for it. She did notice, too, though she gave more heed to his master, that the gentleman was not only a remarkably tall young man, but surprisingly beautiful, having all the fine distinction of the best breeding set off with amiable modesty. He might almost have been a god, his beauty being of that exalted kind that promotes a sure confidence and awakens a lasting love. He was taller than his companion by a foot or more, and of slender build, and he stepped lightly upon his toes that hardly semed to touch the ground that he trod upon. Both Mr. Weston and he were dressed in well-cut suits of Scotch tweed, of the latest fashion, that fitted them extremely well, and each wore a tie of deep claret colour, but Mr. Weston alone wore an overcoat.

They had both noticed Miss Gipps.

The town was still sluggish, sullen and sleepy, and no one was to be seen. The street seemed to be cleared of all humanity, with the exception of Mr. Weston and his companion, whom Mr. Weston addressed as Michael when he first saw him.

The heaviness of the afternoon did not invite a hasty departure, and although the car had already remained so long in the street, Mr. Weston preferred to wait even a little longer before he started the engine.

Nancy Gipps was scarcely out of hearing when Mr. Weston spoke.

' Michael,' he said, ' you must know that Miss Gipps is a good woman.'

Mr. Weston spoke in the easy and friendly manner of a tradesman whose behaviour it was, however great his firm might be, to know all the people and the towns and villages in which he had hopes of selling his goods.

Michael bowed.

' Alas ! ' said Mr. Weston, ' it is not often the case that I can be quite sure of a customer, but I am well aware that if Miss Nancy Gipps had the Mayor's money to spend, she would at once prevent him from buying a great deal of very bad wine, and would give him our good wine to drink instead, and he would live to thank us.'

' He would live happily,' said Michael, ' drinking at all hours our good wine.'

Mr. Weston beckoned with his gloved hand. Michael took his place in the car. The street that had been so empty had now a few people in it.

A girl in a pink frock, who lived an easy and gay life, sauntered by Mr. Milsom's shop and turned for a moment to admire the trousers in the window. Mr. Milsom, who, for some reason or other—perhaps because he had seen a car go by with the word ' wine ' upon it—had sent out to the Rod and Lion for a bottle of burgundy to drink with his cold chicken. Taking the last glass with him in his hand, he entered his shop and peeped out of the window between the trousers. He saw a pretty girl smiling at him. He raised the glass to his lips, and drank her health in a becoming manner.

The girl walked away, and passed scornfully a grocer's assistant in a white apron who stepped out into the road to approve the new arrangement of the shop windows that he had just been dressing. His name was Mr. Tett, and he had long, lean legs, and so high an opinion of himself that he believed his waxed moustache to be the very finest in all the town. He also believed that every young lady to whom he sold starch or potted meat wished him to lead her out into the fields near to the river, where the yellow buttercups grew, and embrace her in those meadows.

When he handed them the parcels he would say in his heart : ' No, dear, you mustn't expect me to act in such a common and vulgar manner.'

This young man looked at the Ford car and sniffed crossly.

The same old gentlewoman who had been thrown against the wall and had broken her leg in the storm was being wheeled by in a bathchair. She was accompanied by her friend—who had also been cast down by the rude winds—and who walked by the side of the chair, holding her hand.

The lady's gardener, a man with an angry look and black gaiters, glaring at every one, pulled his mistress with his back bent as if she weighed near a ton.

Both the ladies looked about them in terror, as if they expected at any moment another burst of wind to rush suddenly up a by-street and cast them down again. Whenever they saw a wall they trembled with fear. They both lived now in continual fear of the wind and of what it might do, and anything they saw move a little unexpectedly they believed to be propelled by that dreadful element. They looked at Mr. Weston's car with gratitude because it wasn't moving.

The Maidenbridge bank manager—a shy and stooping gentleman, who was always putting on a pair of kid gloves that were always a size too small for him—came down the grand steps of the bank. He was walking with Mr. Board, the Mayor of the town. They went by the Ford car, but did not appear to take any notice of it.

The bank manager was speaking in a joking manner to Mr. Board. He told him that he ought to set the young men of the town an example and marry.

'You should marry, Mr. Board,' he said, ' for a man, without a woman—oh, you know the rest.'

Mr. Board lit a cigar. He was more thoughtful than usual that morning. He had suffered from indigestion in the night, and had supposed himself to be dying, and now he thought that a drink might take such nasty night-thoughts away.

The two gentlemen entered the Rod and Lion and went into the private bar.

They found Lily very ready to receive them, though she still went on darning her stocking. She was happy and smiling. Some one had answered her wish, and she expected a merry time. Mr. Board might even slip a five-pound note into her hand and try to kiss her, for old gentlemen were always more merry when they went a-hunting in pairs.

A policeman came by upon the pavement, looking up into the sky as if he saw a thief stealing a chryso-prase from the floor of heaven and wished that he might catch him and have him up before Mr. Board, in the Maidenbridge Town Hall.

A nursemaid—a careless girl, very plump and smiling—followed the policeman, while the child she had charge of tripped over its hoop and fell into the gutter.

The child was nearly run over by a large and luxurious car, that appeared to fill the whole street. Inside the car was Lord Bullman, who had come to invite Mr. Board to dine with him that same even-ing, because he wished to have a good listener for his latest story about a lady and gentleman who lived in London.

' You saw my lord, sir,' said Michael, who liked a little gossip; ' he looked at us as if we were very much in his way, and—if you will pardon my free-dom—he looked as if he never wanted to see us again.'

' He never will,' said Mr. Weston.

Michael was silent.

My lord stopped his car and spoke to the police-man. Mr. Weston still waited, and watched the street as if he looked at a play. He smiled, and made a gesture with his hand as if he pulled the wires that set all these people in motion.

His companion, who didn't like to be silent for long, turned to him.

' I trust that no one '—Michael's voice was gentle

and pleasing—'has insulted you in my absence, Mr. Weston, for in a small provincial town the behaviour of the people towards strangers is not always as kind as it should be.'

Mr. Weston looked down at his boots, that were of the best make.

'A boy,' he said, 'climbed up beside me and peeped into the van.'

'Oh, did he ?' said Michael, and looked over his shoulder.

'Yes,' said Mr. Weston, 'but one look was enough for him ; and then Miss Gipps came by, who read the advertisement.'

'A kind lady,' remarked Michael carelessly.

'Yes,' said Mr. Weston, 'Nancy is a wise virgin who will one day drink my wine.'

'She did not give you an order, or ask to look at the goods ?' inquired Michael.

'She knows their quality,' answered Mr. Weston quietly.

The street was now empty again, and silent. A peace and stillness, almost like death, settled upon the town ; the dull clouds hung lower, and a dimness, that sometimes falls like a cloak upon a day in late autumn, was fallen now.

'The time has come,' said Mr. Weston, 'for us to take the road to Folly Down.'

'Yes,' said Michael, 'that is the village that we were going to visit, and it is certainly fortunate that you have remembered its name.'

'The name is written in my book,' observed Mr. Weston, and started the car.

V

MR. PRING CRACKS A
STONE

THERE is very little, unless he notices the rooks and
the starlings, that is of much interest to the traveller
in a country road in November. And a merchant
whose business it is to travel widely in the world
wouldn't be likely to give much heed to the villages
that he passed by, or to the little cottage children
who ran out of their doors to look at the car and
walked in again disappointedly because it wasn't a
larger one.

Mr. Weston noticed one child—a girl—whom,
in coming round a sharp corner, he unexpectedly ran
over. He looked round to where she lay and bade
her pick herself up and run home, which she did,
laughing, and appeared no worse for the mishap.
This slight incident, however, set Michael a-talking.

' A human girl-child,' he said, ' is a creature set in
a dish for time to feed upon. She wears garters,
frocks, and petticoats, and later, frills and pink
ribbons. She walks out on the seventh day of the
week and sighs for the sight of a pair of holiday
trousers. They meet and embrace, and amuse
themselves as best they may for a few short years,
and then they fall sick and go down to the dead.'

' And what harm is there in that ? ' asked Mr.
Weston, guiding the car carefully round a corner.

' None, sir, that I am aware of,' replied Michael

gaily, ' for mankind is but a changing element, constantly moving, fretted and troubled like the sea, blown upon by all the winds and drawn by all the tides.'

' Yes,' said Mr. Weston sadly, ' I fear they have unfolded a changing affection, but their end was well thought of.'

' Only the poor agree there,' said Michael, laughing. . . .

Although Mr. Weston paid very little attention to the churches or the children that he passed, he took a little more notice of the inns, and even gave himself the trouble to ask Michael whether he supposed that every inn had a stable, and Michael replied a little absent-mindedly that he thought they had.

' I am glad you say so,' replied Mr. Weston. . . .

Mr. Weston's car was a very useful on and though exactly like a great many others, had, now-ever, larger headlights. But the time to light them was not yet come.

On the whole, Mr. Weston was a careful driver, and it was the fault of the child, who had jumped in his way, that she had been so nearly killed. Mr. Weston certainly drove very fast, yet the car never seemed to be, even when it turned the sharpest corners, in the least danger of overturning.

Hardly any one gives much heed to, or even notices, a plain business car that happens to pass along the highway when the evening is closing in and the rooks are going home. But Mr. Pring of Dodder, who was cracking stones with a hammer near to the turn into the narrow chalk lane that led

24

to Folly Down, did happen, after breaking a large stone with a cunning blow, to look up, and he saw the car coming. It appeared to turn, during the moment that he looked at it, into the lane and was gone.

Mr. Pring laid down his hammer gently upon the stones ; he removed his wired glasses, and stepped to the entrance of the lane.

Ten years ago that very day a car that had taken this same corner a little too quickly had overturned into the ditch, killing the driver, whose purse, after the gentleman had been carried away, Mr. Pring was lucky enough to discover in the road. Since then he had always hoped that the same good fortune might come to him again, and as there were two in the car that turned the corner, Mr. Pring hoped for two purses.

He had tried a few sharp flints in the road where he worked, but so far nothing had come of them.

And now, too, instead of a smashed car in the lane, Mr. Pring saw nothing whatever except a lame sheep over the rails that looked as surprised as he.

Mr. Pring rubbed his eyes. He looked at Folly Down hill—the car was already there.

Mr. Pring turned to the stone heap ; he put on his glasses and struck a little stone. The stone cracked in half, and Mr. Pring turned and nodded towards Folly Down.

' If 'tain't the Devil, 'tis God,' he said decidedly, and continued to crack a few more stones before he shouldered his hammer and returned to Dodder for his tea. . . .

From the summit of the hill that Mr. Weston's

car had climbed so swiftly, a view presented itself of the village of Folly Down, and though somewhat a dim one—for the November afternoon was soon to turn to a long evening—yet the thatched cottages, the oak tree upon the green, and even the church tower and the inn signboard, could still be seen.

Gaining so swiftly the top of this hill—so that he had even astonished Mr. Pring—Mr. Weston brought his car to a standstill. Here there was a dry patch of soft mossy grass close to a gate that led into a large field, or rather down, where one lonely horse was standing with his head bent sadly as if he had not moved for many hours.

Mr. Weston looked into the valley. Had he created Folly Down and all the people who dwelt there, he could not have looked at the village in a more interested manner.

For a moment or two he appeared to be lost, as he had been at Maidenbridge, in a fit of the deepest meditation. The only living thing upon the hill that had noticed the arrival of the car was the lonely horse, that had been turned out upon the down because it was too lame to be worked. The horse forgot its lameness. It whinnied, and ambled easily to the gate, looking over with ears pricked up. Sometimes it sniffed as if it smelled the sweetest meadow hay, then suddenly it snorted, turned, pranced in terror, kicked, and galloped away.

'Michael,' said Mr. Weston, after he had regarded the little hamlet of Folly Down with such intensity that, did we not know how important trade is in a civilised country—or, indeed, in any country —might have been thought unduly curious—

26

' Michael, would you be so kind as to give me the book ? '

No sooner was this command uttered than it was obeyed, for Michael stepped into the interior of the van, moving the curtain sufficiently to allow himself to enter, and presently returned with a book that had the look of an ordinary business man's ledger, such as any tradesman might carry upon his travels.

' Before we open the book, Michael,' observed Mr. Weston, ' and before we read the names of those whom we hope to trade with, I will stretch my legs for a few moments and walk upon this pleasant hill.'

VI

MR. WESTON CLIMBS A TUMULUS

M<small>R</small>. W<small>ESTON</small>, for a common tradesman—and the most princely of merchants is only that—possessed a fine and creative imagination. And, although entirely self-taught—for he had risen, as so many important people do, from nothing—he had read much, and had written too. He possessed in a very large degree a poet's fancy, that will at any moment create out of the imagination a new world.

Mr. Weston had once written a prose poem that he had divided into many books, and was naturally surprised when he discovered that the very persons and places that he had but seen in fancy had a real existence in fact. The power of art is magnificent. It can change the dullest sense into the most glorious; it can people a new world in a moment of time ; it can cause a sparkling fountain to flow in the driest desert to solace a thirsty traveller.

Standing upon the barren hill, Mr. Weston wished to see Folly Down as it was in the summer. He had only to wish, and the fancy with which he was gifted would complete the matter.

Mr. Weston now saw Folly Down in its gayer days ; he created the summer anew as he looked down the valley. The hedges were white with sloe blossom, and the willow bushes were in flower ; a

few butterflies were abroad and the bumble bees.
The blackthorn blossoms were shed ; the new green
of the hedges came, and the sweet scent of may
blossom. The may faded, but in the meadows the
deeper colour of the buttercups—those June brides
—took the place of the maiden cowslips until the
hay-mowers came, and then the white and red roses
bloomed in the hedges. Midsummer, that time of
rich sunshine, was soon gone ; the meadows were
yellow again with hawkweed, while in the rougher
fields the ragwort grew in clumps, upon which
the peacock butterflies fed until near drunken with
honey.

Mr. Weston let the summer go. The scented
seasons he had seen in his fancy fled away again and
were gone.

Mr. Weston felt lonely. The same mood that he
remembered having when he was writing his book
came to him again. He climbed a tumulus in the
gathering darkness, and regarded all the earth with
a lonely pity.

A wind awoke from the sea that was but a mile or
two away, and rushed and roared about him. Mr.
Weston took off his hat, and the wind blew his white
hair. He was evidently glad, as any city dweller
would be, to be standing there.

' There are some people,' said Mr. Weston aloud,
' who, I believe, envy my position in the city where
I live, but they are wrong to do so, for I would
willingly exchange all that I am with any simple
child that lives and dies in these gentle valleys, and
is then forgotten.'

Mr. Weston stretched out his hands over the

village of Folly Down. He came down from the mound and returned to the car.

The afternoon dimness sometimes, in a surprising and sudden manner that catches a traveller unawares, changes into the darkness of night. The hills and the Folly Down trees, that a few moments ago could be clearly seen in the valley, now became but the dull, drowsy figures of a strange mystery—the abode of darkness and forgetfulness.

'The ways of nature, in the country,' said Mr. Weston, when he was safely seated in the car again, 'are a little curious, and I should take it kindly, Michael, if you would explain the phenomenon of this sudden darkness, and how it may affect our customers?'

'The darkness of a winter's evening at Folly Down,' replied Michael, 'when heavy sombre clouds droop from the skies so that no stars can be seen, is a thing that pleases rather than troubles the natives, for it introduces to them an entirely new way of life that enters with the first lamp or, it may be, candle.

'With the first lighting of a cottage candle a man becomes an entirely new being, and moves in a totally different world to that of daytime. He is now born into a world whose god is a rushlight, and a man's last moments in this world generally come when the light is extinguished and he creeps into bed.

'Every common appearance that during the day the vulgar sun has shown, becomes changed by candlelight. For now a thousand whimsical shapes, dim shades and shadows, come, that no daytime has ever seen or known. The bright sun of heaven that has made all things upon earth only too real is not now to be feared by the housewife as a telltale, for all is become magic and a pretty cheat. Dust upon a book or in a corner, a straw upon the floor-cloth, show now only as objects of interest. The black stain that the smoke from the lamp has made upon the ceiling becomes colour and is not unlovely. The cheap wallpaper, though wrinkled and torn, has now a right to be so, and is not regarded with dis-pleasure. Nothing after sunset need be looked at too closely, and everything pleases if regarded in a proper evening manner.

'Man is drugged and charmed by this beneficent master whose name is darkness ; he becomes more joyful, and, thank goodness, less like himself. With the first lighting of the lamp, love and hatred, the sole rulers of human life, take a new form and colour. Love becomes more fantastical in the darkness and malice less logical, and both the one and the other are more full of the strange matters that dreams are made of.

'Duration itself has a mind to dance or stand on one leg, for a winter's evening here is often felt to be a period of time as long as a lifetime, and is filled more fully than ever a lifetime can be with unlikely happenings. Even the soft mud of a road in late November, and the little clinging drops of misty rain that may be falling, change their aspect in the dark-ness and become different in character from what they were known to be in the daytime. . . .'

Michael would have said more, only Mr. Weston interrupted him.

'I never before knew you to talk so much as to forget business,' he said. 'You have, indeed, very ably explained the effect of the evening upon the people of Folly Down, but now I would like you to show them our advertisement in the skies.'

Michael climbed upon the car, upon which he arranged a curious network of wires, sustained in the air by two stout rods. As soon as he had managed the wires to his satisfaction, he connected them with the electric arrangements that lit the powerful head-lights which he now extinguished.

That done, he started an electric current that lit up the sky and wrote thereon, in bright and shining letters, ' Mr. Weston's Good Wine.'

VII

ENAMOURED PIGS

MICHAEL stepped down from the car and stood a little way in front of it, in order to see whether each letter of the advertisement showed as clear as it should. He was satisfied that they did, and so returned to the place beside Mr. Weston that was illuminated by a little lamp, and again handed to that gentleman the book that he had asked for.

There was nothing in the least strange or queer in the arrival of these two, unless the reader wishes to feel it so. For why should not these gentlemen, residing for the moment in a free country, set up their advertisement in the sky, and look in their trade account for a few likely customers?

The old horse that was feeding in the field near by came to the gate again and looked curiously at the car.

Mr. Weston opened the book. Only the first page appeared to contain any names at all, and these names were not many, for evidently in the whole compass of the little village of Folly Down, even though he had taken the trouble to advertise his name in the sky, Mr. Weston could not very well expect a large sale for his wine.

But a firm that is pretty well established in the world and has a very large surplus of capital, may be allowed its whim, which in this case was, we may almost say, to take note of a sparrow that, in flying after its mate a little too hastily from a bough to the thatch, chances to fall. And, indeed, any expert in business must acquiesce here, and agree that, though the actual gain in money may be small, it certainly pays the management of a large store to send a representative—though, perhaps, not the only son of the founder—into the less populated villages, where he may study at first hand the needs of simple people in order to ease them of their pennies.

It has often been said, and most wisely, that no man in trade, whether in a large or a little way of business, can know too much about the habits, the manners, and the wants of his customers.

Evidently, before Mr. Weston set out upon his travels he had made careful and detailed enquiries, so that he might know beforehand the kind of people that he was to meet and most probably trade with. He was well aware that no one should be content with the opinion given in a county directory as to what the villages most need and what they will buy.

Mr. Weston read the first name.

' " Mr. Joseph Kiddle."—And who is he ? '

' Mr. Kiddle is a dealer in cattle,' replied Michael, ' who does a very good trade. He buys cows and bulls and little pigs, that he sells again for as much as he can get to the neighbouring farmers ; but amongst all his deals he has one grand and noble ambition, and that is to cheat Mr. Mumby.'

' A high ideal to live for,' said Mr. Weston, smiling ; ' and what is Mr. Mumby ? '

' He is the Folly Down squire,' replied Michael. ' He has the front pew at church, takes the best seat at the inn '—(' I like that better,' said Mr. Weston)

34

—' and he also owns the land and a meek wife. He possesses three elderly and plain maidservants, blames the weather a great many times in the day, and has two sons who prefer fornication to married bliss.'

' And is the selling of cattle at a profit all that Mr. Kiddle does ? ' asked Mr. Weston.

' He is a merry man,' replied Michael, ' and he calls his wife, who is a little strange sometimes, " a lean barrener." His daughters he eyes as if they were plump heifers, and he is never tired of making fun of poor Mr. Bird because he will not drink beer.'

' And what does Mr. Bird drink ? ' enquired Mr. Weston, who naturally wished to take advantage of a chance word that might lead to business.

' Only water from his well,' replied Michael disdainfully.

' But his name is written here as a likely customer,' observed Mr. Weston thoughtfully, ' and I should be glad to know a little more about him.'

' Mr. Bird,' said Michael, ' lives in a very poor way. He feeds the robins with crumbs ; he watches the little running brooks and the foolish daisies, and he longs every morning for the evening to come. Do you wish to know more ? '

' Yes,' said Mr. Weston, ' I do.'

' He is despised, and I will add, if you have no objection, he is rejected of men. His cup, his platter, and his purse are nearly always empty. But even with so many troubles and trials—for his life has been full of them—Mr. Bird might be happy if he were not in love.'

' Ah,' sighed Mr. Weston, ' it is certainly a very

curious thing, that wherever I go upon this round globe I hear that word mentioned. The word has a mild sound ; it is used sweetly in poetry and is sung romantically in hymns ; it is also uttered affectionately in dark lanes behind trees, and sometimes at street corners ; but it appears, for all its mildness, to have something in it very forcible and violent. I am extremely sorry for Mr. Bird, for from your description I believe that he might easily be one of our best customers. It must be a great misfortune to him to be so tormented. But does he do nothing to overrule, or at least to counteract, the ways of so harsh a tyrant ? '

' Mr. Bird,' continued Michael, ' does his best to conquer love ; he preaches Christianity to the beasts of the field. He has already been fortunate enough to convert Mr. Mumby's bull, and only a few weeks ago he began to tell a young sow, that he feeds sometimes with cabbages, the story of its Saviour.'

Mr. Weston laid his hand affectionately upon his companion's knee. Evidently he did not wish to interrupt him rudely.

' But do you know,' he asked, ' whether, supposing that we were fortunate enough to sell any of our goods to Mr. Bird, he would be likely to pay our bill ? '

' The pigs trust him,' replied Michael, ' for only yesterday, when he walked a very long distance upon the downs, hoping to tell the story of the Cross to a fox that he had once seen there, two enamoured pigs that were shortly to farrow followed Mr. Bird home, clambering over stiles, climbing hedges, crossing ploughed fields, wading the watercourses, traversing grassy lanes, until they reached his cottage gate, where he turned to greet them kindly and told them about the Lord. That is, of course, but a solitary incident in the life of Mr. Bird to show how much he is trusted even by the brutes, and though no tradesman can ever be quite sure, yet I feel that if we could persuade Mr. Bird to buy our wine we might trust him too. He is poor, and the poor nearly always remember, having so little credit given to them, that the day of reckoning is sure to come ; and, besides, Mr. Bird is not happy, and so he would be more likely, on that account alone, to remember a debt. Mr. Luke Bird loves Jenny Bunce.'

Mr. Weston shut the heavy book with a bang.

' How often I have to remind you, Michael,' he said a little sternly, ' that in our trade report the women come last. Ours is the only business, you know, that they do not dominate, and I have yet to meet the woman that can tell the difference between white and red port when her eyes are shut. Alas ! I have known more than one of them—excuse my mentioning such trivial circumstances, Michael— to leave a bottle of good Burgundy beside a horrid gas stove until it boiled. Women may enter the House of Lords, but never our whitewashed board-room.'

Mr. Weston appeared to be a little more moved than such a subject warranted, but after a moment or two he became placid again, opened the book, and turned to the next name.

' " Mr. Thomas Bunce," ' he read, ' " of the Angel Inn." '

' His trade is obvious,' said Mr. Weston, rubbing

37

his hands gleefully, ' and it is very much like ours, though it cannot well be supposed that the beer sold at the Angel is so good in quality or so happy in its effects as our good wine. But tell me, Michael, for you know how inquisitive I am, whether honest Mr. Bunce has any peculiar habit or notion that separates him from his fellow-men and gives him character ? '

Michael was silent. He blushed slightly, and looked down at his boots.

' I hardly like to tell you,' he remarked.

' But you may,' said Mr. Weston.

' Mr. Bunce, then, if you must know,' observed Michael, ' has, for a great number of years, been in the habit of blaming some one for all the troubles that come to the village of Folly Down.'

' And who may this some one be,' asked Mr. Weston, ' that Thomas Bunce is so ready to blame for all the sorrows and worries of yonder small village ? '

Michael blushed more deeply than before, and moved as far as his seat would allow him away from his master.

' Mr. Bunce blames God Almighty for every bad thing that is done.'

' He 's a bold man,' said Mr. Weston, and turned to the book again.

' " Mr. Grunter," ' he read, ' " Mr. Meek and Mr. Vosper." '

' These three,' said Michael, ' are people who have a certain importance in Folly Down. Mr. Meek is a very small shopkeeper——'

' Licensed to sell wine ? ' enquired Mr. Weston excitedly.

'Alas ! no,' replied Michael, ' he is only licensed to sell tobacco. And as he wishes others to be contented with what he sells, he shows a good example by being vastly pleased and contented by whatever he hears. Mr. Meek is the best listener in Folly Down. Everything that he hears spoken by man or woman or little child is of interest to him. He is even willing to listen to his own wife, and especially so if she is talking at her doorway, which she often does. Mr. Meek, if he be in company, rarely speaks one word himself, and if he does so it is only to encourage the others to talk the more. He is a little man with a fine strut, and he buttons his coat very tightly.

'Mr. Grunter occupies a high and exalted position in Folly Down. He is the church clerk, and is said also to be an expert lover.'

'A young man in his bloom ? ' suggested Mr. Weston.

'You are very much mistaken,' said Michael ; ' Mr. Grunter is old, he is also uncouth and flabby ; his knees bend outwards as he walks ; he has a large homely face, and his looks, to put them as nicely as I can, do not express wisdom.'

'He might be the greater fool if they did,' said Mr. Weston. ' But what has Mr. Vosper done to distinguish himself before the worms have him ? '

'He has done nothing,' observed Michael, ' except what his wife has told him to do ; but he has a strange fancy concerning the Angel Inn, where he thinks that one day he may meet an important personage.'

39

'A modest ambition,' said Mr. Weston, smiling.
'But kindly tell me, Michael, and that at once, if you
please, what do these three gentlemen drink?'

'All that they can get,' replied Michael readily
enough.

'Honest men,' cried Mr. Weston gleefully.
'We must trade with them at Christmas.'

Mr. Weston looked at the book.

'Either my eyes are grown dim, or else the next
name is written rather small,' he said, 'for I cannot
read it, and I should be obliged, Michael, if you
would decipher it for me.'

Michael leant over Mr. Weston's shoulder and
read aloud : '"The Rev. Nicholas Grobe."'

As soon as Michael had pronounced this name in
his usual clear manner of utterance, Mr. Weston
bowed his head in deep thought. He seemed to be
trying to recollect some incident or other of times
gone by that had at the moment escaped his memory.
He now appeared to remember what he wanted,
and his look showed a certain sadness at the
recollection.

He leaned forward with his head in his hands, as
if following the incident discovered in his thoughts ;
he had gone on to think of some one connected with
it—a friend that he used to have, who, for some
reason or other, had ceased to believe that his friend-
ship could ever have been a real thing, or he real
either.

Mr. Weston's companion always showed the
utmost consideration for his partner's moods—for
the head of the firm would sometimes grow thoughtful—and Michael would always wait patiently, never

even whistling a common catch, until his superior was ready to renew the conversation.

Mr. Weston turned a little from Michael, who fancied that he wiped his eyes, but he soon said gaily enough :

' Ha ! the Rev. Nicholas Grobe. And pray, what are his ideas about life ? '

' Mr. Grobe,' said Michael, looking a little curiously at his master, ' has very different opinions from Mr. Thomas Bunce.'

' I am glad to hear it,' said Mr. Weston.

' You may think it a little strange when I tell you that Mr. Grobe never blames any one, and God less than any, and that for a very simple reason—because he does not believe in Him. As you no doubt understood from the appellation of " Reverend " before his name, Mr. Grobe is the pastor of the village, but in all Folly Down there is only one person who does not believe in God, and he is that man. Mr. Grobe preaches twice every Sunday, but he never names God in his sermons.'

' He must, then,' said Mr. Weston, ' find the Holy Trinity a useful institution.'

' Once he believed in the Founder of Life,' said Michael, ' but he turned from Him, for he could not—and he has often told himself so—believe any more in one who could be so horrid and so cruel.'

' That 's rather strong,' observed Mr. Weston.

' No truer and no stronger than his own experience has been. Mr. Grobe was once wedded to a lovely and sprightly girl. She loved him, though she teased him, most devotedly. She became a mother, but died in a cruel and bloody accident when her child, Tamar, was a little girl.'

'Although Mr. Grobe is an honest man, and an honest man is a noble work,' said Mr. Weston, 'and though after what has happened he says there is no God, yet it must be quite impossible that he should go so far as to say that there is no such thing as Mr. Weston's Good Wine.'

'He drinks London gin,' said Michael.

'Then there is hope of him,' exclaimed Mr. Weston, slapping his knee, 'for if he drinks gin, however moderately, there is no reason why he should not one day, perhaps even this very evening, enjoy a glass of our wine. We have often heard of the like happening before, and I have known many a meek gentleman—a quiet, moderate liver—who has met a sad sorrow in his life, turn to us when all else had failed, and to our wine to comfort him.'

'His own sorrow,' said Michael, 'has opened his eyes to a world of sorrow, and though he sees time flowing like a river and sweeping all things away— sorrow and sadness and joy—yet he cannot deny the certainty that all men are swept away too, and so soon. We may be sure, too, that Mr. Grobe wishes to remember for as long a time as he can his own personal grief, for in his grief is ever contained the thought of her whom he loved.

'Sometimes,' continued Michael, 'during the long autumn evenings, when Mr. Grobe sits surrounded by his books'—('I hope mine is one of them,' said Mr. Weston, and Michael nodded)— 'with gin and tobacco near by, he almost fancies that such a gracious evening can lengthen out interminably, and so he likes to be sure that the lamp—I believe you mention a lamp in your book, sir, as being a guide ; in Mr. Grobe's case, a guide to the gin bottle—is always full of oil.

'Upon such an evening, when the right silence reigns, Mr. Grobe's melancholy feeds upon itself ; his sorrow lingers and hovers in the dark corners of the room that are away from the light. Mr. Grobe then feels his loss, if such an evening be but long enough, as something that can almost be kind and loving to him. The long days, when the sun mounts high in the heavens and sinks but slowly, weary Mr. Grobe. The spring flowers, so virgin-like in their beauty, make him but go out to the fields to weep. The glorious summer, the hot noon of all the seasons, only dooms his steps to falter ; and the harvest saddens him, for that season shows how all things, even a green blade of corn, tend to their end. It is only a long autumn evening that can soothe Mr. Grobe's soul.'

'The very man for our good wine,' said Mr. Weston cheerfully.

VIII

MR. WESTON IS INTRODUCED
TO THE WOMEN

Mr. Weston looked at his book again.

' I see,' he said, ' that Farmer Mumby's two sons are written down here. Their names are John and Martin, and in the margin there are a few notes about them, telling of their pursuits ; but besides pointing guns at rabbits, riding high trotting horses and fast motor bicycles, what else can they do ? '

' You forbade me,' said Michael, ' to mention women.'

' And it was proper, then, that I should,' said Mr. Weston, ' but we may come to them now, for in these modern times they are of some importance to our trade.'

' And so they seem to be to the Mumbys,' said Michael carelessly, ' for besides being the cause of the death of Ada Kiddle, who was drowned in a deep pond, and behaving, until tired of them, in a merry manner with Ada's two sisters, Phœbe and Ann, under the oak tree upon the green, the young Mumbys now begin to boast pleasantly that nothing either in earth or heaven shall prevent them from ravishing Jenny Bunce. But, strange though it may sound, up till this moment they have been prevented.'

' But who has stopped them,' enquired Mr. Weston, ' from having their own way with the girl ? '

'Jenny, herself,' replied Michael willingly, 'who happens to be a good child.'

'I am interested to hear it,' said Mr. Weston, 'and I am interested, too, in the habits and manners of these young men. It is evident to me that, though they have often viewed a girl—and not always decorously—they have not so far even seen the wrapping of a bottle of our wine. I doubt if they have even wished to handle a bottle.'

'They do not suffer from asthma,' remarked Michael, 'that affects the heart and so brings the thought of death into the mind of a man, as Mr. Grobe does. They are not tormented by love, as is Mr. Bird, because they have an easy way out of that wood, for as soon as love pricks them with his arrow, they reply by a similar favour aimed at the nearest girl.'

'But are there no customs in Folly Down,' asked Mr. Weston, 'that are proper to follow ? Pray, do these young men give the maidens anything for what they do to them, or do they mean to marry them ? '

'No,' said Michael, 'they never part with a penny. They have been taught to believe—and German philosophy bears out this belief—that the world lit by the sun in the day and the moon by night was created on purpose that farmers' sons, who ever by their hardy lives and innate cowardice escape all pestilence and war, may have all the women and cigarettes that they need, and pay for nothing.'

'The devil ! ' said Mr. Weston, a little hastily. 'But you know the saying, that there is truth in wine, and even the sight of ours may, if it does no more, give to these young gentlemen a new experience.'

45

'You'll find them hard to please,' observed Michael dubiously.

Mr. Weston frowned a little, but his looks soon cleared and he smiled again when he read :

' " Miss Tamar Grobe." A name I have written myself. Please, tell me about her.'

'With the greatest willingness,' answered Michael, 'for I know her very well. She has a brown birth-mark, about the size of a sixpence, just a little above her navel.'

'You particularise too much, Michael.'

'She is dark ; she has red, pouting lips ; she is neither short nor tall. She has a cherub face and pleasant breasts, well suited to such a maiden. Her ankles are very small, and her gait free though yielding ; and she refuses to leave her father for any one lower than an angel. Would you care to hear any more about her ? '

'As much as you may think proper to tell me,' said Mr. Weston eagerly.

'Tamar is indeed a lovely creature,' continued Michael fervently. 'She has an exquisite white skin, as sweet as a babe's ; her neck and arms and bosom are nearly always bare ; she never pretends to be anything but what she is—a longing girl ; but in her desires, until this evening, as one may expect, she has been unfortunate.'

'How is that ? ' said Mr. Weston ; 'but I think I know.'

'You have guessed aright,' replied Michael, 'for Tamar looks too high. Indeed, she believes that, one adorable evening, an angel will wait for her under the village oak, and that, in his embrace, the evening will become an eternity. She often sighs as she passes the tree, and she sometimes looks in under the boughs, but, instead of the angel, she finds either Martin or John Mumby behaving in a very improper manner with one of the Kiddles.

'Tamar's father can hardly bear her in his sight. He feels that she grows every day more like her mother, whose sad death she caused ; but neither can he bear the thought of her leaving him to go away and be married. And so Tamar wanders in the fields, and often peeps in under the oak tree, where a Kiddle and a Mumby are more likely than not to be embracing——'

'Even when it rains ?' asked Mr. Weston.

'When it rains, the young women visit Mrs. Vosper's cottage. Mrs. Vosper's Christian name is Jane, and her interest in life is concupiscence. She believes it to be God's happiest work, and she sends Mr. Vosper into the back kitchen when anything improper is taking place in her front room.'

'That's kind,' said Mr. Weston.

'Sometimes, in passing down the lanes, for she likes evening walks, Miss Tamar Grobe peeps in through Mrs. Vosper's window, the curtain of which is but an old and torn towel. What Tamar sees makes her sigh silently and wish the more longingly that her angel would come. He will indeed be fortunate if he gets her, for in all the world, with its green meadows, gentle hillsides, and flowing brooks, you will hardly find a maid as lovely as she.

'The grassy downs know the tread of her little feet and feel the light pressure, and there's no tree or bush that would not give all its flowers and leaves

47

—yea, its very sap—to be a man for her sake, because her wishes are so burning. She even imagines it sweet to die in the arms of her lover, for she cannot bear the thought that her body, if it be triumphantly deflowered by his body, should continue its existence upon the earth. She often dreams of perishing utterly in a vast flame of love.'

' I can almost believe,' said Mr. Weston, ' that Tamar Grobe is already inspired by our wine, for, from your description of her, I fancy that all her life is lived in noble intoxication. Surely her beauty is too lively and too free to be endured without the help of our good wine, though even if she has not already purchased, we have only to see her and she will buy.

' But are you sure, Michael, that it is necessary, in such a simple village as Folly Down, to pry so deeply into all the tittle-tattle—the ape-like and the noble, the good and the evil—in order to sell a few dozen to any that will buy ? This seat is as pleasant to rest upon as my chair in the board-room, and I should like your opinion, for we need not hurry.'

' You must know, sir,' replied Michael, ' that it is proper—nay, even necessary—even in our firm, to make all the discoveries that possibly can be made about every one. We have to know, if we are to venture our goods, all the hidden desires and wishes of our prospective customers. We must discover all their passions and indulgences, all their likes and dislikes, all their sorrows and joys, in order to trade with them. We have to pry as deeply as we can into their past manners and customs, and discover also in what direction their future wishes may go.

48

Nothing is more important for our sakes than that we should be prepared for any change of taste or fashion that may happen in the future, so that we may be ever ready to offer to mankind a wine that their pockets, together with their inclinations, and their melancholy as well as their happiness, may wish for.'

'You describe our hopes and aspirations truly, Michael,' said Mr. Weston, looking with pride at his companion, 'for we are not a new firm, and although in one of our advertisements we have spoken of our wine as being new, that is merely said for the sake of young men who reside in universities, and who only approve of their own generation.   But we have done more, Michael, than to please them. We have discovered, by means of a secret process of grafting, the kind of drink that can bring everlasting happiness to the poorest creature upon earth.

'As you know very well, we have discovered that the pennies of the poor have as good a value, if there are enough of them, as the pounds of the rich, who are not, I fear, always as sure as they should be that our wine is the best.   The rich and prosperous, alas ! are so often filled with so many expensive wines that, when they come to ours, they pretend that it tastes a little sour.—You know my poetry, Michael ? '   Michael blushed.

Mr. Weston smiled.   'Do not be alarmed.   I am no Wordsworth—I will not recite to you now, and, besides, I can never remember my best songs. I was but going to mention that, in my book, I have noted and taken into account all the vagaries of human nature from its first beginning, so that my book is really intended to assist us to trade. All the way through my book—but you know it, Michael '—(Michael blushed again)—' I speak of a wine, some of which we carry with us now, that, though we do not advertise it as medicinal, yet, as you very well know, there is no trouble incident to the fretful and changing life of man that this particular wine will not cure for ever.

'We have had customers,' continued Mr. Weston, speaking in a lower tone, ' who have sometimes invited themselves—and I, even I, have always attended them there—into our deepest and most dingy cellar, upon the walls of which are green mould and cobwebs, and upon the floors toads and vipers. To taste this wine of ours that has never seen daylight is the desire of some of the most noble of our customers.'

' And those,' said Michael, ' who go down with you to taste that wine have no booked orders for what they buy. They pay ready cash, and owe us no more.'

' Yes,' said Mr. Weston, ' we allow no credit for that wine.'

IX

MR. WESTON REMEMBERS
A CUSTOMER

Mr. Weston looked up at the sky. He could never admire enough the ingenious electric contrivance, invented by a member of the firm of Messrs. Weston and Company, that could write so ably his name and business upon the dull blackness above.

Mr. Weston regarded the sky for some moments in silence, but some thoughts that evidently amused him were passing in his mind, for now and again he chuckled, and once he nodded, and once he shook his head. In a few moments, however, the subject of his contemplation became known.

'Michael,' he said, with a smile, 'you have awakened in me a rather surprising and altogether unexpected interest in women.'

Michael bowed.

'I fear that I haven't given to them, and especially to the younger and more beautiful, all the study that they deserve. I have always considered women—and I am afraid that I make this only too clear in my book—as being very far inferior to man in purchasing power. But since I saw Miss Gipps go by our car at Maidenbridge and read the name upon it, I have felt that even besides Miss Gipps, there may be others who would spend their means upon good wine if their worldly fortunes allowed of it.

'As you well know, the kind of visit that we are now paying we may be excused for regarding as a little holiday from our more strenuous affairs, and ever since you have begun to tell me so many things of interest about one young woman in Folly Down, you have made me extremely desirous to know more. The surprising ignorance, in the matter of taste and tasting, that some of our men whom we employ upon the road blame women for must be exaggerated, and it may still be possible to teach some of the younger ones the right and proper use of our good wine.

'Most of the ignorance and foolish behaviour no doubt comes from the fact that, only a little time ago, all women were merely the slaves to the cooking-pots. Under such culinary conditions, it is most natural that a true and proper taste for the best should be wanting, and that their only pleasure in life, poor creatures, was to spice the broth, out of which a few hulking brothers or husbands might wish to drink, with a lovely little fungus, like a red blood-drop. I believe'—Mr. Weston smiled— 'my poetry has improved the female intelligence, but even now they hardly understand the importance of a cool cellar.'

'They like the oak-tree bed better,' said Michael.

'And we mustn't blame them,' remarked Mr. Weston. 'But the tree reminds me—— You mentioned Jenny Bunce. I should consider it a kindness if you would tell me a little about her.'

'Jenny is a true country maiden,' said Michael. 'She is seventeen years old. She is just the girl for an honest man to desire, and our best wine is not more delicious than she.'

' Hush, Michael,' whispered Mr. Weston ; ' you must not say so.'

' Her young body,' said Michael, who was no way abashed by the reproof, ' is as plump as a robin's, and her eyes look so naughtily into yours when you meet her that it 's near impossible to refuse their asking. She has a delightfully soft skin, golden-brown hair, and she always sleeps hidden under the bed-clothes. But even though her eyes are so merry, Jenny Bunce is no wanton, and her whole idea of happiness in this life, and in the life to come, is to have a cottage of her own and to be married to a good man.'

' And against this charming girl,' said Mr. Weston, ' an evil plot has been laid.'

' Yes ; Mrs. Vosper has laid the snare,' replied Michael. ' This woman has so often seen the Kiddles used in a natural manner—and, indeed, these maids have ever been a little too willing—that she is satisfied that all is over with them, and now has a mind to see a girl forced, and Mr. Grunter, the supposed lover of Folly Down, blamed for the deed. Mrs. Vosper has the greatest dislike—an inherent dislike—of her own sex, until they grow old enough to be as vindictive as she. Her jealousy has charged her heart with a bitter cruelty, and she goes the way of her kind in having her revenge. Could she see a young girl's beauty clawed and rifled by a company of baboons she would be completely happy, but still she has the good fortune to see that her labours, undertaken in such a good cause, are not altogether in vain.

' She has much on her side, for country men have often grosser manners and less feeling than any orang-outang in an African forest, and Mrs. Vosper believes that a girl's unchastity is the shortest road to despair. She enjoys herself very finely in this manner, being regarded by her husband as a very notable woman, and he, good man—while her front-room doings give her all the sport she wishes for—remains munching his bread and cheese, in all peace and happiness, in the wood-shed, resting himself upon a bag of rotten potatoes.'

'Has Jane Vosper,' enquired Mr. Weston, with a sigh, 'always ministered to the needs of the young in this generous manner ?'

'As a young girl,' said Michael, ' she would walk of an evening demurely round the green, holding her head modestly and looking down at the daisies. But, if any man saw her, she would wander on, taking a turn or two more, and then, with perfect frankness of demeanour, lie down in the oak-tree bed.'

'Country manners,' said Mr. Weston, laughing.

'She lay down under the tree once too often, and had it not been for John Vosper, honest man ! who took her to church, unpleasant things might have been said.

'She is now too old for such amusements, and is most anxious that from what she got gain by—for she caught a man—others should receive only woe. Mrs. Vosper is now a matron in years, and she never speaks to any young girl without introducing into the conversation a certain subject that always causes the young creature that she talks with to become eagerly inquisitive and very thirsty.'

'Ha !' exclaimed Mr. Weston. 'We supply a wine that will quench that thirst.'

'Some are nervous,' said Michael, 'in such matters, and some are almost too eager ; and, if you will believe me, sir, there is no pleasant drink that is more hampered with all kinds of difficulties—and even with serious dangers—than this particular wine that you have mentioned as being very suitable to cool a young girl's desire.

'All about the world there are a large number of men paid to preach—though, to do them justice, they hardly ever heed their own words—against the use of this wine. Indeed, they say that it is no better than poison. It is sneered at, and its effects scorned, so that it brings the victim to contempt and degradation. Mrs. Vosper's idea that this wine is the road to ruin is justified by fact. And, indeed, if this were not so, the good lady would hardly recommend it so kindly to the girls.'

Mr. Weston meditated in silence for some moments. He raised both his hands and moved them before him, as if he covered all Folly Down with them.

'Many have belied our good wine,' he said slowly, 'and it is certainly strange that even those who should know my book the best have the poorest opinion of what we sell. I could give you, Michael, a few quotations—But you 're cold, Michael ! then I will not trouble you.—I will content myself by saying that, in all the careful process of the making of our wine, from the moving of the sods in our great vineyard, no plan has been overlooked, no new and improved system left untried, no expense or labour spared, to perfect its qualities, so that our wine may be a suitable drink for all conditions of men.'

'And women,' murmured Michael.

'But,' said Mr. Weston, who, being an honest tradesman, really believed in his own wares, 'although we are very glad to see so many take an interest in, and wish to taste, our light and less heady vintages, that are fittest to drink—and there are many who know this—in any gentle and green valley about the time of evening, yet there is still a lack of those who order our strongest and oldest wine that brings to the buyer a lasting contentment, and eases his heart for ever from all care and torment.'

Mr. Weston touched his forehead. He was trying to recollect something that his last remark had partly brought to his mind.

'Michael,' he said tenderly, 'did we not once sell a bottle of our rarest wine, that never sees the light of day, to a young creature called Ada, who used to live in Folly Down?'

'We did indeed,' said Michael, 'though I am surprised that you should have remembered her. Ada was the eldest of the Kiddles. A smiling and a happy girl, she could dance and leap like a fawn; her eyes were a deep blue, and her hair as shining as gold. Ada always had a great love for babies. She went out one night in a snowstorm and brought home a lost lamb that had strayed to the downs and was caught in a thicket—but Ada didn't escape Mrs. Vosper.'

'Ha!' exclaimed Mr. Weston, 'I never expected Mrs. Vosper to help us to sell our wine.'

'She certainly gave us her aid in the matter of this bottle,' said Michael coolly, 'for when, one fine day,

Mrs. Vosper was helping to turn the hay in the Kiddles' meadow, Ada worked with her and listened to her conversation.

' Ada worked merrily, and chattered too, and as her frock was unfastened and disclosed her growing maidenhood, Mrs. Vosper was given the opportunity of watching her, and wishing her ravished and dead.

' " And which of the Mumbys do you like best ? " asked Ada, as they worked.

' " Martin be the one for I," Mrs. Vosper made answer, " for I did once see 'e bathing naked in a little brook ; 'is skin be white, and 'e 'ave fine strong legs "—Mrs. Vosper sniggered and looked knowingly at Ada.

' The fair midsummer day turned to evening ; the swallows had fed their second batch of hungry, open mouths, and were tired of flying in and out of Mr. Mumby's cart-shed ; the evening gnats hung in the air as if painted upon it, and Mrs. Vosper and Ada Kiddle stood with a young man under the oak tree.

' They stood near to one another, there in the slow-dying and coloured light of a summer's evening. At this time and season, more than any other, a vision of living beauty, a fair being of delight moves in the twilight. This presence can only be known and loved—for it casts a deep peace around it—by those minds '—('inspired by our wine,' suggested Mr. Weston)—' that are freed from all gross and carnal thoughts and imaginings, and that can merge and deliver themselves into the hand of eternal beauty. Upon such an evening even the Creator of the universe can wish to forget Himself for a season and be born again, in the exquisite loveliness of one lonely daisy.'

' And would that He might so forget Himself ! ' said Mr. Weston sadly.

' Mrs. Vosper told some merry tales,' observed Michael. ' And soon Martin, who wore riding-breeches, took Ada, whose white frock had pleased him, upon his knees. Mrs. Vosper pretended to leave them. Ada escaped, too, for the moment, and the summer stars shone out. . . .'

' And what happened next ? ' asked Mr. Weston.

' Why, you yourself recollected what happened,' replied Michael, ' for no sooner had the fierce winter gales shaken off the last of the leaves from the Folly Down oak, and laid a dead bough across the mossy bed, than Ada Kiddle forwarded to us her request for a bottle of our blackest and strongest wine.'

' I hope she enclosed the price of the bottle with her order ? ' asked Mr. Weston anxiously.

' She certainly did,' replied Michael, ' she sent more than she need have done ; and when they took her out of Mr. Mumby's pond—Ada had been missing three days—she had our receipted bill upon her, as well as the freedom of our hidden cellar, that we always enclose with a bottle of this wine ; so we can demand no more of her.'

' We will visit Ada's grave,' said Mr. Weston gravely, ' for I always remember a good customer.'

MICHAEL MENTIONS THE CROSS

Though Mr. Weston's car had stopped upon the Folly Down hill, yet the lonely down was exactly as still and deathlike as during any other late autumn evening.

Indeed, the car became so lost in the gloom that it was hard to realise that it was in any way connected with the writing upon the sky. The car appeared less real now, and certainly created a great deal less noise than Squire Mumby's horse and trap, when that gentleman returned, merry, from a market dinner, or else from a convivial evening spent in the company of Mr. Board, the Mayor of Maidenbridge, and Lord Bullman.

But no tradesman, and certainly not our Mr. Weston, whose concerns are very important, can afford—though time appeared, in this case, to lie very lightly upon our travellers' hands—to remain for ever upon Folly Down hill.

Even his advertisement, that is written upon the skies to inform the folk what his goods are, may not perhaps be noticed by all who dwell in the village, and so, if the advertiser himself had not decided to go down to his customers, his good wine might have remained for ever in his cellar and never be sold.

Mr. Weston had ever had a firm belief in the romance of trade. He had never written better in

59

his own book than when dealing with the subject—
whether the matter involved was corn, cattle, a place
of burial, a harlot, or a piece of money.

Mr. Weston was romantic himself, as all the best
writers are. He had an idea that, in order to
increase his sales in a country village, it was best to
choose the very properest moment to appear himself
and to offer his goods.

He had wisely chosen the evening to visit Folly
Down, because he believed—and his experiences in
the past went to prove this belief—that most people,
at least in country places, are more willing to venture
their money and to buy drink after darkness has
fallen, than during the lighter hours of the day.

Mr. Weston's education had been a private one,
but he had never ceased to study, during a lifetime
that had been a rather unchanging one, all the
more complicated machinations of trade.

He was well aware that to enter a village when the
evening was come and darkness, was to surround
himself and his coming with a glamour that often,
in a simple country mind, suggests fear. Mr.
Weston knew very well how large a use the gypsies
make of fear when these thieving tribes go a-hawking
of their wares in country places.

' We must frighten them for their own good,' Mr.
Weston had once in early days remarked, ' in order
to make them thirsty. We must entertain them
in a number of ways in order to make them drink.
We must show them signs and wonders, war and
earthquake, fire and tempest, plague and famine,
and all because we wish to draw their attention to
our good wine.

' But if, after these methods are used, the people omit to buy our goods—they are often as blind as bats and as deaf as adders—we must then set on fire their houses, and bang and bellow with a great cannon into their ears, until they do buy.'

' We do our best '—Mr. Weston was speaking at a later board meeting—' to gain their attention. We have sent agents all over the world to shout hell to them and eternal damnation and a fire burning in a lake of fire, naturally supposing that such merry tales ought to make the people drink. We have painted the horror of death, the way of a corpse, the last groans of the sick, so that men may remember our wine. We have taught the bare stones to tell of us and to inform the folk, by their stillness, how once they, too, had the happiness to drink our wine.'

Following the plan of that discourse, though but mildly, Mr. Weston wished to wait for a little upon Folly Down hill, while the light of his advertisement shone above him, and then to descend upon the people before the astonishment of the writing upon the sky had abated.

' For those who have eyes to see must see that,' he said amiably, when he saw how successfully Michael had managed the electric current.

' And why should not we,' he exclaimed, ' terrify the people into buying our wine, as the gypsies frighten them into buying their lace and clothes-pegs ? We, as well as the gypsies, have a mysteri-ous power over the lives of the people, both for good and evil, and this power, if they shut their doors in our faces, they shall feel the effect of.'

' The example of Ada Kiddle should be something for them to go by,' said Michael.

'Why, yes,' observed Mr. Weston, 'and so it should.'

Mr. Weston was thoughtful for a few moments. But soon he said :

' There are two houses in Folly Down, Michael, where honest drink should at least be tasted, if not ordered in quantity, that I should like to know something of before I enter the village. These two houses are the inn and the rectory. Please describe them to me.'

' Folly Down rectory,' answered Michael, ' is a house that stands alone. It is very gloomy. It has windows that will not open, dark sombre walls stained and discoloured by the salt mists that come from the sea, and a vine that almost hides Tamar's window, that is very easy to clamber up. In the brick wall beside the front door there is a bell that, however far it is pulled out, will never ring, unless Jenny Bunce, who is the servant there, knocks her brush against it in the kitchen, and then it rings.

' The rectory has a grand drive that Mr. Grunter weeds with a broken hoe, a lawn that Mr. Grunter mows with a scythe, and an old rat that lives in the garden hedge who has once seen a bishop sneeze. If you wish to reach the inn from the rectory, you find the Folly Down green, and then pass the oak tree, but you must not linger there.'

' And why not ? ' asked Mr. Weston.

' It wouldn't be proper for me to say,' replied Michael. ' But do not, if you wish to reach the inn, take the turning to the left, for that way leads only down a very muddy lane, at the bottom of which is Mr. Bird's cottage.

'The inn is placed upon a little hill. At its entrance is a finely painted signboard of an angel. The inn itself is covered by a good coating of thatch, that is the very best straw in use in this part of the country, and is called "reed." The thatch keeps the house warm in winter and cool in summer, and the ale that is kept in a narrow passage between the kitchen and the parlour is by no means in a common way a bad beverage.'

'When nothing better is to be had,' observed Mr. Weston.

Michael bowed his assent.

'Beside the cool and, let us hope, open doorway of the inn, there grows a wych-elm that, in times gone by, used to prove a great boon to the farmers, who would tie their horses to a convenient bough, while they rested themselves and took a drink inside the house. From the inn, the rectory, as well as the squire's house, that is called Oak-tree Farm, can be seen.

'Oak-tree Farm is the house of the Mumbys. It is a long, low house, sheltered by large elm trees that, though they lean a little, appear never to fall. The house is reached by a steep and stony drive, and often a visitor finds it the easiest to go along a path through the churchyard in order to reach Mr. Mumby's front door.

'Mr. Kiddle lives in a pleasant stone house, set back in a pretty meadow that is his own. He also rents this high down where the old horse feeds.

'From Mr. Kiddle's meadow the oak tree is easy

to be seen—as easily as from Mr. Mumby's fields—
and the sight of the oak tree pleases the young
Kiddles and gives them pleasant thoughts when they
hang their clothes upon the line.

'Mr. Meek lives nearer still to the oak tree. His
shop is opposite to Mr. Grunter's cottage, and the
situation of his house, being so near to the centre of
the village, always gives Mr. Meek the chance to
listen to something, though that something may only
be sounds from the oak-tree bed.'

'A pleasant situation,' said Mr. Weston, 'and I
am already in love with Folly Down. From what I
have myself seen, and from what you have told me,
no place in the round world provides more peace and
joy to its inhabitants than this village. A joy, not
too excessive, but tempered, eased, and sobered by
the necessity of daily labour. With a little of our
wine to drink—and that they could surely afford—
no human lives ought to be more happy. For a
glass of our mildest and least matured should do
much to take away the few blemishes of village life,
and leave only pure joy.'

'One glass—and your written word, sir, your
poetic stories,' murmured Michael.

Mr. Weston softly squeezed his companion's
hand.

'With one glass, and, as you prettily suggest,
with my book in the house, why should not the
people here call their Creator good and themselves
happy? But has anything in the shape of Folly
Down caught your attention, Michael? for I
gather, from your knowledge of it, that you must
have already visited the village.'

'Viewed from this very hill in the daytime,' replied Michael, 'the lanes of Folly Down, beside which are the cottages, form a cross, and where the head of the crucified Saviour should be, there is the church.'

Mr. Weston laid his hand gently upon Michael's.

'I am glad to know whereabouts the church is,' he said mildly, 'for I intend to visit it; but in our family we have long ago ceased to mention the Cross, or the dreadful end of Him who was hanged upon it.'

'Mr. Grobe will not like to hear you say that,' remarked Michael, 'for he is never tired of telling of the death of Jesus. He regards this incident in the history of mankind as most important, and it proves to him how unnatural and how cruel must have been the will of the Father to give His only Son to such a death.'

'Does Mr. Grobe say that?' cried out Mr. Weston, in a tone of astonishment.

'He says and affirms it,' replied Michael. 'For Mr. Grobe cannot believe that a situation so improbable could arise that, in order to give everlasting life to man, the Almighty should send His Son to be so evilly treated. Mr. Grobe felt, more than ever, the injustice of this conduct when his own wife died. But though God went, Jesus lived, and Mr. Grobe believed in Him. He believed Him to be a young man of fine parts, with an imagination that could create an entirely new world, and with so forceful a love that all men could, if they wished, live in this one Man's love and pity—and die in it too.'

'Yes,' said Mr. Weston, with a sigh, 'He was a great poet.'

65

'Almost as great,' said Michael respectfully, 'as His Father.'

Mr. Weston looked pleased.

'Mr. Grobe believes that this Son of Man, who hated all base and mean things, still lives in any heart that will open to Him, and that the heart so wedded to this immortal One, who conquered and subdued death, though it die earthily, will remain His eternally. Mr. Grobe ever speaks of this strange and wonderful Man as though He were his own brother. He comforts and gladdens the sick and the dying, the weary and the sad, with the same Name that was written above the Cross at Golgotha, in Greek, in Latin, and in Hebrew. Mr. Grobe kneels in pity beside the beds of those whose last hour has come, and tells them of a Man—the most loving in all the earth—who died, loving them.'

Mr. Weston bowed his head very low.

'He tells them,' continued Michael, 'how this Man, who was as mortal as they, bore the most dreadful agony in the most praiseworthy manner, praying for His enemies, so that they, too, seeing how He forgave them, might come, though they killed Him, to love Him. No sinner ever dies in Folly Down without the name of Him who loved him so well being spoken and His story being told by his bedside, and no one that Mr. Grobe has ever ministered to has died miserably. And the love that sustains the dying must necessarily give to the dead the rest that can never be taken away.'

'That may well be so,' said Mr. Weston, 'if the last order for wine be placed with the right firm, but even if that has been done, and the wine has been received, the man may be nearly beyond tasting and believe he is drinking vinegar.'

'No one in Folly Down has ever called it so,' said Michael, 'for Mr. Grobe has only been called to minister to the poor and to the simple, who live their lives in a modest manner, and would always believe, even at the last, everything that they are told, and consider anything that they are given to drink as the best.'

'The very readers for my book,' said Mr. Weston. 'I have long wished for such simple readers as you describe. It is impossible, let me tell you, for any one to enjoy good poetry, even if he be created on purpose to praise it, if he find fault with every line that he reads.'

'Those harmless people,' said Michael, 'read nature, too, as if it were a book, and, indeed, it is better than many.'

'Michael,' said Mr. Weston, 'although I know the world had to be before its creation could be described, yet I trust you are not one of those who place nature before art.'

'Indeed I am not,' replied Michael.

'I am glad of it,' said Mr. Weston ; 'and now that I am in a mood for it, may I not recite to you a short chapter ?'

'You might frighten the old horse if you did,' observed Michael ; 'and surely it is nearly time for us to go down into the village, for we have a good many visits to pay, and you wish also to see the church.'

'I have never been inside one before,' said Mr. Weston.

67

Michael looked a little surprised.

' I only like to go,' remarked Mr. Weston, ' where my good wine is drunk. In a condemned cell, in a brothel, in the kennels of a vast city, our wine is drunk to the dregs, but in a church they merely sip.'

' And yet we have had orders,' said Michael.

' And if we fulfil them,' replied Mr. Weston, ' have the buyers ever been known to pay ? '

' Why, no,' said Michael, ' they expect all goods to be given to them.'

' They won't get much from us, then,' said Mr. Weston grimly. ' And now we had better go.'

Michael attended to the lights, the sky became dark, and the head-lights of the car showed the travellers the way to Folly Down.

XI

THE ANGEL

A YEAR after her mother was killed, little Tamar Grobe
fell in love with her angel, seeing him new painted,
one morning in early spring, upon the inn signboard.

The first sunshine was come after the darkness of
winter, and the first lark was singing. Folly Down
was so astonished that the sun should shine again in
real earnest that Mr. Grunter remarked to Mr. Meek
that the day, being so warm and pleasant for the
time of year, must have been sent as a warning to the
wise, and meant, no doubt, that the end of the world
was coming that very night.

Tamar was ten years old. Her frocks were short,
and her legs had as much freedom as ever they
wished. Since her mother's death she had been
very merry and wild, for no thoughts of love had
come to tame her. The little boys of the village she
regarded as mere apes of the field. The sun called
to her and bade her leap and run and tease some one,
and so she escaped her nurse, ran into the garden,
and began to throw stones at Mr. Grunter, who was
weeding the path.

For a while Mr. Grunter observed her behaviour
with equanimity, but when a stone hit the hand that
guided the hoe, he followed her with this weapon,
with which he intended to beat her. Tamar danced
away, climbed through the rectory hedge, disturbing
the rat, and ran along the lane towards the inn.

By the green she met Mrs. Vosper. Mrs.
Vosper saw her chance. Here was a happy innocent in a naughty mood. She drew Tamar to her
and began to fondle her.

'This is St. Valentine's Day,' said Mrs. Vosper,
kissing and still holding Tamar, 'a day when even
the youngest maiden can know, if she chooses, her
future fortune, for the first young man that you see
will be sure to marry you.'

'And what is being married?' asked Tamar.

'Well, now you have asked me something,'
replied Mrs. Vosper, 'but as I bain't no liar, I will
tell you what marriage be.'

Mrs. Vosper drew Tamar in under the oak tree,
and they sat down together upon a mossy root.

''Tis like this to be married,' she said. 'You do
come to crack acorns under this pretty tree, and when
you be tired you do lie down and do stretch out they
bare legs under the green shady leaves. You do
shut thee's eyes as in a cat's sleep, but all of 'ee may
be looked at by any boy who do come by. When
you do see woon thee do fancy 'tis best to whistle
softly. And then do 'ee look up into tree, move
theeself a little and rest pretty, and 'ee may smile. If
you do stay so, he will come. 'E won't do much to
you at first, save only to tease and torment 'ee, but
when stars do shine thee will be happy. In a
month's time 'tis safest to go to church and to give
away bride-cake.

'Now listen to I, Tamar, for thee be woon of they
girls. Do 'ee mind that this be St. Valentine's Day,
and if you look out 'twill be to see him.

'Nothing is more pleasant than the merry games

that 'ee two will have together, and it is always the girl's business to make the boy begin. Thee must make him suppose that it 's all the merest play. If he can only stay and look at 'ee, or sit still beside 'ee and but hold your hand, thee must tickle his neck with a piece of grass and say that you wish he was Jimmy. He will be sure to catch and hold 'ee then. Thee must struggle, but that will only make him the more venturesome, and then thee may say, " Oh ! that bain't nothing to what our Jimmy do do." '

Tamar escaped and ran off. She ran excitedly, she cared not where. She ran to the inn. A young painter, hired by the hour, had, a week or two before, repainted the signboard. He had copied himself when he painted the angel, and had given him a very merry eye, fiery red hair, and a pair of blue trousers.

The first man that Tamar saw—for she believed Mr. Grunter to be a kind of monster and no man— was this painted angel.

Tamar held out her arms to him, and invited him to come down to her. She danced before him, kicking up first one leg and then the other.

' I am going to lie down under the oak tree,' she called out. ' Will you please be so kind as to come and tease me there, and then, when the stars come out, we will be happy and married.'

Tamar kissed both her hands to the angel. She danced for a little longer ; she blushed and ran off. She ran to the oak tree, and at once lay down in the mossy bed.

In the hoary boughs of the oak tree a wood-pigeon was cooing, and now and again there was a pleasant flutter of soft wings, which showed that her mate heeded her. Other country sounds came. A cock crew and Mr. Mumby's bull bellowed joyously. Between the roots of the aged oak the moss, that feels so soon the change of the year, was in flower. Delicate flowers of the most pleasant green tipped each stem.

Little Tamar stroked the moss ; she lay, with her hands under her head, and waited. Her heart was full of a delightful sensation. All her body was trembling, but she knew not why. She looked up at the wood-pigeons, her eyes glistened, and she said softly : ' Oh, I do wish that the angel would come down from the signboard and torment me.'

She stretched, she moved her hands away from her head and held them up towards the boughs. Presently she ran home, with tears in her eyes.

The next morning Tamar ran out, hoping to meet Mrs. Vosper. She saw the lady drawing water at the well and went to greet her. Tamar's eyes were tearful.

' You have deceived me,' she said, ' you only told me a wicked story. I did exactly as you bid me, and the first man I saw was Mr. Bunce's angel. I went to the oak tree to lie down, but he never came to tickle me.'

' Perhaps you covered your knees with your frock and he didn't see you,' suggested Mrs. Vosper.

' Oh, no, I didn't,' exclaimed Tamar, who was really crying now ; ' I lay down exactly as you said I was to, and only Mr. Grunter came by, and he never noticed.'

Tamar looked up at Mrs. Vosper.

' I don't like you,' she said, ' but I love my angel.'
And she ran home in a hurry.

Tamar soon grew to be a wayward, dark thing,
with one high ambition that permitted her to love no
mortal man.   She ranged the countryside, for she
never knew when she might not expect to meet her
angel in some lonely valley.   She knew every shepherd, every path in the fields, and every little hill.
Often she would stray away from Folly Down
rectory upon moonlight nights, and even during dark
winter evenings.   Sometimes she would stop and
look at her own shadow, that the sun or moon would
cast upon the turf.   She would look curiously at it
—the shadow, the figure of a girl.

Her father was a lonely man.   He nursed his
sorrow, and he never heeded what Tamar did.   A
lady, who lived a few miles away from Folly Down,
and whose name was Miss Pettifer, would blame Mr.
Grobe roundly for neglecting his daughter.

' You ought to send her to school,' she said
defiantly, ' where Tamar could play hockey, learn
to behave herself, and talk French.'

Miss Pettifer began to breathe quickly, which
showed that she was getting angry.

' If you let her run about these hills in the way she
does,' she told Mr. Grobe, ' who can say what might
not happen !   I wouldn't be in the least surprised
to hear that the girl had fallen in love with a hay-
trusser—or a badger.   Or she might set up house-
keeping with an old raven in a tree-top.   If a girl is
not taught to play hockey, she might be found in a
wood, talking to a serpent.'

' She wouldn't be the first woman who has done

that,' Mr. Grobe had replied. 'But now, Miss Pettifer, I have my sermon to write.'

Sometimes, when summer was in Folly Down, Tamar would rise early and run out into the first sweetness of a new day. She would visit the oak tree, drawn there by the cooing of the wood-pigeons.

She would lie down in the bed ; she would press her lips against the tree, with an ardour that showed well with what an agony of passion she would receive her lover when he at last came to her.

XII

TAMAR TAKES A BATH

IT is very often the case that in a lonely country place, where there is little to do and less to talk about, a mistress and her maid acquire the most intimate knowledge of one another. Neither the lady nor her handmaid can hold a single secret in her heart that the other does not wot of. They see one another a great many times in the day, and nothing ever happens to the one that can be hid from the other.

Jenny Bunce, the servant at the rectory, knew well enough that ever since Tamar was a little girl she had expected a wonderful man from the skies to come down one dark night and to carry her off to the oak tree and to stay with her there.

In a country way of thinking, any one who came down from the skies must, of course, belong to the heavenly family who lived there. And so Jenny believed that the angel that Tamar expected would most likely be one of God's cousins. She used to deplore the fact that her father, Landlord Bunce, could never mention God unless he blamed Him for something.

'Our daddy shouldn't blame folk that 'e don't know and haven't never seen,' Jenny once said; 'and besides, all t'other folk in the sky mayn't be so bad. None of they have never bought drink from daddy and gone off, same as John Mumby do, wi'out paying for it. . . .'

Tamar would speak of her angel in the grandest manner, and so impressed was Jenny with his resplendent magnificence that she viewed her mistress as a being very far above the level of the Mumbys and the Kiddles, and she had almost a mind to worship her.

Tamar loved her angel passionately. Her love burned with a fiery heat within her heart. She lived in her hope. She felt a vision of happiness that, even though it was so far removed from the ordinary varieties of things felt or seen, can feed a life with gladness.

Ordinary love, such as mere mortals give to one another, Tamar was wont, in her talks with Jenny, to discredit, so that the handmaid, feeling that other grand matters were possible, held aloof herself, as a compliment to her mistress, from village gallantries. And Tamar, seeing her maid so inclined, praised her resolution.

But now that Mrs. Vosper had a mind to push Jenny into the arms of a man, Jenny was always compelled, when she met her in the road, to listen to her insidious whispers.

Mrs. Vosper was most discreet, and would approach Jenny softly, ' having,' she would say, ' a tale of importance to tell.'

' And there bain't no maid who do dress like 'ee, some one do say,' she would whisper, ' and some one 'ave a nice gift 'e do keep for thee.'

Jenny would blush and hurry to Mr. Meek's to buy the lemons that Tamar had sent her for, and as she would move away Mrs. Vosper would call out : ' Tain't nothing no harm that I do mean. . . .'

Folly Down rectory was an old house that had never reached modern ideas, and Mr. Grobe was the last man in the world to wish to alter its original formation. There was no bathroom at the rectory, and in the winter-time, in order to save Jenny from having to uncover herself—for she lay deep in her bed—too early in the morning, Tamar would usually take her bath beside a good fire in her bedroom, after tea.

Jenny, a most cautious maiden as regards the outside world, would prepare the room for this event very carefully, drawing down the blinds and pulling the curtains. The window was high in the house, and nothing could possibly have been seen, even by the most inquisitive, from the ground outside, but that was not the quarter from which Jenny expected prying eyes when she drew down the blinds.

She expected the naughty peeping to come down from above, and when she saw a star twinkle she drew the curtains quickly, for she fancied it might be Tamar's angel.

While Mr. Weston was conversing pleasantly with his companion upon the top of Folly Down hill, Jenny Bunce in her black frock, and wearing the daintiest and cleanest of white aprons, was carrying a can of hot water to Tamar's room. She went, of course, by the back stairs, which is the proper way for any servant to go.

Jenny knocked and was admitted, for Tamar was already there. She had taken off her frock and was sitting thoughtfully by the fire. Tamar's hands lay idly in her lap, and she looked meditatively at a large flame that spread up the wide chimney, like a tree.

Jenny poured the hot water into the bath; she attended to one thing and then to another, as though she had a mind to find employment in the room for all the evening. Tamar still looked into the fire, and Jenny, having completed every available task, looked sadly at the door. Tamar noticed her hesitation.

' You may stay here if you wish, Jenny,' she said, ' for I know you always want to talk.'

Jenny certainly did. She always had a great number of questions to ask her young mistress, and besides, she always regarded her extreme cleanliness as something rather amazing to witness—a ritual that was hardly ever submitted to amongst her friends, unless they were to be married the next day.

Jenny, too, had always a hope that Tamar's angel might descend down the chimney, and such a coming Jenny always wished she might be there to see. She always wondered, too, how Tamar managed to slip from her clothes as easily as she did. And how she could stand up so boldly before the furniture with not one shred to cover the beauty of her entire nakedness Jenny could never tell, and she would gasp with wonderment at such a sight.

' Don't 'ee never mind,' asked Jenny, who would always watch her mistress in the bath for a minute or two before she spoke to her; ' don't 'ee never mind showing all of 'eeself, as thee be doing, to the clock ? ' Jenny's eyes grew larger and more incredulous as she examined the beauties of her mistress.

The clock was a pretty one. It was in a case decorated by harebells, and had been a wedding gift from Tamar's father to her mother, for his favourite flower was a harebell. It ticked in an ordinary manner that couldn't, even in the wildest imagination, have been called amorous.

' Why, no, Jenny,' replied Tamar, ' I don't mind the clock seeing me ; and, indeed, why should a girl be ashamed of her own skin, for God made us so ? '

' But 'E did only mean our hands and faces to be seen bare,' said Jenny, ' and our daddy do say that 'tis all 'Is fault that what we be like elsewhere should be made at all.'

' But, Jenny,' enquired Tamar, ' if we were only face and hands, how could we dress ourselves in pretty clothes ? It wouldn't be at all pleasant for us if we were only wooden elsewhere.'

' But we should,' said Jenny decidedly, ' cover all our wickedness, that daddy do blame God for making, wi' all the clothes we can.'

Tamar wrapped herself in a large bath-towel. She stepped near to the fire and smiled at Jenny. Jenny came nearer and looked at the clock. She was pleased that her mistress had covered herself.

' You may sit down, Jenny,' said Tamar. ' And now, please, tell me the news.'

' Oh,' replied Jenny, ' there bain't much for me to tell, only Mrs. Vosper 'ave been at me again. She 's been telling me about they boys, and some one be saying that 'e 'll hang 'isself if I don't come out and meet 'e under oak tree.'

' Jenny,' said Tamar, ' you know my father wouldn't like to hear you speak so, and you shouldn't talk to Mrs. Vosper if she says such things.'

' But I must talk to some one,' observed Jenny.

'You had far better speak to any man who is fond of you than to Mrs. Vosper. Jenny, why do you not allow poor Mr. Bird to talk with you? He looks so longingly at you when you walk across the green.'

'Oh, but it wouldn't do for I to marry 'e,' said Jenny, 'for every one do laugh at 'is ways, and Squire Mumby do shout to Mr. Bird same as to a dog when 'e do order him out of field.'

'But if other people are rude to him,' reasoned Tamar, 'that doesn't show that Mr. Bird isn't a gentleman.'

'Oh yes, it do,' replied Jenny decidedly, 'and besides, our daddy do say that Mr. Bird bain't no drinker, no more than the Almighty be.'

'Mr. Bunce ought not to say so,' remarked Tamar.

'Oh, but 'e do,' said Jenny. ''E do blame 'E for all temperance, and 'e do say 'tis 'Is fault that Mr. Bird do only talk to the lambs and to the hedge-sparrows. And 'e bain't no man to do that.'

'But what can you know about a man, Jenny?'

'I know everything,' said Jenny. 'There bain't nothing that Mrs. Vosper haven't told I all about, and Mr. Bird 's too religious to be naughty.'

'I doubt that,' said Tamar reflectively, 'for I feel sure that those who live in the presence of the Most High would be the most delightful lovers.'

'If they be first taught by we girls,' said Jenny, 'for Mrs. Vosper do say that men-folk be always faint-hearted.'

'Of course, all this is nothing to me,' said Tamar, who, having dried herself, was beginning to dress; 'but of this I certainly feel sure, that even an angel, who must be more religious than Mr. Bird, can please a girl.'

Tamar dressed herself slowly ; she brushed her hair before a glass.

Jenny watched her now with entire satisfaction. Her mistress had appeared to her as a kind of strange monster in her bath, and now that she was out of it and clothed, Jenny thought better of her.

With Tamar turned from her and looking into the glass, Jenny grew bolder.

' Mrs. Vosper says,' said Jenny, ' that the happiest moments in a girl's life are over so quickly that afterwards one can never remember the joy of them.'

' Isn't it possible,' said Tamar, looking into the glass and blushing, ' to stretch out such moments into long hours ? '

' Not for me, miss,' said Jenny, with a sigh ; ' at least, Mrs. Vosper be always saying that they fancy matters be soon over and so I needn't be frightened.'

' But a night can be very long for lovers, Jenny.'

' Not out of doors, miss,' replied the handmaid.

Tamar turned, and sat looking into the fire. The flaming tree had died down. Tamar stretched both her hands over the fire. She wished to see, rising out of the hot coals again, that tree of flame. But the fire was sluggish, and refused to rise for her pleasure.

If Tamar doubted at all about the coming of her angel, she doubted in the winter. In the spring, when the gorse bushes became as yellow as the sun's beams, she believed in his coming. In the summer the warmth of the coloured days made her feel certain that her lover must be near. But now she only had the fire to tell her pretty tales.

Would all her days, she wondered, be passed in Folly Down, in the company only of shepherds, and perhaps a badger, as Miss Pettifer had hinted? Would her years gather, weeping, about her and find her, as their number increased, still a maid? Would they, and later years as forlorn as they, lead her on into the darkness? Tamar hid her face in her hands.

Jenny began to tidy the room. She deplored the fact that her mistress so soon renounced and gave over a conversation that, had she been with any one else, would have meant long hours of amiable talk.

Jenny looked at Tamar's back. No other servant, she felt sure, could have so charming a mistress, and certainly never see her—with such queerly mixed feelings of fear and admiration—unclothed.

But Miss Tamar might have gone on talking a little longer.

Jenny was at liberty to go to her home that evening. But she did not wish to go there. She had done all she could in Tamar's room, but now, as Tamar was so silent, she believed that her mistress wished her to go away.

Jenny stood still and listened. The gate of the rectory backyard shut. Some one had knocked at the back door.

Jenny went out of the room and ran down the stairs in a hurry.

Outside in the darkness there was Mrs. Vosper.

XIII

MRS. VOSPER CHOOSES
HER PREY

Mrs. Vosper lived very high in the excitement of life. She lived upon the mountain called Lust. And there she fed happily upon the act of the beast, that is likewise—as we are taught by the wise, as well as by Mr. Bunce—the act of God.

But Mrs. Vosper hated her own sex, and she wished to do two things with them—to bring them into trouble, and to amuse herself by watching their undoing.

She had the same dislike for virginity that her betters have always had, though for a different reason, for Mrs. Vosper believed that virginity was a happy state because it brought no troubles, and she wished all women—and especially the young ones—to be brought to woe.

Mrs. Vosper had early learned the amiable behaviour of a spider, but she was even more of an artist than it, for the dull fly would not do for her ; it must be a feeling one. She would pass over the more ordinary and common kind of village girl, leaving their manners to chance, that was often no kinder than she. Mrs. Vosper let these go, with but a hint or two, they being but poor little trout, with meek bellies, who would never be brave enough to struggle when hooked, but would allow themselves to be landed, and only lie upon the grass gasping foolishly.

These simple ones would be caught so easily by any one, that even Mr. Meek would hardly have taken the trouble to blame Mr. Grunter for what happened.

As soon as ever they arrived at Folly Down, Mrs. Vosper chose the Kiddles as her prey. Ada was chosen first, for she was the eldest, and the event of her end certainly proved that Mrs. Vosper was a clever woman, who knew a girl who could not bear to face her shame.

Ada had always, as a very little child, been extremely interested in all the creatures of the earth that increase and multiply. She had an enquiring mind and a happy heart, and her forehead would pucker when she grew thoughtful. No one of all those who wore white at Whitsun was more fitted by nature's hand to rejoice in her life beside these tender lilies that grow in the silent valleys.

Ada was afraid of nothing ; she could never believe that anything would hurt her, and she would run into Mr. Mumby's field to pluck the yellow flags while the bull—a ragged heathen, and great-grandfather to the one that Mr. Bird converted to Christianity—was there.

Ada had the happiest and the gayest laugh that could be imagined ; the laugh of a very girl, and hair that the sun loved to kiss and the wind to blow. She was always the first in the meadows when the cowslips came, and ran so fast from one group to another that, in less than a moment, her hands were filled with yellow flowers.

Ada was interested in everything that she saw. Boys interested her, and the ducks too. She compared their habits and their pastimes, and watched any little boy to see what he did, and the ducks to see what they did.

Her father, Mr. Kiddle, had been brought up to fancy that young maidens were only of use to their mothers ; but as soon as Ada was ten, Mr. Kiddle discovered that she was useful to him too, for she could overtake a cow that was going the wrong way, in a moment, and turn it into the right path in spite of its horns.

Not only after the cows did Ada run, but she would overtake the biggest boys, too, even upon a Sunday when every maiden is dressed in her prettiest clothes.

'Ada do run,' said Mr. Kiddle to Mr. Bunce, one Sabbath evening, ' and there bain't no stopping her. She be growing a big maid, and 'tain't proper, so her poor mother do say, for she to show so much.'

'When one of they pretty maids do run or do leap,' replied Mr. Bunce sadly, ' something be going to happen, and there be some one who should be blamed for it.'

'Yes,' said Mr. Kiddle, ' 'tis only too true what thee do say, landlord, for all they running ways do lead to oak-tree bed.'

'Then some one,' said Mr. Bunce, ' should be ashamed of 'Imself.'

Ada's merry running ways reddened her cheeks and made her so joyous and so free that the old owl from the church tower nodded kindly at her as she ran up the church path to swing on the church yew.

Once—and we think it proper to record it here—

a rather strange conversation occurred upon the
road between Mr. Kiddle and a stranger that fore-
boded no good to Ada, although at the time Mr.
Kiddle took little or no notice of it.

The dealer had bought three cows at a July sale, to
which, as the day was a Saturday and her holiday, Mr.
Kiddle had taken Ada.   The drover that Mr. Kiddle
usually employed was not at hand when he was
wanted, and so the dealer decided to do without him.
There was Ada to go in front of the cows, and he
himself could follow behind with the horse and trap,
and so keep the stock going in the right road to
Folly Down.

Ada was proud of her charge.   She walked boldly
in front of the cows, dressed in her best summer frock
and wearing a hat with a pretty pink ribbon.   She
carried a stick, with which she threatened the cows if
they happened to venture their horns too near to her.
She walked grandly, giving to her little body a fine
air of consequence ; and when they passed through
a village Ada called to all the little girls she saw—
some older than herself—to get out of the way if
they did not wish to be tossed over the trees.

In order to be more ready to dispute the passage
with his beasts, should they, goaded by the flies, wish
to return by the way they had come, Mr. Kiddle had
dismounted from his cart and led the horse, holding
the whip in his hand.

The day was very hot, and Mr. Kiddle, clad in his
market coat that was made of the thickest material,
would often stop the horse to wipe his forehead with
his red handkerchief, and once, as he did so, a cow
that Ada had frightened with a tap upon its nose with

her stick, bolted past him and would have been lost
had not a strange man, who must have been walking
a little way behind, unknown to Mr. Kiddle, turned
the creature again.   When the cow was safely on the
right way the stranger walked beside Mr. Kiddle,
who thought he recognised him as a travelling tinker,
although he had forgotten his name.

He was an old man with a long beard, whose
clothes were rags ; but Mr. Kiddle had all the way
wished to tell some one how proud he was of Ada,
who did all the running, so he was glad to have even
a tinker to talk to.

They were travelling along the main road that
went near to Folly Down, and a little way ahead of
them there happened to be a turning to the left hand
that might tempt the cows.

'Surely,' said the tinker, pointing with his out-
stretched hand to this lane, 'the cows will go down
there.   See how the flies tease them ;   they will
never pass such a pleasant green path as that.'

Mr. Kiddle laughed.

'Why,' he said, 'don't 'ee see me little maid, who
be standing there to keep them out of it ?   She be
waving her stick and telling the beasts to go right.'

'I see no maiden,' said Mr. Kiddle's companion,
'and I hear no girl's voice calling to the cows.'

'Be thee blind and deaf ?' asked Mr. Kiddle.

'No, no ; I can see and hear better than most
men,' replied the tinker.

'How many cows be there, then ?' asked the
dealer, as Ada cleverly turned them up the chalky
lane that led to Folly Down.

'You are laughing at me,' replied the tinker, who

continued his way along the turnpike road, while
Mr. Kiddle led his horse after the cows.

' Your three cows have, strange to say, taken the
right turning, but I see no child.'

' What do it mean ? ' asked Mr. Kiddle, when he
told this strange story at the inn.

' No good,' replied Landlord Bunce, ' no good for
Ada.'

Even before Ada Kiddle left the village school
Mrs. Vosper began to notice her ; and one summer
day, when Ada was skipping upon the green, Mrs.
Vosper pointed out her firm, strong legs to young
Martin Mumby.

Another day Mrs. Vosper stopped Ada and began
to talk to her about the little lambs and the daisies,
and soon she spoke of the ducks and the boys.

Time passes very swiftly in Folly Down with such
amiable people as Mrs. Vosper to talk with, and very
soon, though Ada ran as swiftly as ever, a certain
drowsiness would oppress her, and she would prefer
to listen to Mrs. Vosper than to pick flowers upon
the hillside.

When Ada was captured, after a merry race and a
few maiden-like endeavours to save herself that were
not successful, Phœbe soon followed as the spoil of
Martin too, and within a year Mrs. Vosper was telling more stories to Ann.

Ann Kiddle showed a little more care of herself,
and didn't give herself up at almost the first assault
as her sisters had done, though in so doing she
only provided more entertainment to Master John
Mumby, who, shielding himself safely behind Mr.
Grunter's supposed reputation for such affairs, very

soon——after a struggle or two——brought the young lady to heel upon Mrs. Vosper's sofa, while Mrs. Vosper looked through the keyhole, but blamed herself for not having brought her glasses out with her when she left the pair together.

When the Kiddles were all settled, Mrs. Vosper looked expectantly round Folly Down, believing, as it was proper she should, that the fun of the fair need never be said to be over while any young girl lived.

Jenny Bunce, the only daughter of the innkeeper, and the servant of the rectory, was the next to be chosen.

As soon as she chose her out, Mrs. Vosper commenced her beguilements. But she found Jenny suspicious and queer, and for a reason indeed that Mrs. Vosper had not expected, for whenever Mrs. Vosper suggested certain doings that, she said, always gave a girl pleasure, Jenny would look strangely and fearfully into the sky and would say to herself that she feared Miss Tamar's angel might be listening or else looking, and that she wasn't sure whether the mention of such affairs would please him or not.

Jenny's holding back, after their happiness with the Kiddles had been so easy, gave to the Mumbys a very keen appetite for the feast that one day they knew should be theirs. But waiting in such homely matters wasn't pleasant to them, for they liked to win at the first throw, especially as every one fancied that it was Mr. Grunter who did it, and that they, being gentlemen of honour, went to the town for their pleasure.

Martin would sometimes, even in the daytime,

greet Mrs. Vosper when she was drawing her water
at the well, and press her to bring Jenny to him.   He
had even, he said with an oath, done what he had
never done and never had need to do : visited the
church and listened to one of Mr. Grobe's ' God-
forsaken ' sermons—a remark nearer to the truth
than the young man wotted of—and only for the
reason of sitting near to Miss Jenny, in the hope
that she might respond to any merry gesture he
would make explaining his passion and what he
meant to do.

But she gave no heed to him, and never looked
about her at all, unless it were to look at a bearded
saint in the window whose hands were certainly
incapable of making any indecent signals.

' Who would have expected such a thing ? '
Martin Mumby said.   ' That a little slut like that,
a mere servant, should give Mr. Grunter so much
trouble ! '

' 'Twill be all the more fun when she do come
round,' was Mrs. Vosper's reply.

Mrs. Vosper tried her best, but Jenny still held
back shyly, looking into the sky fearfully if anything
more foolish than usual was said.

But the morning before the wine merchant
arrived at Folly Down, Martin Mumby said to Mrs.
Vosper : ' We mean to have her this evening.
Nothing shall stop us.   It will be very dark ; there
will be no stars or moon or any other light in the sky.
If you do not find some way to bring Jenny to the
oak tree to-night, you and Vosper will be turned out
of your cottage and into the road by Christmas.'

Mrs. Vosper was pleased to hear this.   Evidently

the Mumbys meant business at last. But she pretended to be horrified.

'If doing thik be what 'ee do mean,' she said, dropping the bucket she was going to fill at her well with a clatter, ' 'tain't no good for I to blame they kind of ways upon Mr. Grunter.'

'And why not?' demanded Martin.

'The poor man be too wold for wars and battles, and all the village do know, and parson too, how plump and strong be Jenny Bunce.'

'Do you bring her to us,' said Martin, ' and if she be the pretty ewe lamb that Kiddle do call her, 'twill be fun for all.'

'Oh, rich folks be naughty ones!' laughed Mrs. Vosper.

XIV

MRS. VOSPER TELLS A STORY

MRS. VOSPER took Jenny's hand and drew her out into the darkness. The back door of the Folly Down rectory shut of itself behind her.

Mrs. Vosper had chosen the right moment, for Jenny was in a suitable mood to be betrayed. She felt careless and a little tired this evening. She knew that something was going to happen, because, when she was running upstairs to change her dress that afternoon, she slipped and fell.

' A wedding,' said Jenny, picking herself up, ' or a funeral, but which of the two it do mean I bain't sure.'

And a little later, in scrubbing her face with her flannel, she spilled some soapy water upon her black frock.

' Oh, I don't trouble,' she said, looking at the spot on her dress; ' I don't trouble if all of I be spoiled. I bain't one to wait for no angel to marry me, and Mrs. Vosper do say 'tain't no good for no girl to go out wi' Mr. Bird, 'e would dare do nothing, only kiss 'ee.'

Jenny looked at herself in the glass.

' 'Tis what we girls be made for,' she murmured.

But out of doors Jenny was a little more wary, and Mrs. Vosper, being wary too, was careful at first to speak of nothing that could frighten her.

' 'Tis nice to be out,' she said, ' when a maid bain't afraid of the darkness.'

' Oh, I bain't afraid of nothing in Folly Down,' replied Jenny, ' and I be only out for a little time.'

Mrs. Vosper drew her down a narrow side path and through the garden gate.

'Martin Mumby don't wish to offend 'ee,' she said, 'but 'e have caught a little live bird, and 'e did a-fancy that Jenny Bunce mid like a peep at the pretty thing. 'Tain't no common bird, but 'tis one wi' pink feathers.'

Mrs. Vosper took Jenny's arm and led her along.

'Oh, well,' sighed Jenny, 'I may as well go along wi' Mrs. Vosper. . . .'

The dull air of a November night, when one steps into it from a lit room, is often breathed with fear, as if it hides odd things in the darkness. The heavy clouds, though unseen now, that were grey and heavy all the daytime, at night press upon the heads of the folk who are abroad, like the soft damp clay upon the coffins of the shrouded dead.

If a girl be out in the November darkness, she must perforce breathe this thick and heavy air with a strange foreboding and walk fearfully, as if she were moving into the jaws of a huge snake that lies at the end of the lane, ready to devour her.

At such a time the very fear that she feels helps a girl to her own destruction, if the forces of evil be abroad. For other powers besides those of mere wayward desire move about her, though unseen. Hands are stretched out of dark corners, that are not human hands. The darkness is all eyes, and when she treads 'tis upon a mandrake that screeches—and an owl passes above. The girl recalls in the darkness the tales that have been told—stories of the visitation of a vampire from the places of the dead. A word has been listened to, that a strange beast has been heard to cry by some and seen to howl by others as it moped under Mr. Mumby's barn wall.

Jenny trembled, but yet she went on. Mrs. Vosper held her, moving slowly in the darkness, as if she did not mind which way she took. She even stood still for a few moments, as if to give Jenny confidence in her ; and in order to beguile the time and to lead Jenny's ideas in the right direction, she began to talk in a merry tone and to tell Jenny about her own early marriage.

' I were married at sixteen,' said Mrs. Vosper, holding Jenny nearer to her, ' and I did beg hard to lie alone thik night.'

Jenny laughed.

' Ah ! I thought 'twould amuse 'ee to hear,' whispered Mrs. Vosper ; ' 'tis a tale I 've never told before, though I mind 'en well enough. 'Twas late, too, when dancing folk was gone shouting and singing, who did all jump and go like big fleas, in parlour —'twas then that I did begin to cry, and did take up me little Prayer Book, that were a Sunday School present, and sit with 'en in me lap before fire. I were a poor little maid, an' me bosom did pant and shake. 'Twas a pretty Prayer Book for a young maid to hold in 's lap so safe. Ah, what strange things we poor maidens do care for ! I did wait and cry, for no man had never done nothing, only kiss me cheek under oak tree.

' And then Vosper did come in from wood-shed. " 'Tis best thee be moving now, married maiden," he said ; and I did carry me little Prayer Book upstairs, still a-crying. 'Twas then I did kneel down by bedside, same as me poor mother 'ave taught. " Stop that whining," Vosper did shout, for 'e had drunk a pretty good drop, "and strip off they clothes, will 'ee?"

'"No man shan't touch me," I said, taking off what I did wear, and creeping into bed, "for Prayer Book will save I from wickedness," and I did lie out wi' Prayer Book in me lap still.

'Ha, ha!' laughed Mrs. Vosper, 'they men bain't afraid of religion. Do 'ee see,' she said, 'there be some one in lane, and I do believe 'tis wold Grunter?'

They passed the large figure of a man standing in the lane like a misplanted tree. He uttered no remark, and gave no heed to a polite reminder from Mrs. Vosper as to what he was said to do out of doors.

' 'E bain't no talker,' she whispered to Jenny; 'Mr. Grunter bain't no talker, and 'is work be silent too.'

Jenny laughed gaily. She knew that, although her father laid the blame of all the Folly Down troubles upon a high One, the folk of the village all blamed Mr. Grunter when anything happened to the girls.

' 'Tis a pretty bird,' said Mrs. Vosper, holding Jenny's arm tightly, 'that Martin Mumby 'ave to give 'ee.'

'Be 'en in a cage?' asked Jenny.

'Why, no,' replied Mrs. Vosper, 'but thee mid 'ave a cage made for 'im, if thee be minded.'

Jenny was willing enough to believe Mrs. Vosper. She walked happily; her fears of the darkness were gone; she wished to see the little bird that she was promised, and meant, as soon as Martin Mumby gave it her, to take it home and feed it in the rectory kitchen with cake crumbs.

Without her being aware of it, Mrs. Vosper was leading Jenny nearer and nearer to the oak tree upon the green.

XV

JENNY CALLS FOR HELP

THE evening was a suitable one for the mischief that was intended, and the oak tree a proper covering for the act.

The tree was an ancient one, and its leaves, that whispered in the moonlight, could tell many a tale of what had happened underneath the boughs of some great and kingly ancestor. There the blood had been shed of many a young girl, dying to pacify the wrath of an angry god, the garlanded priests using their sharp knives, after they had taken toll of the victim in the orthodox manner.

But this tree was the last of them. There was no hope for this tree if it were cut down, for Mr. Mumby's pigs had eaten all the acorns, and no tender branch was budding. If anything happened to the Folly Down oak to destroy it, it would die like a man.

The Mumbys were the chosen priests of the evening, and the plotters knew well enough that a lie or two could easily lay all the blame upon Mr. Grunter. ' Even though the old fool doesn't like war and fighting, no one in Folly Down will believe him,' Martin Mumby had said to his brother.

John Mumby was the elder of the two young gentlemen. He had a handsome, mean face, and a sly look. He always behaved in the grand bullying manner that the sons of large country farmers so

exactly copy from the rich and the mighty who own
the land, as they have always owned it, and give beer
and promises, as they have always given them, to the
earnest voters of happy England during an election.

Both these young gentlemen had the same excel-
lent ideas about life. They beheld with a vast and
awful admiration the doings of the great, and Martin
was never tired of telling a wonderful story of how
when Lord Bullman, being a little confused, after
lunch, as regards the different forms of life around
him, and seeing his loader running for more ammuni-
tion, thought he was a hare and shot him with his
last cartridge. Martin Mumby, riding by, had been
invited to take the keeper's place, and did so with
honour, keeping, however, very near to his lordship.

Before Jenny came out, Martin and John Mumby
were standing under the oak tree, smoking cigarettes
and waiting, with some impatience, for the arrival of
their victim.

Mrs. Vosper led Jenny to the oak tree.

In Folly Down there is a custom, which in most
cases is followed, of the young men and the young
women talking a little together before they begin
really to amuse themselves. In nearly every village
in the world this is thought to be proper, the conversation always beginning in as harmless a manner
as may be.

As soon as Jenny came nearer, John Mumby hid
himself behind the oak tree, and Martin enquired of
Jenny whether she had seen Ann Kiddle lately.

' Oh, she ! ' said Jenny, ' 'tain't often that I do go
about wi' she.'

' They Kiddles do never leave no man alone,'

observed Mrs. Vosper, ' and folk do say that wold
Grunter 'ave been busy again, both wi' the one and
t'other of them.'

Martin Mumby stepped nearer to Jenny. She
asked him whether he had the little bird that Mrs.
Vosper had spoken about.

' Oh yes,' replied Martin, ' I have the little bird.'

Sometimes in the darkness a girl's shape can be
far more provocative than when her form is seen in
the light of day. Jenny's voice, the dimness of her
body, the certainty that, as she was there, his desires
would be satisfied, made Martin the more eager to
begin. He threw a half-burnt cigarette upon the
grass. But there were steps passing, and some one
laughed. In Mr. Meek's cottage a light had come
in the upper window. A little farther away a bucket
clattered. Luke Bird had gone to his well to fetch
a little water.

After filling his bucket, Luke Bird held his lantern
over the water. He thought he saw the face of
Jenny in the water. She was smiling up at him, and
he wondered, supposing her to be at the rectory,
what she was doing. She might be making a meat
pie for supper.

Luke had always liked meat pies, but as he
couldn't cook pastry he never had one. Mr.
Grobe, he thought, was a happy man to be able to
eat Jenny's meat pies ! She would cut up the meat
seriously, and then roll out the flour, and presently
there would be a very pleasant smell of the pie baking.

Some one screamed.

' A girl,' thought Luke ; ' but no girl comes
to me.'

Under the oak tree Martin Mumby touched Jenny.

'What be doing?' she asked.

A cough came from the farther side of the green.

'That be wold Grunter,' said Mrs. Vosper, grasping Jenny's arm. Jenny screamed, and John Mumby came out of the darkness and stood beside her.

'Wold Grunter be at work wi' 'ee,' laughed Mrs. Vosper. ''Tis only Grunter who do hold 'ee so close.'

Village sounds that come in the darkness need an interpreter. A scream, a call, a laugh, a sob, may be so slight a matter that few who happen to hear them would regard them as being of the least importance.

Mr. Meek heard Jenny scream when he was on his way to the inn, and was glad to hear it. He hoped that the scream might become a nice story one day. Squire Mumby, on his way to the inn too, heard a struggle going on under the oak, but he supposed that the boys might be chasing a tom cat, and so he passed by, taking no notice.

Jenny struggled and freed herself, but John Mumby took her firmly in his arms and carried her to the mossy bed under the tree.

John Mumby held Jenny down; he pressed his hand over her mouth. She bit his hand.

Jenny cried. She even called out to God for help. This call of hers set John Mumby a-laughing. Mrs. Vosper crept nearer, but Martin ordered her off.

These strong young men were used to holding live things that struggled for freedom.

Martin began to tease Jenny.

99

'Here's a pretty maid come out to see a little sparrow,' he said jeeringly.

Jenny cried out again, naming Some One who is said to be the Protector of innocence.

'Maybe He'll come to save you,' laughed Martin. John cursed his brother.

'What be waiting for?' he asked him.

'Grunter be busy,' sniggered Mrs. Vosper.

A loud cry came out of the darkness where Mr. Grunter was standing.

'World be ending,' shouted Mr. Grunter, 'and God be writing 'Is t'other name in sky.'

Martin released Jenny and looked up towards the northern sky. He could only stare blankly at what he saw, for what, indeed, could have been more unexpected than writings written there?

When Mr. Grunter had called, Martin only supposed that the Shelton policeman, in a fit of curious absent-mindedness, had walked towards Folly Down, and certainly the end of the world was near as likely to come as he. Although Martin Mumby could ride a horse, he wasn't in other ways one of the bravest.

He looked at the sky and trembled. But John reassured him.

'It's nothing,' he said. 'It's only a name.'

Mrs. Vosper was more annoyed than frightened at the interruption. She had witnessed the beginning of a play, and she very much wished to see the end of it.

''Tain't true,' she whispered, 'what wold Grunter do say, for 'tis writ in Bible that there mid be a sound of trumpets before world do end.'

But Jenny had crept away, and was gone.

XVI

THE REVEREND NICHOLAS GROBE

EVER since his wife died, the Reverend Nicholas Grobe had looked at the world in a sorrowful manner.

He allowed his beard to grow, and one morning, when he trimmed it with a pair of scissors, he saw to his surprise that it was grey.

To most people Mr. Grobe's behaviour was both gentle and loving, and he had worn the same black tie for twenty years. The days that are, to many, so rough and rude, passed by very easily for him, for sorrow is a good leveller, at least when the first burst of it is over.

Mr. Grobe had had a better reason than most men have for going into the Church of England.

The Folly Down living was in the gift of the Grobe family, and for a great number of years had been occupied by one of them. One day, when his profession was being discussed, Mr. Grobe's father enquired of Nicholas whether he preferred figs or thistles.

Nicholas understood the question, for the Folly Down rectory possessed a fine kitchen-garden wall, against which a fig tree grew, which, being in such a sunny place, ripened good figs.

' Thank you, sir,' replied Master Nicholas, ' I prefer figs ' : and so he went to Cambridge.

As a general rule, Mr. Grobe took tea with his daughter. He had done so on the evening when our story commenced; and when the young lady left him to take her bath, Mr. Grobe entered his study and closed the door quietly behind him.

Mr. Grobe never hurried over what he did. He filled his pipe slowly and lit it with a spill that he took from a silver cup he kept upon the mantelpiece, which he had somehow or other managed to win at Cambridge. This done, he settled himself in his chair before the fire, and allowed himself to contemplate, in a mild manner, the affairs of his people—that strange collection of human creatures that formed the population of Folly Down.

They were entirely unreal, for the most part, and, with two or three exceptions, they lived lives of moderate happiness.

All paths lead to the churchyard. Squire Mumby, though he went towards the inn, was really going in the opposite direction ; and Mr. Meek's granddaughter, Letty, had only that very morning, as if to show the place where all living things went, crawled through the churchyard gate and sat straddle-legged upon a grave, pretending that she was mounted upon a very fine horse. Mr. Grobe had seen her and allowed the child to stay, for she seemed to be happy.

Mr. Grobe liked the long hours of a winter's evening. He resembled the poet, William Cowper, in his love for them. He used to wish that these peaceful hours were everlasting, for in them he could wonder about God, even though he did not now believe in Him.

The domestic sounds of an evening have a way of

telling a peaceful gentleman, who doesn't always sit and stare at his clock, how the time goes. Mr. Grobe knew very well the evening sounds at the rectory. He knew Jenny's movements, and the quick hurry she was always in to shut the back door when she turned out the cat. Jenny would always clamber upstairs as if the stairs were a mountain that she was in danger of falling off, as, indeed, she sometimes did, and she would sometimes stop and talk to a can of water as if it were alive. It was easy enough for Mr. Grobe to tell Tamar's step in the passage from Jenny's, for there was a determination in the way that Tamar walked. A firm tread she had, a tread that told that she wouldn't be contented with a little, and that any one who made love to her must be without fear.

Besides the girls, the rats would scamper, too, in the old walls of the house, that were roomy enough to harbour an army of these creatures. They preferred the evening time for their romps, so much so, that Richard Grobe, the last rector and uncle to Nicholas, would amuse himself by loading an old horse pistol and shooting leaden bullets into the walls when the rats stampeded.

' Would you carry off my sermons to make your dirty nests ? ' he would shout angrily, and, waving the pistol, he would shoot a bullet into the wall.

But he must have at last bethought him that even rats deserve more kindness, for when one came out of a hole and cleaned its whiskers upon the hearthrug, Mr. Richard Grobe begged its pardon in Latin—for he was a scholar—for all past offences, and put the pistol to his own forehead and shot himself.

Death is a great master among the artists; though he can be so common and vulgar as to kill every one, yet he can give each experiment of his such a new colour that, seen by a husband or wife or brother who survives, the blow falls so heavily as to be regarded as utterly unnatural.

Mrs. Nicholas Grobe had died with terrible suddenness one Christmas time. She, as well as little Tamar, was very fond of looking into shop windows, and especially so when the shops were trimmed for the Christ's holiday. Tamar, gazing into one window where Christmas cards were exhibited, called to her mother, who was near by, to come and look.

In the window was a large card upon which an angel was painted. He looked a very nice young man, with fine white wings. His hair was gold, and Tamar worshipped him. She had a sixpence that her father had given her to spend, and she bought the angel.

At the railway station a porter brushed past her, and the card fell upon the line. Tamar at once, with a cry, jumped after it as a passing express rushed in. Her mother jumped too to save her, and succeeded in pushing the child out of danger, though the express caught her own foot under it, and she died bloodily.

Tamar had killed her mother because she loved an angel.

Years went by, but Mr. Grobe still pondered over this unnecessary accident. It seemed so useless and silly. Why should Tamar have jumped after the Christmas card exactly at the moment when the express rushed by? Had the train been five seconds later, they would both have been saved. What did God do to stop that train?

One person, after Mrs. Grobe's death, came to ask for her, expecting to find her alive. This was Hugh, her brother. He had run away from an office, and had gone on, by one means or another, until he reached the wilds of Tibet, and remained there, hearing nothing from home, except that his pretty sister had married a clergyman. One morning, when the air was still and cold, he rested on the grass in Tibet, looking at a wonderful red flower, and as he looked at the flower, he longed to kiss his sister Alice. With this idea in his heart, he left his solitude and at length arrived at Folly Down, in the springtime, and more than a year after her accident.

It was a pleasant evening in May, and masses of bluebells coloured every little copse when young Hugh found his way up the chalk lane and then descended the Folly Down hill. He was happy because he had come so far to kiss Alice, and now he knew he was near to her.

His long journey had seemed so small a matter with so perfect a creature, whose lips were like red poppy flowers, at the end of it. She had always been a little naughtily inclined, even to a mild brother, and after the kiss, when her good husband was safe in his study, they could walk affectionately upon the downs, and even rest a little if the grass were dry.

At the bottom of the lane, and near to the green, Hugh came upon Mrs. Vosper, who was watching eagerly the clothes hung up by the Kiddles upon their line, and was even counting the garments, commenting upon each as she did so, in an interesting manner.

Hugh, who hadn't noticed the rectory when he descended the hill, harmlessly enquired of Mrs. Vosper where Mrs. Grobe lived.

Mrs. Vosper had just said to herself that ' girls be girls, though they be Kiddles.' She now turned, with a sly grin, to the gentleman who had spoken to her.

' The lady do bide in a pretty home,' she said, and pointed to the churchyard.

' She is in church, is she ? ' asked Hugh. ' A week-day service, perhaps, but the church doors look to be fast closed.'

' Thee 'll soon see where she do bide, if thee go up there,' said Mrs. Vosper, smiling ; and as soon as Hugh was gone, she nodded to the Kiddles' clothes and remarked merrily, ' 'Twas a good thing she's doings were put a stop to by they little worms.'

Hugh didn't stay long in Folly Down. He saw her grave, and got no kiss out of that. He made the best of his way to Tibet once more, and soon found a grave there for himself.

But it hardly needed this incident—for he was told about the visitor by Mrs. Vosper some weeks after Hugh was gone—to remind Mr. Grobe, day in and day out, where his wife had gone to.

She had been exactly the wife to make the kind of man he was—a man of harmless mien—entirely happy. She had with her all the wild, naughty ways of a spoilt child that knew nothing, only love, and he loved her the more, of course, because that was all that she cared for. She was never tired of laughing at him, and he, good man, liked to be laughed at. Her husband, with all the fear of his own happiness, amused her; and the people of Folly Down amused her too, and especially the babies. Her own Tamar —perhaps because Tamar was her own baby—she hardly noticed, but the other brats that she visited appeared so surprised to be living, so odd and so sulky, as if they would have been far better pleased to have been pigs than babies, that Alice Grobe was never tired of laughing at them.

But she was, even with all her laughter and naughty ways, just the one to be—more often than she knew—a saving help in time of trouble, and she was just beginning to teach Tamar the best way to tease and torment her father when she died.

Of course, the people of the village had watched Mrs. Grobe, to see what she did, as soon as she came to live amongst them, but they did not have much to say about her until after she was gone. It was then that her behaviour was spoken of, though not often very kindly, although she had, during her time at Folly Down, certainly saved the life of one man.

The man was, curiously enough, Mr. Grunter, though this was before he made a name as a lover, and in the days when he was only spoken of as, and thought himself to be, nothing.

'I be nothing,' said Mr. Grunter to his own garden gate-post, 'and so I mid hang meself.'

Mr. Grunter was a man who kept his word. He found a rope in his wood-shed and proceeded to the oak tree. The hour was late; the summer stars were out, and no one could have been more surprised than Mr. Grunter when, on looking up to find the right bough to tie the rope to, he saw Alice Grobe, nestled amorously in a fork of the tree. Mr.

Grunter could only stare at her, for she appeared to be wearing only one garment, and that a transparent one.

Mrs. Grobe, who had a very ready discernment, knew what he had come to do, and instead of fondling the bough again, she caressed Mr. Grunter.

No one could have been more astonished at such a proceeding—for the lady was as near naked as could be—than the would-be suicide. He let the rope drop.

'Well, Mr. Grunter,' laughed Alice, 'I'm a woman, aren't I? and a woman is better than the gallows-tree.'

Mr. Grunter regarded her in a very awkward manner, and with some fear too, and when she slipped away from him, he could only mutter, as he turned to go home, ' I did go out to murder meself, and I do walk home an adulterer, or next best to 'en.'

At his own gate he stopped and looked at the post.

' Perhaps 'tis news to 'ee,' he said, ' that a lady be made the same outside as a poor 'oman. . . .'

Mr. Grobe looked into the fire ; he had put into it an old log, and the flames from the coals curled about the wood that was very dry. He watched the flames, beholding how they clung round the wood, licked it, sprang up once again, and wound themselves about it. He heard a knock at the back door ; there were steps outside in the lane, and then the clock upon the mantelpiece struck six.

Time was moving as it usually moved upon a long November evening, moving all too quickly for him.

Mr. Grobe began to wonder at what evening hour, had he any choice in the matter, he would prefer time to stay, so that his thoughts, that at those times were not all unhappy, might stay with him.

He wouldn't wish to choose too late an hour for the longest one. He preferred to be meditatively inclined, rather than sleepily, when time stopped. He wanted to choose the time when the tobacco tasted the sweetest, and when the deeper night hadn't put its hand upon the fire.

He wouldn't wish any thought, however long and pleasing, to remind him that bed-time was come ; ' bed-time ' that, in the way of symbolism, might be called ' grave-time ' too.

He might even, he thought, if the time halted at the right hour, sit and brood during the long evening, and discover his lost God, and even bring Him into that very room, and sit Him upon that chair and get Him to talk about the weather out-of-doors.

Alice was in her grave, and the Almighty in His, but the lamplight always cast a timid doubt upon His burial ; and if a doubt lay there, then why, even she might come to him again, if He came.

Such feelings, even if they be but poetry and a lie—and, for that matter, a lie may be as immortal as a truth—occupied Mr. Grobe and gave to his thoughts an everlasting trend. A time of quietude that is full of the right contentment, can solace, just as the fierce agony, the vast joy of passion, can arm each participator with so holy an ecstasy that the valley of the shadow is passed in a moment, and the yellow sun is seen rising over the mountains of eternity.

But even with death defeated in one manner or another, modest death still has his set duties to perform, and immortality, viewed in passion or solitude, can only be but the patches of sunlight seen upon a dull, hot summer's day, when thin, soft clouds are above. But these patches should at least console us a little for the loss of ourselves.

Folly Down rectory was very silent now, and even the rats, as if each had taken to its hole a Latin grammar to study stolen from the late Richard Grobe, were utterly still.

'Perhaps,' thought Mr. Grobe, 'the clock may stop at seven,' for that hour he regarded as the most happy.

He would try to forget that Tamar had killed his wife. He wished his daughter the happiness that she longed for. He hoped an angel would come to her, 'for, after all,' and Mr. Grobe smiled, 'such things have happened before in the world.'

XVII

THE ANGEL INN

Mr. Thomas Bunce, the landlord of the Angel Inn at Folly Down, was a gentleman who, by the appearance of him, could be merry in all his parts. His nose was a little one, but his grin was wide ; his girth was wide too, and his eyes used to wink only to amuse themselves.

If one looked at him for long enough it was possible to get the idea that some one had cut a face in an old eighteen-gallon barrel that had been left to the mercy of the weather out-of-doors for a great number of years, and then set it upon legs, and being pleased with his work, had named the thing Mr. Thomas Bunce.

Mr. Bunce was merry ; he was merry because he had his own method and means of getting rid of all the troubles of the world. His way was to blame God for them all.

It was said in Folly Down that Mr. Bunce had started life as a sow gelder—a profession that his father had followed very honourably—but had later, out of respect for the Church, taken service as butler to a rich Dean.

' You must be a father to the maidens,' said Dean Ashborne, when Bunce entered his service, ' for though God is good, I am afraid that women are very bad. You must check their naughtiness.'

' Now with pigs——' Bunce was beginning, but the Dean mildly interrupted him.

'You must tell me if these young women mis-
behave before you ; they will probably do so if you
are not firm with them.'

A few weeks later Mr. Bunce appeared before
his master.

'You told me that God was good,' said Mr.
Bunce, ' but Bessy, who is very bad, complains that
something happened to her in church during sermon
time, and no one else would dare——'

Dean Ashborne held up his hand gravely.

' Bunce, you had better marry Bessy,' he said.

At the door Bunce shouted the parting word :

' 'Tis 'Is doing, and that I do know.'

' All things are,' answered the Dean, and waved
a good-bye.

Besides possessing a nature that blamed, Thomas
Bunce also owned a nature that questioned. He
questioned the right of troubles being brought
home to him that were said to have happened in
church, and he also questioned the right of Mr. Luke
Bird to love his daughter Jenny—who arrived as a
consequence.

But honest Bunce had married Bessy for two
reasons more important than the mere matter of
Jenny being expected.

Bessy's home was in the same village as his when
he worked at his former trade, and he soon discovered
that no one could pickle onions better than she, and
also that she possessed a grandfather clock.

This clock, when they were married, was brought
to the Angel Inn, which Bunce had purchased. It
was indeed a wonderful clock, with a splendid sun
painted upon it, that shone at all hours, but never

shone too hot. The clock had belonged to Bessy's grandfather, Mr. Holly of Shelton, who, in his old age, did nothing else but watch the pendulum swing, and nod in time with it. The clock was called Mr. Holly out of respect to Mrs. Bunce's grandfather, for that old gentleman was widely remembered in the neighbourhood as a person of consequence. It had ever been regarded as a compliment of the highest kind if Bessy, during Mr. Holly's last years, invited a friend to walk into the cottage in order to watch the nodding ways of her grandfather, who would begin as soon as he descended the shaky stairs from his attic, and continue to nod in time with the clock until he fell asleep. Mr. Holly didn't nod in vain, for he left behind a firm impression in Shelton that he was both a deserving and a thoughtful man.

Mr. Bunce was pleased with the clock when it came, but he soon grew suspicious of it, because it went so slowly during the daytime, and so fast in the evening, which was, of course, the best time that he had for selling his drink and being happy with his friends. As soon as his suspicions were aroused, he watched the clock most carefully, in order to see that no one came into the room to tamper with it.

When the inn opened at six o'clock, the hands moved in their usual slow daytime manner, but when Squire Mumby and Mr. Kiddle were come, and perhaps Mr. Grunter and Mr. Meek, and jests and tales and good beer were going, then the clock—and who could Mr. Bunce blame for that, unless it were God ? —raced round so fast, the minutes after the hours, that, in the shortest time imaginable, the house would

have to be closed. Then Mr. Bunce was forced to
lock the door, reluctantly enough we may be sure,
behind the bulky form of Mr. Mumby, who needed
time for his drink, and to stand dolefully and listen
to the steps outside that were soon departed down
the lane.

But while the evening stayed, Thomas Bunce's
smile—a grin it often was when he stooped to draw
the ale from the barrel in order to give the cup into
Dealer Kiddle's hand—was a pleasure to see, and
Mr. Bunce's rolling oaths, that grew rounder and
deeper as the time went on, were a pleasure to
hear.

' 'Tain't fair to move on folk's clocks,' Mr. Bunce
had once said to Squire Mumby, when the hands all
too gently came near to ten.

' Perhaps Grunter may have touched the clock, or
Luke Bird may have crept in, unnoticed,' suggested
Mr. Kiddle.

' Oh, 'e ! ' replied Mr. Bunce angrily, ' and what
do 'ee think thik Bird said to I woon Sunday ? '

' How should I know,' replied the dealer, ' unless
you tell me ? '

' Why, I heard him say this,' shouted Bunce,
' that if only landlord had been born a goat he might
have been saved.'

The Angel Inn parlour was no meagre place.
There was no paltry narrowness about it, for it possessed a larger circumference than any of the neighbouring village taverns could boast of.

In those happy past times, when England was free
and men could drink, and no gentleman was ever
sent to prison, half a dozen squires, whose horses

were held by ragged boys in the lane, would sit and drink and talk bawdily—being away from their wives—for as long as they chose.

The wide, open hearth at the Angel, still the same as in those days, had a tale to tell of Squire Teedon, who owned Shelton Grange, and who, one Christmas Eve, carried into the Angel parlour a large sack full of tom-cats and threw them to roast alive upon a faggot of dry furze, to the immense entertainment of all the party assembled. One protest—for one of the cats happened to be hers—was received from Mrs. Tobiah, the stout landlady, who had never been known in all her life to refuse a gentleman a certain favour, and so wasn't afraid of them. Mrs. Tobiah remarked that Squire Teedon should be sat in the fire himself for doing such a deed, though, as soon as Mr. Teedon put his arm about her and kissed her becomingly, she smiled and said that she 'wouldn't, for the world, that any part of such a fine fellow should be burnt,' and proceeded to listen, with as much pleasure as the rest, to the sizzling of the cats' fur.

The Angel parlour was hardly changed since those happy days, and even the very pewter mugs used were the same. The room possessed, as in those old days, the same genial appearance, and always welcomed a traveller.

Of all the furniture at an inn the pictures, hung upon the parlour walls, are the most interestedly regarded by any customer; for as the drink goes down, so the pictures become distincter, until the figures or scenes depicted become more and more alive : King Edward draws his weapon—a sword—and holds it aloft ; a lion wags its tail when about to spring.

Over the great fireplace at the Angel Inn a large picture hung, that portrayed Columbus, in a black velvet dress and finely starched ruffles, discovering America. This painting was very proper and life-like. Columbus was kneeling upon the deck of his ship, and thanking God—(Landlord Bunce always thought him a great fool, though he never liked to say so, for the picture was his)—for bringing him and his sailors to their journey's end, or, at least, so near to it that he could rope his ship to a large American fir tree. That was the grandest picture in the room, but there was another.

The other was charmingly sweet and Victorian. It was a picture of a young lady with a mild contour, wearing a long nightgown trimmed with deep lace, and holding a rose in her right hand.

There was always a proper precedence to use in the important matter of a customer's gazing at these two pictures.

During the first part of a merry evening, when strong, sturdy, martial, and adventurous thoughts prevailed in the mind, Columbus would be looked at, because he was a sailor and a man, and the second anchor, that the sailors were about to let go into a frothy wave, would be properly admired. But as time went on, the drink changed these excited and noble feelings into more gentle and amorous ones, so that those present would glance slyly, hoping none noticed, at the young lady's nightdress. Soon such looks would grow bolder, and certain of the company would even, ere the evening ended, come to regard the great mariner as but a dull fellow who would have done much better and served his country in a far wiser manner had he discovered a few maidens instead of a continent.

For what greater pleasure could there be—and Mr. Meek's thoughts, because he never spoke them aloud, always went the fastest—than in imagining such a young lady walking, in that very same night-dress that reached to the toes, through the haycocks upon a summer's evening. Mr. Meek would see himself, though in a glass darkly, inviting her to stay and rest with him upon the hay, for the stars now shone, while he, good man, would bethink him of an evening hymn suitable to such an occasion.

There were two pleasant settles placed beside the fire in the Angel parlour, and a stout oaken table was near and between them, upon which Mr. Bunce placed the mugs that he filled so glibly.

Only on the rarest occasions did his wife enter the parlour, for Mrs. Thomas Bunce hardly ever came out of the kitchen. She loved the vinegar as much as Mr. Bunce loved the onions that she pickled in it. Her husband had a way, too, of reminding her of things, and of how she had once said that she had been visited, in a very strange manner, in a church.

' 'Tis perhaps,' Mr. Bunce would remark, if his lady happened to put her head in at the parlour door, ' a good thing in some ways for many a poor plain woman that He bain't particular.'

She would retire at once, and would stand beside a stained and shaky table and peel onions till she cried. Mr. Bunce had certainly never exaggerated her plainness in his remarks, for her face that might once have been pretty was now thin and pinched, and her jaws seemed to be the exact counterpart of a pair of nut-crackers.

But Mrs. Bunce would always try to look happy when her daughter Jenny came to see her, and then she wiped her eyes that had been weeping onion tears, with a greasy towel.

When November comes and shuts out, all too rudely, the last days of summer, locking the door after them and hiding the key in the grass under a primrose root, so that the spring may have a cold hunt for it, there were always those in Folly Down who could turn for comfort to the parlour at the Angel.

In the safety of this parlour, exempt from the world's cares, there would be always something of a merry or sad kind to be listened to when the door was opened ; some tale or other that at least was compounded of words for the most part, though sometimes signs were used, and these had always a country meaning that those who had eyes to see with could understand. But if nothing was said or hinted at, the grandfather clock was sure to be ticking, for even if Dealer Kiddle's tongue was silent the clock ticked. And, besides the clock, there would be Mr. Meek to be noticed, buttoning his coat in order to keep all the warmth in him that he got out of the fire. It was Mr. Meek's nature to receive what he could get, and, above all things, he delighted in receiving something that he hadn't paid for. He was always surprised (far more so than Henry Fielding when, as he narrates in his *Voyage to Lisbon*, he was charged for wind in his bill) that he, good Meek, was never charged by Mr. Bunce for flame. Had he been landlord, a charge would certainly have been made for that item—though, perhaps, no direct one—for during the winter, in order to recompense himself for heating his shop with an oil stove, Mr. Meek always raised the price of tape and black currant jam.

Now and again, at the inn, Mr. Meek would look slyly at Mr. Bunce, as if he were trying to make up his mind whether the landlord were a conscious benefactor to his kind or a mere fool in business. But at least, whichever it was, Mr. Meek wished to receive all the benefit for as long a time as he could, and so he would open his coat to the fire and button it again a dozen times of an evening, and he hardly ever opened his mouth to speak, for fear lest the stolen warmth should escape at that aperture.

The right people were usually met at the Angel— the proper companions of a quickly passing, though long, winter's evening—who knew well enough that the good God was in His heaven and that naughty young women were upon the earth, and that both the one and the others had been brought into being so that Mr. Bunce might have some one to blame, and Mr. Grunter something to meddle with.

The drugged, solid air of the Angel Inn parlour became more and more human as the evening progressed. The empty, wide spaces without, all the firmament and all the stars, were what they pleased to be. They had the black night as a companion, but Grunter, Kiddle, Meek, and Squire Mumby had the lamp and the fire. And the blue smoke of Mr. Mumby's pipe, rising in rings, proved that life thus lived was happiness, and that all those stars, together with their Creator, were but a monster depravity in the black sky.

All news that came to the inn was welcome ; indeed, any word was welcome, for, with a decent allowance of beer in the pate, no sound, let alone no word, need pass unnoticed.

A cow, named there by Kiddle, became a blessed, a hallowed creature, though it was but a lame one ; and a simple pig, that had eaten its own young for its breakfast, became a creature with an ingenious and soul-awakening appetite.   All the world outside and all that happened there would be changed into an odd fantasy as the beer flowed, and its inhabitants—those living and those dead—would become but puppets that could be jerked just as one chose into the inn, and thrown out again when their tales were told.

Thus it was that a beetle that, by its destiny, happened to crawl over Mr. Kiddle's great hand, provoked mirth and laughter, and even, what was more strange, a wise remark from Mr. Meek, as the dealer shook the beetle off his hand into the burning coals, that ' the insect was given a nice warm bed for which it hadn't paid a farthing.'

Then it was that reality, that foe to joy, was sent a-packing, and the wayward mind of man, that loves its pleasantries and will listen to anything so long as it be foolishly spoken, toyed with its own shadow that mimicked the substance, and so smiled at the senseless labours of the day.

At the Angel Inn the fable of the new birth had its believers, for, indeed, in Mr. Bunce's parlour folk became new-born and wore a cloth of another colour, for even Mr. Grunter's old boots took a new hue to them, and the caked mud upon them became humanised.   The hand that held the mug to the gross lips was changed. It was no more the work-ridden hand that had delved with the spade all the hours of the day ; the hand had a higher calling now, it served at a festival. The terrible urge of ever-recurring toil was here laid aside—for all such toil of an ordinary man in this world of rivalry makes the blood bitter— and the honest company can now at least be reminded, by some black spider asleep upon the ceiling, of those wise beasts, the gods, who reflect, but never stir, who ever lie still and allow the sunlight to warm them and the cold stars to cool, through all eternity.

And now that this November day has slipped into its grave, Thomas Bunce sets a match to his parlour fire. And we—we will have no garish sunshine in our story, but only a long evening to prepare us for the everlasting night.

XVIII

MR. KIDDLE HOPES TO DEAL

It happened sometimes that Mr. James Vosper, the husband of the lady whose interest in life we have already described, would do a brave thing. Indeed, no husband had more need of a little courage, for ever since she had compelled him, by threats, to go to church—and that wedding eve, it was the poor man who held a Prayer Book in his hand and not she—he had been but a slave and worse used than a dog.

Even though he believed all his wife said, even against the exact evidence of his own eyes, about Mr. Grunter, and always repeated it, as she told him to do, yet obedience to her wishes made his life no easier. She refused him sugar in his tea, and though he had always liked clean ways, he was forced to feed literally in the dirt.

Mr. Vosper's only hope was the Angel Inn, and his only act of courage was to get himself there. But this act he rarely accomplished, and if he did venture, he would enter the inn in a dejected manner, like a pariah dog who creeps under a rich man's table to feed upon the crumbs. But, once there, the genial warmth of the place would cause Mr. Vosper to forget in some measure his usage at home, and he would venture a remark, saying, of course, what he supposed his wife would like him to say, though he would first touch his forehead with his finger and look humbly at his master, Mr. Mumby, for whom he worked as a day labourer.

Mr. Vosper's countenance was a small one, and his frame small too, and his look, if you could get at it through the hair that nearly covered his face, was both mild and forgiving.

There was a queer fancy in Mr. Vosper's mind, and this may account for his one act of courage. This fancy may have been acquired by his sitting so long of an evening in the darkness of his wood-shed, for he was rarely allowed a candle there, while the parlour company were amusing each other. Mr. Vosper's fancy, bred of the darkness, was nothing less than that, to his thinking, the Angel Inn was paradise, and that if he could only choose the right evening, he might meet God there. But so far, though he ventured as often as he was able, yet he had never been lucky enough to meet any one who might, by a bold stretching of the imagination, be called the Father. And so Mr. Vosper—who really only wanted to tell God what a fine wife he had, and to ask a small question—would join a little in the conversation, and then wander out disappointedly into the night.

He had now made another sally, for anger had given him courage. Mrs. Vosper had this evening spoken to him more rudely than ever, nipping him in a very vital spot—his pride—for she had informed him that he was too great a fool even to load a waggon. This was a great insult, because it was a true one, for never, either in haytime or harvest, did any waggon loaded by Mr. Vosper arrive intact at the rickyard. And if any load turned over in the lane,

that load would be sure to be his. The knowledge
that he couldn't, however much he tried—and he had
tried for near forty years—load a haycart, was a sore
trial to this good man, and, did he meet God at the
inn—who, Mr. Vosper felt sure, must understand
farming—he hoped to lead Him aside and whisper
his question.

The company at the inn were now seated, and
each one, as was proper, looked at Columbus, who
prayed still.

Mr. Mumby, being the owner of many a fair acre
—indeed, the whole of Folly Down was his—had, of
course, the place of honour near the fire. Squire
Mumby was seventy, and he carried his years well.
He liked country conversation, being a direct descendant of Mr. Justice Shallow, and his cheek-
bones would stick out and shine, and his moustache
would curl, and his dull eyes become merry when
any village doings—that were not proper ones—
were mentioned.

Opposite to Mr. Mumby, a cunning, blinking eye
and a red, blotched face expressed, more truly than
any statement of fact could do, that Mr. Kiddle dealt
in cattle. Besides his looks, Mr. Kiddle showed his
profession in his speech, for if he had any remark to
make, he would begin with a stifled shout, 'Whoo-
ho-whoop!' as if he were directing all the cows in
the world into his own field.

As a marked contrast to the demeanour of the
dealer, Mr. Meek, the Folly Down shopkeeper, had
a look that was both modest and simple, and deceived many when he weighed up the rice. Mr.
Meek sat like a mild sundew, drawing into himself

the warmth of the fire and the talk, that was often warm too.

As soon as the company were assembled, the grandfather clock told them the time—it was half-past six.

The evening had settled in very quietly for all present, like many another after a day in which no accident of importance, or any especial piece of good fortune, had happened. Squire Mumby had slept as usual, with his daily paper in his hand, after his midday dinner, while the cat purred upon the hearth ; and Kiddle, having visited his stock and set a price upon them to show a handsome profit, had returned home again.

But even though nothing unusual had happened, there had been that day a curious feeling of expect-ancy in the air of Folly Down, so that Kiddle even, passing an old barn in a field, had peeped in through a chink in the boards, in order to see if his wife, who after the death of Ada had become melancholy, might not be hanging there. Even though she was not, Mr. Kiddle still felt that something was going to happen, and he supposed it possible that a calf with six legs might be born of the lame cow.

Mr. Mumby hadn't looked at Columbus when he came into the inn ; he had an important matter in his mind that would not permit him to look at a mere picture. He wished to make a purchase.

The purchase that he wished to make was nothing else than a fine bull calf that he had seen that very morning in Mr. Kiddle's field ; and to show what was in his mind, without committing himself, Mr. Mumby had merely remarked as he entered,

' 'Tain't no old bull that I be in want of '—and the talk turned to Mr. Grunter.

No one so far had appeared to notice Mr. Vosper, who had reached to no eminence in village life— though this evening was to raise him a little ; but he now both wished to be heard and seen, for fear that he might be so far forgotten and dismissed from all minds as to be actually trodden upon.

Mr. Vosper touched his forehead to Mr. Mumby; he coughed; he slowly counted his fingers; he spoke.

' 'Tis a strange fancy to consider,' said Mr. Vosper, ' that all they pretty Folly Down maidens do take up wi' wold Grunter.'

' A bull,' remarked Mr. Mumby, ' be a bull, and Grunter, I do fancy, be a man.'

' An old woon,' replied Mr. Vosper respectfully.

Mr. Meek leaned forward in his chair ; he held his coat apart ; he drew it together and buttoned it tightly ; he sucked and swallowed as if, besides the warmth, he had also buttoned in Vosper's last words.

Mr. Vosper coughed and spat. He had scented onions, and believed that Landlord Bunce was coming, and he wished to be seen and recognised. Vosper was right in his conjecture. Some one was swearing in the passage, and Mr. Thomas Bunce rolled into the parlour. He had been busy in his shed, and he now carried a large bag of onions into the kitchen—the way there was through the parlour —where Bessy Bunce stood ready to peel them.

Mr. Bunce always arrived in this rolling manner, as if the inn, that was a strong enough old house, were a ship riding a gale. As soon as he had safely delivered his onions, Thomas Bunce placed a jug of drink that Mr. Mumby had ordered upon the parlour table. He welcomed his guests, shouting out each name and nodding at the owners, and then turned and looked suspiciously at the grandfather clock. He was aware of its naughty manners, and believed that it would soon begin to go faster.

Mr. Vosper was now grown more resolute, and was beginning to feel himself a man. He had strengthened his thoughts by counting his fingers. Even though he couldn't load a waggon properly he believed he could count. He had discovered this fact in the darkness of his wood-shed. He had counted his fingers there, and correctly, so that he could inform himself that he was not entirely without faculties so long as his two hands remained to prove it.

'I bain't nor good at loading,' Mr. Vosper had told himself, 'but I can count.'

He told himself so now, and he spoke the more boldly.

'Me wife do blame Grunter for all that a bull do do, an' there bain't nor maid in village that 'e 'aven't followed down lane, so me woman do say, to do 'is own will wi' 'em.'

Thomas Bunce had listened. He now observed Vosper curiously, and rolled near to him, regarding him importantly, as if he wished to ask him a serious question. Bunce touched Mr. Vosper, he shook his coat, he wished to have all his attention.

'Listen to I,' said Mr. Bunce, 'for 'tain't often that thee do talk here, and folk do say that all of thee's evening time be spent in wood-shed.'

'I be here now,' murmured Mr. Vosper.

Mr. Bunce held up his hand.

' There bain't much that thee can do,' he said, 'and when thee do load a waggon, 'tis only to turn 'en over, and though thee do count thee be only a fool.'

Mr. Vosper nodded.

' But a fool who be married,' remarked Mr. Bunce, ' can sometimes answer like a wise man.'

Mr. Vosper was going to speak, but the landlord again held up his hand.

' I do ask this of thee,' said Mr. Bunce. ' Be so good as to speak and to tell we who 'tis that should be blamed for baby who do crawl on dealer's doorstep, and who do belong to Phœbe Kiddle, and bain't no more like wold Grunter than a kitten be like a pig ? '

' 'Tis Grunter's,' replied Mr. Vosper stoutly.

' No, 'tain't,' said Mr. Bunce, holding his head higher than he was wont to do as he spoke, ' 'tis God's.'

The company were silent. They looked astonished, for though they knew that the landlord's habit was to blame God for the many accidents in life, yet this particular trouble that had come to the Kiddles he hadn't so far laid to the Almighty's charge.

Mr. Kiddle, who up to that moment had been turning over in his mind the best way to get the better of the rich Mumby in the matter of the bull calf that he had to sell, now turned hurriedly to Mr. Bunce, a little aghast at his suggestion.

' I do know 'tis true, for she's baby do crawl,' he said, ' that our Phœbe have had a maid's misfortune, but I did never know till this moment that landlord do blame 'E in skies for they sort of dealings.'

' Maybe 'E bain't up in clouds this evening time,' remarked Mr. Vosper prophetically, ' and 'E may want a word wi' we folk.'

Mr. Meek started. He was aware that the flame from Mr. Bunce's coal was not the only favour that he had received for nothing. He had been told as a child that God gave things away, but he never believed it. God being wise, as Mr. Meek supposed Him to be, would always expect a price to be paid for goods supplied. The summer sun a few months ago had ripened Mr. Meek's green peas, and the rains had watered them. The Shelton doctor, an honest man, was wont to carry round his own bills. 'Suppose,' thought Mr. Meek, ' God took to copying the doctor and brought a bill to me ? '

Mr. Mumby looked at Mr. Kiddle. He believed him, and not without reason, to be a very sly man. He supposed that he would try to use the turn that the conversation had taken to get the better of his friend in a deal. Perhaps he might be going to affirm that God was related in the same fatherly manner to his bull calf, as well as to Phœbe's baby, as Mr. Bunce would have it. Squire Mumby smiled. He was pleased to have discovered what the dealer was after. He nodded at Mr. Bunce.

' You may drink,' he said.

Mr. Bunce swayed to the mug ; he raised it to his lips and drank. Mr. Bunce looked uneasily at the clock ; he sat down beside Mr. Meek, and turned his back to Mr. Vosper.

' All here do know,' said Mr. Bunce, slowly moving his right hand before his face in circles, ' that the leaves be fallen and that the water brooks be running ; that the swallows be gone ; that harvest haytime and the hot summer days be over too.'

' That be true,' remarked Mr. Kiddle, ' and now

that winter is come, Squire Mumby be going to buy bull calf for fifteen pounds.'

'Twelve pounds ten,' grumbled Mr. Mumby, 'I will give and no more.'

Mr. Bunce held up his hand.

'There be a time for dealing and a time for talking,' he said.

'A maid,' he continued, making a gesture as if to push his interrupters aside, 'do walk out upon a summer's evening; she do step pretty, and what she do wear do show what she be—woon of they girls. She mid be any woon of they—Phœbe, Ann Kiddle, or maybe Miss Tamar. Folk who do chance to be out do see she a-coming, and do know, even though she do walk at the end of lane, that she be a maiden. She be there like she be made, she do step free, and her frock be a blue woon. There bain't no fear in her eyes, for all the green lane do seem to be her father's own housen. She do know Mumby's old barn, and Folly Down hill bain't nor stranger to she. Many a morning, when larks do sing, maiden have risen from she's bed to peep through window, and then she do gaze and fancy she's own pretty face in looking-glass. She do smile at herself, but she don't know why she be glad, and her mother do call and tell she not to loiter up there. Maiden do walk out on a Sunday, and she do feel what she be, and any man, however old, do look when she be passing.'

Mr. Meek shivered. He hoped that look wouldn't be charged for in his account.

'The sun do shine hot in summer, and 'tis playtime for the evening gnats, and maiden do walk lonely in lane. Than she do step upon green where daisy flowers do grow, and she do lie down under oak tree to watch they same little gnats a-dancing.'

'They bain't stinging gnats, I do hope?' said Mr. Vosper.

Mr. Bunce shook his head.

'Maiden do lie out pretty,' he said, 'and all she do wear be seen.'

Mr. Bunce turned to his friends. He wished them to see this young creature as he was seeing her. Mr. Mumby nodded as if he understood him.

'A thunder-clap do come,' said Mr. Bunce, 'the skies do open, a cloud do cover she, and maiden be hid——'

'By wold Grunter,' observed Mr. Vosper calmly, 'and me 'oman do say '—Mr. Vosper stood up to be the better heard—'that if a maid be afraid to be a-doing time she be young, her winter years will come, when oak-tree bed be damp and wormy, and do she lie there then and dance or sing? If she do, 'tis but to pester the folk wi' wold silly manners.'

'But who be to blame?' asked Squire Mumby, staring hard at Columbus, for he believed he might be the one who knew; 'who be to blame for they doings?'

'In Folly Down,' said Mr. Kiddle, 'we do blame Grunter.'

'At Angel Inn,' shouted Landlord Bunce angrily, 'we do blame God.'

Mr. Vosper shifted a little uneasily in his seat. It wouldn't matter so much, he felt, if Grunter, who was expected at any moment to enter the inn, was listening outside the door, but suppose the Other One happened to be there? Mr. Grunter was well aware of what was being said about him, and he approved of it, but why had Mr. Bunce shouted so loudly?

Vosper had come to the inn, hoping to meet a certain Person there; but if that Person heard His Name so taken in vain, Vosper might never learn what was wrong with the loading.

Mr. Mumby was uneasy too, for, although he was a very strong man, and by no means likely to come to any harm in a row, he liked a discussion to be peaceable, and always deprecated any risen wave of anger that might break into a conversation. Mr. Mumby shook his pocket. His money jingled in it, and that sound stilled the wrath of Mr. Bunce.

' I do mind once,' said Squire Mumby, who hoped to make peace with a story, ' when Farmer Pardy of Honeyfield and his head carter, John, were both of them blamed for finding a young woman walking in the fields and for lying she down in green grass. Each one, Pardy and John, did swear 'twas t'other, and the chairman upon the bench, Lord Bullman, did say that whoever opened court-house door first and came in should say who 'twas.'

' And who did open 'en? ' asked Mr. Bunce.

' Carter John's wife,' replied Mr. Mumby, ' and she did point to her husband.'

Mr. Meek smiled; he held out a hand to the fire to steal a flame to button into his coat.

The story changed the thoughts of the party. Mr Kiddle turned a little and glanced timidly at the young woman who was wearing a nightdress. She reminded him that he had daughters. He had drunk four pints, and he began now to think of his girls, instead of the hoped-for deal with Mr. Mumby. The long nightgown had melted his heart, and he wished to get for his own girls all the sympathy that the inn could give. He looked flabby ; the red blotches upon his cheeks were darker, and his nose was shining and sentimental.

' Much do happen,' said Mr. Kiddle, ' even in little Folly Down, that do astonish a poor man. A cow mid take a wrong turning and fall into ditch, and money will be lost over she. Maidens be born into a man's house, and their own mother do look into barn for a rope to hang sheself wi'. Once poor mother were a maiden, as plump as may be, and now she do look for a deep pond.'

Mr. Kiddle slowly shook his head.

' Phœbe and Ann,' he said sorrowfully, and staring without any shame now at the pink cheeks of the young lady, ' our Phœbe and Ann do always sing in church choir. Ann do kneel next to Mr. Grobe when he be a-praying.'

' No harm could come of that,' said Mr. Mumby, ' and no one has ever blamed Mr. Grobe, for 'tis God above, so landlord do say, or Grunter below who have done it.'

Mr. Kiddle still looked at the pretty picture.

' We do all know Grunter,' he said, ' but none of we have seen God at any time.'

' But that bain't nor reason,' broke in Mr. Bunce, ' why we shouldn't blame Him ? '

Farmer Mumby didn't reply ; he could only stare at the door that was slowly opening.

' 'Tis only Grunter,' exclaimed Bunce. ' 'Tain't t'other——'

XIX

TIME STOPS

The gentleman who now presented himself to the Angel Inn company wore whiskers, together with a fringe of beard. He had a great white face, a placid look, and he never laughed or smiled. He was not a stout man, although his body was large ; and though he could dig well, he walked awkwardly. Mr. Grunter had the appearance of a man who waited through shine and shower, in peaceful abstraction, for his last day to come.

Any one who had heard of Mr. Grunter without seeing him would probably have expected, by the many tales told of him, that when he appeared before them for the first time they would see a very different kind of man. For Mr. Grunter had none of those winning and amorous characteristics that are said to go—though this is by no means always the case— with a merry and a naughty life.

But appearances are often deceptive, and certainly more so in matters of a wanton nature than in any other kind of affair, and Folly Down was justly convinced—for Mrs. Vosper had been plain enough in her talk, as an eye-witness would be—that no trouble came to any unmarried girl in Folly Down without Mr. Grunter having deserved the blame.

Mr. Grunter was an obscure character ; he was queer ; he was a cold, clammy old man. He looked as though he had spent all his leisure hours, preferably in the winter-time, in standing in cold and damp lanes looking at nothing and thinking of less.

Though Folly Down knew better, we know that Mr. Grunter, though he took but a mild and detached interest in the event, waited in the lanes for the end of the world. This consolation—and some might call it so—Mr. Grunter considered to be near at hand, and for good reason, for he had once overheard Mr. Luke Bird informing Mr. Mumby's geese that the end of all things was at hand.

The geese had happened to stray, towards the end of a hot June afternoon, to the side of a little hill. They were but a goose and a gander with six fluffy goslings, that were guarded with the utmost care by their parents. Mr. Grunter, as chance would have it, happened to be at work on the side of the hill, cutting nettles with a scythe, having been invited to do so by Mr. Mumby, who had advised honest Grunter to do a little work for the sake of his health. Mr. Grunter had laid down his scythe, and was resting for a moment behind a gorse bush, when he perceived, to his astonishment, Mr. Luke Bird approaching the geese in a slow and considerate manner, so that Mr. Grunter was sure that Luke had something important to say to them.

Mr. Bird was no coward. He had seen the white geese upon the hill, with the little brown goslings, and he saw in a vision what a fine show they would make if all the geese that would ever come into the world hereafter were accepted, after regeneration, into the fields of heaven.

'What a happy place heaven would be,' thought Mr. Bird, ' for such a multitude of geese.' And he filled a little phial that he carried in his pocket with some ditch-water, and cautiously approached the geese with a view to baptising the first family of them.

Mr. Bird knew that the geese were more than half converted already, for they had belonged, in Mrs. Grobe's lifetime, to the rectory garden, and had only been given to Mr. Mumby when that lady died.

Luke Bird went near to the geese, but he soon perceived that he must choose another way than baptism —immersion would have been better, but alas! Luke was no Baptist—did he wish to fill heaven with geese. For no sooner was he come near than the goose and gander fluttered their wings, showing by many signs their hatred of religion, arching their necks and opening their beaks, and expressing only too surely their contempt for Christianity. Mr. Bird was forced to retire. The geese followed him noisily, but Luke suddenly turned upon them and, waving his arms, told them that the end of the world was at hand.

Jeremy Taylor writes in his Essay upon Contentedness that ' He that threw a stone at a dog, and hit his cruel step-mother, said, that although he intended it otherwise, yet the stone was not quite lost.' And so it happened to Luke Bird, for, though the geese only turned and bit at the grass when he spoke to them, Mr. Grunter received the word into his heart, and each day after that afternoon he expected the world to end. That was Mr. Grunter's belief, but the people of the Folly Down world believed other things of Mr. Grunter.

One can easily understand—for even in London such people are looked at—that a Folly Down man with a reputation for wantonness would be gazed at with inquisitiveness, as well as with pleasure, by those who sat around Mr. Bunce's happy board. When he entered, Squire Mumby, a chief amongst them, welcomed Mr. Grunter with a friendly nod, and informed him in a very few words of the turn that the conversation had taken, and of the difficult problem that the company there assembled had set themselves to solve.

Mr. Grunter gave no heed to him; he seemed not even to hear what the squire said, but only, in his usual awkward manner, sat down—as if he were un-decided till the very last moment which way to put himself—upon the same settle as Mr. Meek, who eyed him a little curiously, hoping, no doubt, to see some sign in his outward appearance that might help to prove as true all the fine stories that Folly Down gave such credence to.

'We be asking,' said Squire Mumby in a louder tone than that he had first used, and at the same time leaning forward a little so as to catch Mr. Grunter's attention, 'whether 'tis God or your own carnal body who do hurt they maidens.'

Mr. Grunter wasn't the sort of man who either hears or understands very readily—indeed, he only attended to spoken words in his own way and in his own time—and he hadn't listened.

'Whoo!' called Mr. Kiddle, pointing to Mr. Grunter with his right hand, 'Whoo-whoop! Be 'en thee or t'other who do lay out they girls?'

Mr. Grunter smiled.

Mr. Vosper wished to speak too.

'Me 'oman do say'—he moved nearer to Mr.

Grunter—' 'tis all thee's doings, but landlord do say 'tis gentleman farmer's antics, and we do know 'E bain't always in the skies.'

Mr. Grunter looked up at the ceiling as though he saw the blue sky there. He then regarded Mr. Mumby, looking him all over in a peaceful and complaisant manner, and said calmly, as though he were speaking of a small April shower that he expected to follow the dry weather of March :

' It be coming, what Bird do tell they geese of—the end of the world.'

No one paid the least heed to Mr. Grunter's remark, for every one had expected that he would entirely disregard the question put to him, setting it aside as if it had never been asked. But Squire Mumby wished to be heard again.

' Whoever do enter Angel Inn next,' he said importantly, raising his mug to his lips, 'will tell all of us who be to blame.'

Mr. Grunter looked pleased to know it, for now whatever was said in Folly Down was sure to be about him, and so he took all that was said and all that happened in the same mild and contented manner and did not feel ashamed.

It was at this very moment—an important one in our story—following a three minutes' silence that was in itself a very strange thing in that house, that Mr. Thomas Bunce chanced to look at the grand-father clock. He did so because the unnatural silence that came over the company—an angel is said to be walking near when such a silence happens—had disclosed the astonishing fact that the clock was not ticking.

Mr. Bunce was sure that the clock was wound. He knew that the heavy pendulum was in proper order, though no one nodded to it now; and yet the clock had stopped.

Except for the picture of Columbus and the young and seductive lady in the nightdress, the great clock with its yellow sun—a humble celandine, perhaps, as Wordsworth would have informed us, might have inspired the artist—was the most often looked upon with timely interest, amongst all the inn furniture, by Mr. Bunce's visitors.

No policeman, supposing that one of them had happened to call to see that the right and lawful hours were kept at Folly Down inn, could ever have found fault with that timepiece. The clock was truthful; it was even more honourable than that; it was always two minutes in advance of its prouder relation, that was set high above mankind, in the Shelton church tower.

Mr. Bunce stared hard at the clock. He wished to be sure.

All was silent again.

' Time be stopped,' exclaimed Mr. Bunce excitedly.

' And eternity have begun,' said Mr. Grunter.

When a very strange and unlooked-for event suddenly happens, such as that of a judge, who is fond of his joke, divesting himself of wig and gown and changing places with the prisoner in the dock, whom he is hanging, and then seeing the black cap put on for his benefit this time, we may expect even the most decorous of famous barristers to stare a little. And, just as in such a court every eye would look, so at the Angel Inn, when Mr. Bunce spoke so excitedly, every one turned to the clock, and all listened and wondered whether its ticking would be renewed.

Mr. Bunce's exclamation and Mr. Grunter's rejoinder were received, as we may well imagine, with intense surprise, though the word ' eternity ' that Mr. Grunter had used had never been spoken by Mr. Bird. Mr. Bird had told the geese that the end of the world was coming, and he had often spoken to a straying donkey about heaven and hell, but he had never told any beast or fowl what the ages would be called when time was ended. Mr. Grunter had heard the word, though not spoken by Luke, but explained in moving terms by the Reverend Nicholas Grobe in the Folly Down church pulpit, and for a good reason too.

Mr. Grobe, who was obliged to leave God out of his sermons as soon as his great sorrow forbade the belief in Him, was forced, in order to get the right bass note in his talk, to put something as dreadful in place of that Name, and so he told his hearers of Time, as man knows it in his short and fleeting years, and of Eternity, about which man can know nothing.

' Mr. Grobe did always say that Eternity would come when clocks do all stop,' said Mr. Grunter in a loud voice, for he was proud of the fact that he had remembered so well this word of Mr. Grobe's, the meaning of which now appeared clear to him.

Mr. Grunter, finding that he alone was talking, still continued.

' Words and names,' he said, ' though they be different, do all mean the same. There be writers in heaven same as there be writers upon earth, and sometimes folk in heaven as well as folk on earth do forget what they be called, and if a name bain't God or Eternity, 'tis Weston.'

Mr. Kiddle looked at the young lady in the picture as if he expected her to begin to walk, and to do so she must needs raise her nightdress a little.

'Though time be stopped,' he remarked—and he wasn't the sort of man to be disturbed by riots, subterranean fires, or breakage of mirrors—'our deal bain't ended, and 'tis thirteen pound ten that I will take for fine young bull who be lusty enough to leap oak tree on Folly Down green.'

''Twill always be a very small bull,' observed Squire Mumby, nodding, so as to exclude all yielding thoughts, at Columbus. 'An' a small bull bain't no more use than a mouse to my large cows.'

Mr. Meek opened his coat and buttoned it again hurriedly. The fire was burning a little low. Mr. Meek frowned. He was never very well pleased when the conversation was about beasts, and sometimes he would go as far as to interrupt the gentlemen with a little chirping cough, like a grasshopper's. Mr. Vosper heard the cough, and knowing what Mr. Meek's feelings were if a bull was mentioned, spoke too.

'It bain't proper,' said Mr. Vosper, touching his forehead with his first forefinger, 'to talk about bulls wi' Mr. Grunter in the room.'

'Vosper do say true,' agreed Squire Mumby, 'an' so Kiddle had best keep 'is own small calf while he be a-growing, for while Grunter do sit on settle 'tis women we should talk of.'

No one in the room appeared to be the least surprised that, though the clock had ceased to tick and time was stopped, all should go on exactly as before : that Mr. Kiddle should wish to deal, and that Mr. Meek should wish, by a little cough, to bring the talk back again to women. Indeed, the word spoken by Mr. Grunter had been but a word, and Eternity, for all the company knew to the contrary, might be as pleasant to live in as Time.

To look at Mr. Grunter was to be assured that nothing very devastating had happened. His look was the same, his fringe of beard and his white cheeks were no different now than they had been during the rule of Time. A large interest, like a fine pink halo, always surrounds a man, however old and plain he be, who has the reputation of being very merry in a certain way. And so all who were present, as though to establish themselves in the new order of being, looked at Mr. Grunter, whose large white face appeared at this moment to be larger and whiter than ever.

'Vosper do speak truly,' said Landlord Bunce, rolling across the parlour, 'for now that time be stopped, and we who be here are like to talk for ever, 'tis well that we do choose an everlastin' subject, and that subject be they women, though '—and Mr. Bunce stood still—' 'tis God we mid blame for all their foolishness.'

'True, landlord,' murmured Mr. Vosper, 'but 'tis a folly they do share wi' wold Grunter.'

Although the pendulum had ceased to swing, and the hands of the old clock, with its yellow sun still shining, had ceased to move, and a strange feeling had entered that parlour, as if Time himself, being tired of the continual burden of changing matter, had halted and stood still, yet there was nothing to prevent a sound from outside from reaching the ears of those who sat in the tavern.

In the old days the artless trotting of a horse had always given rise to the question—and a very natural one, to be sure—as to whether young Squire Dashwood or merry Mr. Teedon, the heir to a barony, was outside in the lane. But now, in these latter days, the hum of an automobile had taken the place—for all human things change—of the trotting of a horse.

All outside movement that supposes a new arrival and an addition to the company within doors is hearkened to with suspense by those who sit at an inn, for who can say for certain whether it will be the honest presence of Mr. Sheet the pig-dealer who will open the door, or else it may be Mr. Thomas the sweep, and the surprise of seeing him instead of the other will give just the shock that keeps life a-going and makes all things possible.

Deep in the country it is recognised more than ever as a fact that there are some people, whether for art or fancy—and that they best can tell—who move in a mysterious way. Not very many days before our story opens, the sound of some one crawling to the door had been heard at the inn. It was Mr. Vosper, who had taken this means of escaping the eyes of his wife, who, he knew, watched the inn yard very closely—and no bishop, we can well imagine, would be likely to enter paradise in so contrite and humble a manner.

The humming sound ceased. A car had stopped at the inn gate.

' 'Tis butcher Giles,' said Mr. Kiddle, ' who do come at all times and hours, and no one don't know when 'e be expected.'

' No, no,' remarked Mr. Vosper, 'tain't butcher who be outside in lane, for 'is motor do rattle and bang. 'Tis Jim Coleman, who do bring out herrings and bananas and do visit we.'

' Whoever it be,' said Mr. Mumby in a loud voice, in imitation of Lord Bullman, ' who do first enter here, he be the one to say whether 'tis God or Grunter who do hurt they pretty maidens.'

Since the grandfather clock had stopped ticking, Landlord Bunce had been more than usually silent. A doubt had come to him then that made him a little uneasy, for he began to wonder whether, after all, he had been right in always blaming God for all the troubles that came. If Folly Down was right, then he was wrong. He had certainly never asked this question face to face with God ; neither had he, for that matter, directly asked Mr. Grunter.

Mr. Bunce never liked to offend a customer. Any one else might ask Mr. Grunter, and even if Grunter approved of the sport he mightn't approve of a direct question being put to him by Landlord Bunce. Perhaps a way might be found to decide it that wouldn't offend Mr. Grunter. Perhaps a new-comer, as Mr. Mumby suggested, might know.

All listened for the click of the inn gate. Had a pin been dropped upon the floor Mr. Meek would have jumped.

' I be sure 'tis Jim Coleman,' observed Mr.

Vosper, feeling that something had to be said to break the uneasy silence of uncertainty.

' I do hope none of me stock be broke out,' murmured Mr. Kiddle, looking nervously about him.

At that moment, though no click of the gate had been heard and no sound of a footstep in the yard, the parlour door opened widely.

' Mr. Weston's Good Wine.'

XX

A LOST RELATIVE

THE landlord of a free house—for Mr. Bunce owned the Angel Inn—was the right and proper party to listen attentively to any offer that came to him to make a purchase in the way of his trade.

The gentleman who had opened the parlour door so suddenly had notified his business there in a manner the most intelligible to our honest landlord, for his first words, pronounced so distinctly—' Mr. Weston's Good Wine'—explained clearly enough that he travelled in a very good line.

Mr. Weston was quite alone when he entered the room. Evidently his friend and companion, Michael, had gone elsewhere.

Although a tradesman in a tavern parlour is no uncommon sight, go where you will, here or there about the world, yet those who used to sit and drink at the Folly Down inn had always an interested eye for any man, tradesman or other, who came for the first time into that house.

Nothing, of course, could be thought more natural and proper than thus to take an interest in a stranger. Whether the interest were for good or ill was another matter, for a countryman is by nature a suspicious person, and he feels at enmity with any one whom he sees for the first time, be he whom you will.

When Mr. Weston was first seen standing in the inn doorway, telling his business, Mr. Vosper, who was the nearest man to the door, moved a little hurriedly from his seat and found a place for himself upon the settle beside Mr. Kiddle. Being seated there, and at a safe distance from Mr. Weston, he regarded that gentleman very inquisitively.

As soon as he had spoken, Mr. Weston came farther into the parlour, and seated himself in a very friendly manner beside Mr. Bunce, whom—and it needed no enquiry to be sure of this—Mr. Weston knew to be the landlord.

It has often been said—and with truth, too—that a good trader is never at a loss to know, in any company, the right behaviour to use in order to increase his sales.

Mr. Weston appeared to be happy and easy at the inn. He even nodded at Columbus in a good-humoured manner, as though Columbus were thanking him in his prayer, and—what was more strange, too, for Mr. Weston had a manly look—he was also noticed by Mr. Meek to peep slyly at the young lady in the nightgown, as if he knew more about her than he wished to tell.

By the way he settled himself so comfortably, Mr. Weston might have been born at an inn, or at least in the environs of one, for his looks plainly showed how pleased he was to be there. He exhibited the most gracious manners, such as we venture to hope may be copied, after reading this book, by the chiefs of all our great houses of trade.

Mr. Weston, having looked and admired the pictures, began to regard the company happily too, being pleased to see honest folk enjoying themselves in their own way.

It was curious, too, to note with what unanimous approbation every one in the company regarded Mr. Weston. Each one saw him as something more than a mere stranger come in for a moment, for each, as soon as Mr. Weston had seated himself, supposed him to be a lost relative.

Squire Mumby at once saw a distinct resemblance —the way he smiled, perhaps—between Mr. Weston and a distant cousin of his, an undertaker, who had once treated him so generously at the Maidenbridge Rod and Lion to one whisky after another, and all of them double ones, so that before an hour was past Mr. Mumby believed that he heard the larks sing and the cuckoo call, though the month was December.

The parlour fire burned up brightly when Mr. Weston entered the inn, and after stealing a flame, Mr. Meek looked at the new-comer too, and as he looked he remembered a picture of his own father, a worthy barber of Portstown, who, as Mr. Meek had often been told by his mother when he visited her, now resided in heaven. Mr. Weston had the same rugged look and genial, compassionate eyes.

Landlord Bunce had only to view Mr. Weston standing in the doorway in order to be reminded of his brother James, of whom he had always been very fond. But unfortunately James Bunce, who in times past had returned his brother's affection, had been forced to leave the country because he had taken a young lady once too often to the Stonebridge fair, who would have called him to account when her child came had not James fled to America.

No sooner had Mr. Bunce looked at Mr. Weston than he believed him to be his brother James returned from his travels, for the young lady, Miss Merrythought, was lately married. James was grown older; that was but natural; but he had the same jovial look and open countenance.

Dealer Kiddle had stared too, stared so hard that he could almost have sworn that Mr. Weston was his Uncle Rutter, risen from the dead—a man who had never in all his life been known to miss a good bargain, and who had once bought a second-hand wooden cross for a shilling, that he kept for his own grave.

'Our Father,' murmured Mr. Vosper, and was glad that no one had overheard him.

But although each man thought he knew Mr. Weston, Grunter was the only one who dared to tell him so.

'Thee bain't John Weston, be 'ee?' he enquired, 'me wife's brother, who did court twelve maidens in woon year, and all were mothers by the next? There be a photograph of John, hung up in cottage, who were chief singer in church choir, and thee do exactly resemble him.'

'I am glad to hear it,' said Mr. Weston.

Mr. Meek laughed.

Whether or no the presence of Mr. Weston there created a new world of pleasant thoughts and feelings, it is impossible to say. Yet a vision, or what seemed to be one, overcame Mr. Vosper at that moment, though he certainly wasn't used to dreaming while awake. He felt himself to be riding safely upon the very top of a monstrous load of hay, while the waggon below him rumbled and creaked and safely turned the dangerous corner into Mr. Mumby's rickyard, to the vast astonishment of all who were present there.

A strange fancy, too, came to Mr. Kiddle, for he felt more sure than ever before in his life that, in a very little while, perhaps that very evening, he would sell to Mr. Mumby, at a fine profit and with honour, not the bull calf alone but two plump heifers from his pastures, and that one of them would have a little calf running by its side.

Mr. Grunter, too, became suddenly happily aware that a former possession of his—an old boot that he had mislaid in rather strange circumstances—was restored to him by the mediation and help of Mr. Weston.

At that very same time, too, Squire Mumby and Mr. Meek looked at one another, and though they were very different men and were certainly not in the least sentimental in their habits of thought any more than a lamb or a lion, yet they began to drink now out of the same mug.

Out of all the company, Mr. Bunce alone retained his natural thoughts, wishing to know a little more of this tradesman's goods before he ordered any bottles.

' And what kind of taste has your wine ? ' asked Mr. Bunce of the merchant.

' It is like nectar,' replied Mr. Weston.

The sound of that word pleased Mr. Bunce. He rolled out to the dark and narrow passage where the barrels were kept and drew for the stranger—who had called for it—a mug of bitter ale.

Mr. Bunce sat opposite to him. He studied his features with great care, for he did not wish to be deceived or to be cheated. Mr. Weston accepted this cautious scrutiny in very good part, and he certainly didn't look the kind of man to be ashamed of anything that he had ever done.

The landlord, after looking at Mr. Weston for a little while, felt ready to speak.

' Even though I do not often sell wine,' he said, ' unless there happens to be a funeral or a wedding, I should be glad to know the strength of your wine and its bouquet ? '

' My wine,' said Mr. Weston, in a low tone and leaning forward towards Mr. Bunce, ' is as strong as death and as sweet as love.'

' You know how to praise what you sell,' remarked Mr. Bunce, looking steadily into Mr. Weston's eyes, ' but I never like to hurry about giving an order.'

' There is no need for you to hurry this evening,' replied Mr. Weston, looking at the grandfather clock.

' No, no, there bain't no need to hurry,' said Dealer Kiddle and Mr. Vosper in one voice, ' for time be stopped.'

' And Eternity have come,' muttered Mr. Grunter.

Mr. Weston smiled blandly, as though Time were nothing to him and Eternity his usual wear. He looked around him as if he were pleased by Mr. Grunter's muttered word ; he even smiled at the pretty girl in the nightdress, whom he had named Mary.

Indeed, if we—and a writer has, as Mr. Weston himself knows, a privilege in this matter—may be permitted for a moment to look into this wine merchant's heart, we may be sure that Mr. Grunter's disclosure was very much welcomed. For Mr. Weston couldn't help recollecting then how, in a childish fit of mischief, he had once planted a long snaky root in his mother's flower plot that grew in the summer-time into a horrid patch of nettles that deserved only to be utterly burnt and destroyed.

'But tell me, gentlemen, what was the question,' asked the wine merchant, looking round upon the company, 'that you were going to ask of the first stranger that entered this friendly tavern ? '

Every countryman knows that walls have very long ears. No one at the Angel Inn was in the least surprised that Mr. Weston was aware of what had been spoken about. But homely talk amongst them-selves was a very different matter to repeating what had been said to a stranger, however much he looked like a near relative.

But one amongst them was at least expected to have courage. This was Squire Mumby, who, be-cause he was a landed gentleman and a very large taxpayer, had acquired the right, by virtue of all the customs of the house, to tell any tale boldly.

'Landlord Bunce differs from us all,' said Mr. Mumby in an important tone ; ' he blames God for all the trouble.'

'Oh, he blames God, does he ? ' observed Mr. Weston, smiling.

'Yes, he does,' affirmed Squire Mumby. 'He lays all earthly sorrows at His door, and here in Folly Down he blames Him for getting the Kiddle maidens into trouble, but I must add—and it's proper that I should '—(Mr. Weston was noticed to bow)—' that all Folly Down, and I think rightly so, blames Grunter.'

Mr. Grunter's large white face expanded even larger than usual when Mr. Weston turned to him.

' Please tell me,' asked Mr. Weston, looking from Mr. Grunter to Mr. Vosper, ' for I have written some village stories myself, all about it.'

' I can tell 'ee,' said honest Vosper, ' for me wold 'oman be cattish, and do go about for to seek out they doings.'

' Oh, I 'm not the only country writer, then,' remarked Mr. Weston, with a slight frown.

' She bain't nor fool like that ; she bain't no writer,' said Mr. Vosper, who believed that Mr. Weston was hinting dark things against his wife ; ' she be only interested in what all maids do like to do since world first rolled into a ball like a pig's louse.'

Vosper paused for breath.

' Please continue,' said Mr. Weston.

' 'Tis she's story I be telling,' said Mr. Vosper, wishing to relieve himself of all responsibility. ' She do say how she were gathering sticks woon day in field, and in a ground near by there was seated a maid, and not far off she there was wold Grunter— and thik were the second time of doing, too.'

' What was Mr. Grunter doing ? ' enquired Mr. Weston.

' Taking off his boots,' replied Mr. Vosper mildly.

' 'Tis 'is way of beginning,' explained Mr. Kiddle. Mr. Weston turned to the last speaker.

' The name of one of your daughters,' he said, smiling, ' is Phœbe. Please tell me all about her.'

' 'Tain't for I to tell 'ee so much,' replied Mr. Kiddle, ' for though I do know a little about stock, a maid's matters bain't so easy to examine.'

' A father,' remarked Mr. Bunce, ' I do mean an earthly father, bain't nor judge of 'is own maiden, though his near neighbour mid be, and when I do see Phœbe Kiddle lift her skirts to cross brook by stepping stones, I do spy a nice rounded leg to blame God for.'

Mr. Kiddle looked at Mr. Bunce with astonishment.

' Surely,' he said, ' thee don't dare to blame 'E for anything that have happened in our family ? '

' Oh yes, I do,' replied Mr. Bunce, ' for all things be 'Is doings.'

Mr. Weston hid his face in his mug and took a very deep draught. He tipped the mug slowly, and at last set it down empty upon the table.

While Mr. Weston was drinking, some one had spoken, and each man looked at his neighbour, thinking that it were he. The words had been spoken directly after Mr. Bunce had made his remark, and were heard plainly enough by every one in the room :

' I form the light, and create darkness : I make peace, and create evil : I, the Lord, do all these things '

Mr. Kiddle looked at once at Columbus. Mr. Kiddle had never said a prayer in his life, but Columbus seemed to be praying, and so perhaps it was he whose prayer was being replied to.

On the other hand, Mr. Meek had looked at Mary —and we may as well take Mr. Weston's name for her ; they were strange words for her to say, no doubt, but still one never knows when a young woman wears her night attire what she will talk about. Mr. Meek believed the words were spoken by Mary.

Mr. Weston was aware that a little uneasiness had

been caused by the words of one who couldn't be seen, and so, wishing to bring matters back to plainer grounds, he asked, happily enough, speaking to the company in general :

' Haven't you anything to tell me about Ann Kiddle ? '

' Grunter 'ave,' grumbled Mr. Vosper.

Mr. Grunter's white face looked at that moment to be a little sad. He was not a man of much conversation, but perhaps he thought the more, and was most likely contemplating philosophically how soon, how very soon, the joyful moments of dalliance fade and perish. He must, at that very moment, have come to a sound and sane conclusion.

' A maiden bain't beer,' said Mr. Grunter.

' There ! ' cried Thomas Bunce, striking the table with his fist, ' Grunter do say it. 'Tain't 'e, but God, who be up to they naughty fancies.'

Mr. Bunce stood boldly up in the middle of the room and held up his hand.

' I do now ask, before you all,' he said, ' this gentleman, whose name be Mr. Weston and who do sell wine, which be to blame ? '

' He will certainly tell us, for all tradesmen know so much,' observed Squire Mumby, ' who is the naughty one.'

Mr. Weston paid for his beer. He stood up beside Mr. Bunce, placing his hand upon the landlord's shoulder and gently compelling him to sit down again, while he himself remained standing.

' There are, I believe,' said Mr. Weston, raising his voice a little, that, though deep, was pleasant to hear, ' certain gentlemen who reside in this country who are initiated in colleges and other places in the manners and ways of the God you speak of. These men are called ministers.'

' Some are deans,' said Mr. Bunce.

' I am aware of it,' continued Mr. Weston, bowing politely to the landlord and thanking him for his timely information. ' But though some are deans, as Mr. Bunce tells me, yet the majority are called ministers. I myself '—here Mr. Weston looked down modestly at a spittoon that was filled with clean sawdust—' I myself have mentioned in a little work of my own how these ministers originated. They are all of them the sons of Levi.'

' In Folly Down,' said Mr. Kiddle gently, ' they would have been called the sons of Grunter.'

Mr. Weston looked at Kiddle smilingly.

' I will remember your suggestion,' he said gratefully, ' if ever I revise my book. But now I must proceed.

' A certain portion of these pastors are gentlemen ; the remainder, a more common kind, are called priests or dissenters—I take my information from the country directory. The gentlemen pastors receive a stipend from the State as regulated by the rise and fall of the price of——'

' Not women, I hope ? ' said Mr. Kiddle, in a shocked tone.

' No, only wheat.' Mr. Weston touched his mug, which Landlord Bunce at once filled. ' These gentlemen, so endowed and secured against want, are said to be the most correctly informed as to the ways and habits of God, and so if we wish to receive a true answer to Mr. Bunce's question—a question that he has a good right to ask—we should enquire of the Reverend Nicholas Grobe.'

Mr. Weston sat down. Dealer Kiddle clapped his hands. He had once heard Lord Bullman speak in the same high manner.

Landlord Bunce rose excitedly.

' I will visit Mr. Grobe at once,' he said, ' for, as time be stopped and no moments bain't passing, wold Bess mid now and again leave her pickling of they onions and serve drink to parlour company.'

Mr. Weston softly took out of his pocket a neatly bound notebook.

' Before you go, landlord,' he said, in a winning tone, ' will you allow me to put your name down for a dozen bottles of our good wine.'

Mr. Bunce had one arm in his overcoat.

' If I become a winebibber, Mr. Weston,' he said, ' and do get tipsy wi' drinking, who be I to blame then ? '

Mr. Weston laughed.

XXI

MRS. VOSPER'S COTTAGE

As soon as Jenny Bunce was escaped from her ravishers and had tidied herself a little in the lane, she wondered what she had better do next, and where she should go.

She was a young woman who had no wish to give up what belonged to her merely because an unforeseen accident had happened. That evening was her own to do as she chose with, for, by the law of service in country places, one evening a week is the property of the servant.

Jenny might, of course, have gone home, but she knew that if she entered the inn her father would at once request her to draw the drinks for the men, and her mother would beg her to peel the onions for pickling, and she had just then no particular wish to perform either of these tasks.

Her outing this evening had begun excitingly, but the excitement wasn't altogether unexpected, for nearly every woman who had spoken to her since she was a child, not to mention Mrs. Vosper, had informed her that—her mother had said that if she took off her hat in church something might happen to her— in some mysterious manner those creatures that are called men and wear trousers could hurt a nice, well-behaved girl. Jenny asked her mother about her hat.

' And suppose I did take 'en off in church ? ' she said naughtily.

' Why, anything might happen to you—a nasty thing might fall from the roof and creep up your leg,' replied Mrs. Bunce, shuddering. . . .

Jenny stood still in the darkness of the lane and wondered where to go. Her heart beat quickly and her limbs trembled, for she wasn't altogether recovered from her late adventure.

She considered. Was it late or early ? She supposed that she had been out for some while. The proper time for her to return to Folly Down rectory was ten o'clock. Was it near that hour, or past ? While she was being enticed there by Mrs. Vosper, and while she was being held under the oak tree, time perhaps had run on faster than she knew, and the Shelton clock might strike ten at any moment.

Curiously enough, the rude treatment that Jenny had received at the hands of men had awakened her wishes in a manner that she least expected, and now she began, strange though this may sound, to want Mr. Luke Bird.

She certainly surprised herself by this wish, but with her bosom panting in the darkness and her thoughts on fire, she was sure enough that she wanted—a husband.

So far Jenny had looked upon a man, together with the oddity that village women so slyly hinted at and sniggered about, as only being a rather large and extremely silly waxwork doll. She had been so sure of this that, when once as a child she had come upon James Barker, who was ninety years old, asleep in the sun, with his chin and nose amongst the nettles, she gave him a good tug, pulled him over, and began to undress him, believing him to be a grotesque doll that should be put to bed in a proper manner. No one in all the world had a more mild and doll-like expression than Mr. Bird, and Jenny now longed to undress him as she had once undressed Mr. Barker.

'Oh,' sighed Jenny, 'I do so want Luke Bird!'

Jenny Bunce waited and listened. She heard the Shelton clock begin to strike ; she counted its strokes. The clock struck seven. Jenny was surprised ; she had supposed, at least, that the clock would strike eight or nine times.

Would Luke Bird come to her and take her away at once to his cottage? She would gladly go with him if he came, and very likely some good man would join their hands in marriage before they went to bed. Who knows?

But Luke didn't come, and Jenny felt herself to be growing desperate. She must go somewhere. She decided to go to Mrs. Vosper's cottage and talk to the Kiddles. Though it was not actually raining, the evening was damp, and both Phœbe and Ann Kiddle were sure to be there.

In the thick darkness, on her way to Mrs. Vosper's cottage, Jenny met some one in the lane. At first she thought this some one might be Mr. Bird, but coming nearer, she heard a sigh, and the being she brushed against proved to be her young mistress.

Tamar was expectant and happy. She was, indeed, more lively than Jenny, whose heart-beats were now quieted. She kissed Jenny fervently upon the lips, so that Jenny turned a little away.

'You mustn't be surprised to meet me, Jenny,' said Tamar. 'You know that I like to walk in the dark lanes, and I do believe that, this very evening,

wonderful things are going to happen. I met Mr.
Grunter, and he had seen something.'

'Oh, 'e be always seeing what 'e shouldn't,'
laughed Jenny.

Tamar blushed in the darkness.

'A bright light, Mr. Grunter said, shone in the
sky, and at the very same moment that the light came
there were screams from under the oak tree, as if a
girl were being hurt there.'

''Tweren't nothing,' said Jenny.

'But, Jenny,' exclaimed Tamar, 'I have a strange
feeling in my heart that I know to be a true one. I
believe that this evening a beautiful young man is
walking about the village, who has come down from
heaven.'

Jenny gasped.

'I mean,' said Tamar, 'to go presently to the oak
tree to see if an angel is waiting for me.'

'Oh,' exclaimed Jenny, 'oh, Miss Tamar, you
must be careful.'

'Yes, I know, Jenny,' whispered Tamar, 'I know
I must be careful to please him, and I want you to tell
me all about it.'

'But I know nothing, miss,' replied Jenny.

'I must know everything,' said Tamar eagerly,
'before I go to the oak tree, where I shall find him
waiting.'

Jenny was thoughtful.

'Mrs. Vosper do know a lot,' she said, 'and
Phœbe and Ann Kiddle be proud to talk of such
doings.'

'But I don't want to go into Mrs. Vosper's cottage,' whispered Tamar, 'for I might meet Mr.

Grunter there, and though I 'm not afraid of any one
out of doors——'

'Oh, he bain't nothing to be afraid of,' laughed
Jenny.

'He is blamed for doing so much here.'

'Not by our daddy,' remarked Jenny.

'I am such an ignorant girl, you know,' said
Tamar sadly, 'and perhaps Miss Pettifer was right
when she said that if I went to Lord Bullman's school
for girls at Wemborne I should learn a great deal
that I should find very useful.'

'Well, you have told me something,' exclaimed
Jenny, 'for I never knew that there were schools anywhere that did teach such doings. But bain't none
of they Wemborne teachers ashamed to tell so much?'

Tamar sighed ; she hardly heeded Jenny's words.

'If only I had gone to Wemborne,' she murmured, 'I might know now how to please my angel.'

Tamar was silent. She had never been approached
in the way of love, and she had no wish to appear
too ignorant and foolish before her waiting lover.

Jenny Bunce wished very much to help her mistress.

'Though I be sure Mrs. Vosper's bain't so good
as a school to learn about things, still they be always
talking there,' Jenny said gravely.   'And if 'ee did
stay outside window, thee could hear all they do tell.'

'Very well, Jenny,' said Tamar.

They began to walk together along the dark lane
towards Mrs. Vosper's cottage. Jenny was the one
now who seemed unhappy.

'What 's the matter ? ' asked Tamar.

'I were only thinking,' said Jenny, 'how lonely
Mr. Bird must be at night-time. 'E be but a poor

simple man to bide alone, for there bain't no pigs nor
geese for 'e to preach to all the long dark hours, and I
be afraid that if 'e do bide so lonely, 'e won't know
how to behave to a maid who do have a mind to him.'

' Oh, Jenny,' asked Tamar nervously, ' I hope you
wouldn't have that sort of fear about an angel ? '

' Just give 'e the chance,' said Jenny, remember-
ing how Tamar had looked in her bath.

As soon as they reached Mrs. Vosper's cottage,
Jenny Bunce knocked at the door and went in.
Tamar crept near too, and peeped through the win-
dow. Two young women were talking gaily to-
gether in Mrs. Vosper's parlour ; one of them was
Phœbe Kiddle, and the other was Ann.

Ann was fair. A large, comely creature, though a
little heavy in her movements, she had gentle innocent eyes, a fine white forehead, thick lips, and a loud
laugh. She laughed boisterously at almost everything that was said, and when she laughed she
stretched out her arms and her legs, so that the chair
she sat upon always seemed too small for her.

Phœbe was smaller. She was as plump as her sister
and more desirable, and at nearly every movement
something invisible seemed to tickle her leg. She
never allowed her skirt to remain as a skirt should,
but every time she laughed she leaned her head forward almost into her lap, as if she were anxious to hide
her body from the naughty prying eyes of the world.

Mrs. Vosper's cottage was dark and dismal. It was
sheltered by a high bank behind it as well as by a
large hedge in front, and her parlour, the only decent
room in the house, was lighted by a lamp that gave
the feeblest light. All the year round Mrs. Vosper's

room was decorated as if for Christmas. There were
paper flowers, and long pink paper streamers hung
in every direction about the room. There were so
many of these streamers that they looked like a
spider's web, and it was right and proper that they
should, for into her web when it rained Mrs. Vosper
had ever enticed one or other of the Kiddles. Indeed,
she never thought of any maid as being really captured until she came there. For, whatever amusement
might go on in the oak-tree bed, Mrs. Vosper found
it hard to believe anything could hurt a girl there.

'They out-of-doors matters,' she would say,
'bain't the real thing, for snakes do crawl and winds
do blow, and no chap be sure what 'e be doing.
'Tis best to bide indoors. No maid do wish to be
watched by sparrows.'

Mrs. Vosper had often invited Jenny Bunce to
visit her, but Jenny had always refused, and certainly, after what had happened that evening, the landlord's daughter was the very last young woman in the
world that Mrs. Vosper expected to enter her web.
But Mrs. Vosper was always ready for any of nature's
surprises, and she welcomed Jenny most affectionately.

Mrs. Vosper was always glad to learn, and she saw
at once that nature even out-reached her in her
favourite game. For here was Jenny Bunce, so lately
escaped from her enemies, not fled to the rectory to
tell her mistress about it all, but drawn by a force
that certainly seemed here to need no assistance from
Mrs. Vosper, into the very place the most likely for
the almost immediate and final settlement of the
first affair.

Mrs. Vosper wished at once to put Jenny entirely

at her ease, even though a little rudeness had been shown to her under the oak tree, and as whatever occurred in Folly Down under the shady cover of darkness—and who expects to see a light shine in the sky?—was laid to the score of Mr. Grunter, Mrs. Vosper remarked feelingly to Jenny, in the village way of expression, that any young woman who was touched by him always, of course, forgave him his trespasses.

'No woon don't never blame 'e,' said Mrs. Vosper, 'for 'e don't know what 'e do do. 'E be a poor man who bain't got no other occupation to keep him out of mischief than tormenting the maidens. 'E be only church clerk and gravedigger, and all do know that folk don't die, nor yet services be said, every hour in the week. Some work—and we all want to be a-doing—must be found for poor Grunter when church bell bain't tolling nor ringing, and what can a poor man do who have never learnt to plough nor to sow? All he can do be to catch and tease a maid. Wi' others it may be different, but Mr. Grunter must always be forgiven.'

Mrs. Vosper took up her knitting. Jenny laughed. But she was not there for her own amusement alone, and so she spoke to Phœbe Kiddle.

'How do all they fancy manners begin?' she asked; 'what be 'en that a girl do say when she wants to be naughty?'

''Tain't nothing to be said,' replied Phœbe, ''tis only the maid who be tantalised and teased.'

'But what does happen first?' asked Jenny, sitting down in a chair near the window.

''E don't kiss 'e at once,' replied Phœbe.

Phœbe pulled at her skirt, perhaps to show that

165

any forward movement must be managed by the lady. She leant near to Jenny and laughed.

' 'E do look up into tree, and then 'e do start swearing about Luke Bird or some one, or 'e do say how much money 'e have saved in post-office, and while 'e do talk something be happening and happiness do come. He mid be saying that envelopes be dear, while all the world be lost and gone, and every leaf upon oak tree be a baby looking at 'ee. " Hay-cutter be broke down in field," 'e do whisper, though thee do forget all they things. 'Tis as if a wild creature, who do talk like a fool, did hold 'ee. 'Tis as if cold death grinned at 'ee, but 'ee don't never heed him. Thee do burn in a fire and they baby leaves be a-laughing. And then 'e be a-talking again and do ask whether strap gaiters be proper to wear in church Sundays, or whether father did say what price barren cows were in Maidenbridge market. 'E do talk as if nothing hadn't happened, and 'twas 'e all the time who wouldn't take no for an answer.'

The ivy outside the window rustled.

' 'Tis nice to know about things,' said Jenny, ' and I do suppose Ann do know a little, too, and maybe she can tell how folk do begin to be bad.'

' They fancies do begin wi' looking,' said Ann, stretching out her wonderful limbs that appeared almost to fill the little room. ' A man has a snake's eye that can draw we to 'im. A maid do think she be running away, and the wind do rustle the leaves, but she do draw nearer to 'e and never farther away. 'Tis 'is looking that can't be turned from. They eyes be ever asking, and 'tis we who must go they eyes' way.'

' 'Tis a wonder,' said Jenny virtuously, ' that such

wickedness be allowed to happen, for if all the world were only a long street, wi' nothing worse than shop windows to look at, we girls would all be as good as clergymen.'

' But 'tain't always looking, 'tis touching too,' said Ann, going nearer to the window, ' for when I be touched all things do happen.'

' And so they should happen,' said Mrs. Vosper, ' for all the world be made for happiness.'

The ivy outside the window rustled again. Tamar left the window and was gone.

The three young girls leaned near to one another so that their heads almost touched. They told many tales to one another ; they chatted and laughed, and now and again one of them would lean back, as if she couldn't hold her own merriment, and shake with laughter. The more exciting their tales became, the lower were their voices in telling them. They were soon speaking in whispers.

' John's skin be the softest,' said Ann.

' Oh, but Martin be the one to please 'ee best,' whispered Phœbe.

Even though these names were spoken so low, Mrs. Vosper heard what was said.

' 'Tis all wold Grunter's doings that thee be telling of,' she remarked loudly ; ' 'tain't no woon, only Grunter, who be about such work.'

The girls leant together again, for both the Kiddles had much to say to Jenny. They were telling her about amorous delights, and advising her to begin to enjoy them. And Jenny would blush, hide her face, and wish to be married that very evening to Luke Bird.

Very soon Phœbe and Ann saw that their counsel

was not being regarded, for all they said only made Jenny the more eager to be taken into the arms of a young man who would both nourish and marry her. And soon a feeling of uneasiness, that comes so strangely sometimes into human affairs, crept into that room.

At first when the girls were at Mrs. Vosper's the atmosphere of the room appeared to be gay enough, as it used to be when they came there in rainy and damp weather. The paper roses that decorated the picture of King Edward VII. and his gracious spouse, that at first had looked so gay, were now drooped, and sooty stains from the lamp clung to them. The pink paper streamers, that had often entangled the guests when their frolics exceeded the proper reach of decorum, now hung dusty and untidy. Neither were these signs that showed where moth and rust do corrupt, all, for though the fire burned and the room was close and frowsy, yet a chill as from the tomb now filled it.

The girls were silent. Something had joined their conversation that hadn't been invited. Their laughter received a check, and they felt ashamed.

Even Mrs. Vosper, old rogue that she was, couldn't prevent her evil heart from beating more slowly and coldly, for she, too, was forced to breathe the air that was charged with a something unutterable. Shame and the fear of shame had joined the party.

Phœbe Kiddle was soon again to become a mother, and Ann was in trouble too. They had laughed for a little, but now, when their merriment left them, they looked blank and fearful.

' Most nights,' said Phœbe, ' when we 've been

talking and laughing, all the evening be gone. 'Tis then near bedtime, and we go away happy, but time do go slow to-night.'

Ann Kiddle looked at Mrs. Vosper. Mrs. Vosper was knitting a dress for Mrs. Meek. Mrs. Meek had given her the wool, and would also pay for her labour. Mrs. Vosper knitted easily and quickly, as all wicked old women can knit. She could knit with her eyes shut ; she could knit without heeding at all what she was doing.

' She 've finished a whole sleeve while we 've been talking,' said Ann, ' and yet time has gone very slow.'

Jenny Bunce said that she soon ought to be going.

Phœbe and Ann looked at her enviously. They knew well enough, for everything that happens is known in a village, that up to that evening Jenny had escaped the snares that had netted them so easily. They knew, too—and this knowledge gave them an even greater pang for their own folly—that Jenny Bunce had only to hold up one finger to Luke Bird in order to be led to church. But they had always been true to Mrs. Vosper ; they had always blamed Mr. Grunter, and had always lied about the young men.

The chill feeling became a clammy damp that wound in cold coils about the girls, encircling their hearts so that they began to wish themselves dead. Phœbe shivered ; she became aware that something tickled her. She was a girl who was extremely nervous about anything that crawled, and she knew well enough that almost anything might creep up between the stones of Mrs. Vosper's floor. That was why she always pulled up her skirt. She was always afraid of something or other crawling over her skin. She was

sure now that a cold worm was creeping upon her.
She felt the thing move again; she screamed, and tore
at her clothes. She snatched at something, and a large
centipede fell off her and wriggled under the grate.

'Oh, I bain't well,' she sobbed ; 'something do
pain, and I bain't well.'

''Twas all they summer fields,' she cried, 'and no
girl should walk there.'

''Twas they green shady leaves,' whimpered Ann,
looking curiously at herself, as if she wondered that
such a large, splendid creature could be really crying.

'What be howling for ?' called out Mrs. Vosper
angrily, while she knitted the faster. 'All doings
be happiness to a girl.'

'Jenny Bunce be lucky,' moaned Phœbe. 'She
don't know nothing of they summer fields.'

'Oh yes, I do,' said Jenny, who did not wish to be
thought too ignorant in the presence of so knowing
a lady as Mrs. Vosper.

'I could tell you something if I liked, too,'she said.

Ann was happier. She hoped that Jenny had
really something to tell that even the prying ears of
Folly Down had no knowledge of. Jenny told her
story disjointedly ; she did not wish too much to be
made of it ; she only desired to show that she had
had experiences.

'The butterflies were about, and they hedge-roses,
and I did prick me finger reaching up for a rose,
when some one did catch hold of me.'

'Wold Grunter,' said Mrs. Vosper.

''Twas evening time, and I never troubled who
'twere, but I soon let 'e know that Jenny bain't a soft
woon, and I did run to oak tree.'

' To lie down in mossy bed ; 'twas well done of
'ee,' said Mrs. Vosper.

' I did climb tree,' observed Jenny curtly, ' and
Luke Bird, who did come by, did see I up there, and
did fancy that I were a creature from heaven.   But
'e didn't think so for long, for when I threw oak galls
at him, 'e did say I were a white monkey out of hell.
But as soon as he stood back a little I began to climb
down tree.'

The Kiddles looked at Jenny with envious malice.
They saw that her story was going to end happily.
Folly Down must have judged wrongly when it said
that Jenny Bunce had never cared for Luke Bird.

Mrs. Vosper looked angrily at Jenny, too.   This
was not the proper way that things should happen.
In this story the girl seemed the mistress of the affair,
to do or not do as she pleased.   If young girls acted
as they wished, where would her pleasure come in,
or nature's either ? she wondered.   If young girls
listened to themselves instead of to their wise elders,
they might even grow to prefer happiness to squalor,
and gaiety to degradation.

' Thee only climbed down to be seen,' said Phœbe,
pointing a finger at Jenny.

' I won't say no more,' complained Jenny, ' and I did
only say that I bain't to be caught hold of just anyhow.'

Mrs. Vosper looked up from her knitting.

' If thee can talk of such wickedness, Jenny
Bunce,' she said, ' why didn't 'e let some folk do as
they were minded, under tree to-night ? '

' I don't fancy being forced,' answered Jenny.

Jenny spoke loudly, even angrily, and Mrs.
Vosper looked alarmed.

'What be shouting for?' she grumbled. 'How be we to know that some one don't bide outside in the darkness?'

'I thought I heard a step outside,' whispered Phœbe.

Ann shivered.

''Twas as if Jenny did want to tell,' she muttered. 'She were always a little liar and tell-tom at school.'

'I bain't telling no lie,' said Jenny hotly, 'and I don't trouble if God 'Isself do hear what I say.' She raised her voice. ''Tweren't wold Grunter, and I don't care who do know 'en. 'Twas they——'

Mrs. Vosper jumped up. She covered Jenny's mouth with her large hand. She looked anxiously at the window, as if she thought the Shelton police-man might be standing outside and listening to what was being said.

'There's that same step again,' said Phœbe.

'Some one walking in the lane,' said Ann.

The young woman listened, and Mrs. Vosper laid down her knitting and listened too.

The footsteps continued to be heard. They were easy and leisured steps, the slow, measured steps of a peace-loving gentleman who walks in his new-made garden in the cool of the day.

The cottage gate opened and was carefully shut again.

A knock came at Mrs. Vosper's door. Mrs. Vosper went to the door at once; she hoped that the Mumbys were come to finish their work with Jenny Bunce, but a voice in the doorway said:

'Mr. Weston's Good Wine.'

XXII

A PRETTY BEAST

BESIDE a little copse of willows that was reached by one of the prettiest of the Folly Down lanes, and close to a pleasant well of clear spring water, there lived Mr. Luke Bird.

Luke Bird's hut had more the appearance of an arbour than a cottage, and was the very place, no doubt, where good Christian lost his roll, and no arbour upon earth could have been more suited to meditation, that blessed handmaid of all true religion, than Mr. Bird's.

There is no kind of bush growing in the fields that can give more gentle feelings to man, or move more tender and gracious thoughts in his heart, than the willow tree. 'The moon owns it. The leaves, bruised and boiled in wine, subdue lust in men and women. The flowers have an admirable faculty in drying up humours, being a medicine without any sharpness or corrosion ; you may boil them in red wine and drink freely. It is a fine cooling tree.'

No one, and least of all so sensitive a young man as Luke Bird, could dwell in such a place without soon finding himself in perfect harmony with his surroundings. The gentle shade of the cool willows in summer, their kindly shelter against the north wind in the winter, informed Luke Bird that God was kind.

Luke had been unfortunate in his life, for he had once been a clerk in a brewery. But that, though bad enough, is not the worst that we have to tell of him. He had also tried to bring the hearts of the people of a little village called Dodder to God. And even that is not all. He had wished to marry Rose Pring, and he had tried to marry Winnie. But in nothing, neither in religion nor in love, nor in his clerkship, had he been a success.

Luke Bird had been turned away from his work because he had once had the courage to preach a little sermon in office time to Sir James Hop, the rich owner of the brewery, upon the evils of drink. Sir James, who was a member of Parliament, and should at that very moment have been addressing a meeting of his supporters in the Maidenbridge town hall, listened with extreme politeness to Luke, and as soon as the young man had finished, he was kind enough to explain to him, in the mildest tone—whereas Luke had used the warmest—that far the greater part of the liquid called beer is made of pure water, and that, if simple-minded people liked to buy water at six-pence a pint, the drinking of it could do no harm to themselves, but a great deal of good to the firm that sold it.

Sir James also explained that man is a free agent, moving here or there in his own time as he chooses, and dwelling as a rule in a house where, if there isn't a tap in the back kitchen, there is usually a well in the garden. Sir James invited Luke to sit down, and looked at him pityingly, even taking his hand as though he were his own son.

' I am growing an old man,' Sir James said, ' and every day that I live I am more than ever convinced that all men are fools. The Bible says so, and it is certainly true. Nothing will ever prevent people from spending their money foolishly, and I do a very kind thing, for which the country has awarded me a knighthood, in providing a vegetable water, still or bitter, that a man may drink in great quantities and be little the worse for. I do more than that. I keep many a conservative working-man—and I know a little about the mentality of my followers—in the public-houses and away from their homes, where they must always be a horrible trouble to their families.'

To this gentle and persuasive speech Mr. Bird replied a little ungraciously, by saying that whatever else there was besides water in the beer must be poison. But this accusation did not in the least perturb the urbanity of Sir James.

'And why not poison?' he said, smiling, 'for Goethe remarks in his maxims " that life would be utterly impossible to most men if they allowed themselves no drug to neutralise and quiet their distresses." We produce a very mild poison at a very reasonable price, and you must remember, Bird, that the more people pay for a thing the better they like it. We must always charge something, for we cannot cheat our shareholders, who have lent us their money. The more poison we put into the beer the better for our customers, for sometimes, by our means, they are entirely released from all earthly troubles.

'And now, Mr. Bird, I am afraid I must leave you, but if ever you do me the honour to call at my house —you know it is the largest in the town—you may be sure you will be given no beer there.'

The next day Luke was sent about his business.

He at once went to Dodder, but he was unfortunate there too. He talked to the people of things that they had never heard of before and so had no mind to hear now. He talked of a book called the Bible that had once, when it was in Latin, frightened the people into good behaviour. But as soon as this book was translated into the vulgar tongue the people feared it no more ; it was become a King Log to them, and they treated it with the contempt that so many modern Anglican bishops say it deserves.

The people of Dodder would have none of Mr. Bird and none of the Bible. Luke was driven back to the town again, and came to Winnie. He gave her a ring. But the very evening after Winnie had received his present she ran off with a rag-and-bone merchant, named Mr. Kimbo.

Sometimes misfortunes sour and debase the heart of man, but this did not happen with Luke Bird, for, with all his misadventures, he still remained simple and innocent.

He had a sensitive, pleasant, and intelligent face, a friendly and unsuspicious smile, a reddish-brown moustache, and he darned his own trousers.

One disappointment leading on to another, and that to another too, led Luke to believe that a rich brewer is anti-Christ, that young women are less faithful than fleas, and that country people lack souls.

Luke had saved four hundred pounds, and he went to live at Folly Down. There he repaired with his own hands the little cottage that had once been a basket-maker's, but had for many years been occupied by no one. Luke lived upon butter as yellow as guineas, and new bread and well water. He lived

176

beside the willows contentedly enough, but alas ! he soon wished for something to do ; he wished to do good. He wasn't proud ; indeed, he was a very humble young man, but he couldn't help believing that even he, humble as he was, could do some one a kindness.

The great idea of what he might do—at least, the first thought of it—came to Luke Bird one summer evening as he sat in his little parlour, while the soft wind, laden with the delicious scent of meadow and down, filled the room, entering in by the open door. All was peaceful and quiet in the willow copse. Not a leaf stirred. Luke wanted others to love him, and to be happy as he was happy.

He remembered that at Dodder the only creatures who had looked at him with affection were the sheep and the cows and the little singing birds. He remembered that once at Dodder, when he was eating his dinner out-of-doors, a robin had perched upon his shoulder, and had even eaten crumbs out of his hand.

' The creatures are kind and loving to one another,' thought Luke, ' they are different from man.'

Suddenly as he sat there and looked out of his door, he felt convinced that it was the beasts of the field and the fowls of the air that God's Son came down to save. It was they and they alone who possessed souls. The certainty of this new belief filled Luke with hope. God had sent His only Son to be born in a stable, so that the most innocent and simple creatures, the oxen and asses, should have the first chance of salvation.

Luke pictured the scene in his heart : those quiet creatures whose sweet breath rose in holy adoration of the Divine Child—that was more likely a calf or foal than a human child—graciously accepted Him as their Lord. It was man, that unholy beast, that liar to the uttermost, who, with his gross conceit, must needs steal from the rightful heirs the birthright of heaven. With a wicked, an indecent success too, for all earthly animals must appear very much the same in the eyes of the All-Father.

No sooner had Luke conceived this idea, than he at once remembered many incidents as well as passages in Holy Writ that went a long way to prove his new thesis.

To begin with, God's Son is called a lamb a great many times in the Bible, and so, perhaps, He was really one. All through the Bible beasts are written of that show the utmost intelligence and virtue. Noah's dove, Balaam's ass, the ravens that fed the prophet, the bears that devoured the naughty children, are but a few of the many cases—and my readers may add to them—wherein the sense and discernment of the creature far exceeds that of his unjust tyrant and false master, man.

'Besides all that,' thought Luke, 'by the proper law of retribution and recompense, the harmless beasts of the field and the fowls of the air that are so badly used by man '—Luke had witnessed the battue in which Lord Bullman had taken so distinguished a part—' would naturally expect to be better used by God.'

Such thoughts, so exciting and illuminating, occupied Luke's mind during the first summer that came after he had reached Folly Down. He both clearly and forcefully realised how salvation must be accepted by the beasts, by the total subjugation of the will of the creature to the will of the Creator. By the blind faith and trust in a Supreme Power that nothing can disturb, by the belief that says, 'Though He destroy me, yet will I trust in Him.'

That summer and winter went by; the early spring came, and then May. Luke sat at his door, as he had done when he first decided who were the rightful heirs of salvation. There had been a thunderstorm in the day, and a sweet and refreshing rain was falling upon the young willow leaves. Luke looked out of his door. The evening stillness was delightful. No evil sound marred the peace and harmony of nature. He saw nothing that was not gracious, consoling, and beautiful. But he could not stay in such a garden while any beast or bird could be saved by means of his preaching, and that very evening Luke Bird went out into the fields to convert Squire Mumby's bull to Christianity.

The bull was a fine Devon, and possessed the finest pair of horns imaginable. It had won the first prize at three local shows, and was an extremely fierce creature, with a great metal ring fastened in its nose.

Mr. Bird approached it timidly, and when he came near enough he told it, in the most simple words possible, the story of Jesus.

The bull had observed Luke approach with signs of anger. Luke was a stranger to it, and it had no love for strangers. But as soon as Luke had told his story the bull became instantly docile, though a moment before it had bellowed fiercely and tossed up the dirt with its sharp horns.

Luke continued his tale. He spoke most mildly.

He told the bull of the rich pastures in heaven that have neither wall nor hedge, but reach across the whole of the sky, where any creature may wander at will. Luke had only spoken for a little while, and the huge creature, bending his knees first, as if in prayer, soon afterwards lay down and gazed attentively at the evangelist, while its great fierce eyes had become almost kind.

Luke didn't loiter in the field after giving his first sermon, that had been so gratefully listened to. He was a humble young man, and he knew that it was not his presence, but rather the Name that he had spoken, that had calmed the bull. He had no wish to remain longer than necessary. He thought it best that the word should work in his new convert without the near presence of a man. So Luke walked away slowly to the gate of the field, looking back now and again to see if the bull were still lying down.

Once safely in the lane, Mr. Bird returned happily to his little cottage. He was so well pleased with his success that the next morning he arose at cockcrow, and brushing the early dew with his feet, he walked along a footpath that led to the down and visited a field of newly-sown corn and spoke to the rooks.

He told the rooks that all they had to do in order to be saved was to believe the Gospels. The rooks neither cawed nor flew away, which showed that they heeded what he said. One that was perched upon a tree, in order to give warning to the others, evidently regarded Luke as a friend to the birds, while the others merely went on picking at the newly-sown grains of corn that Mr. Mumby's workmen had drilled the day before.

Mr. Bird was now very happy. He loved all the creatures, and even felt more satisfied with his fellow-men, because he knew now that when they died and were buried they would never be heard of again. He even forgave them, in the name of the beasts of the field, because he knew how short their time was.

And now, of course, Luke Bird's cottage gate was ever open to his new converts, who were also his dearest friends. The red-breasted robin entered there, and if a stray donkey passed that way it would be sure to receive a little sermon, Luke's blessing, and a thistle. All beasts that came were welcomed, and even Mr. Mumby's young pigs, that rooted in the grassy lanes and were not very helpful in a garden, would receive a kindly word and a cabbage.

But an event, alas! we are sorry to say, happened to Mr. Bird, during the summer that came before Mr. Weston's visit to Folly Down, that changed Luke's happiness into sadness.

He had let his thoughts wander, which he never should have done. And when he first began to preach to the creatures, he had raised one up in his heart—the fairest, indeed, amongst them all—that he hoped one day to find perched upon the boughs of the village oak, and intended to carry home with him to be his wife. This one would, of course, be a female creature that would lie in his bosom and he in hers, and they would both cherish and adore one another for ever. Thus it was, even though he had foolishly supposed that his new-found happiness was so lasting, that love, which had ever been Luke's torment in life, awoke in him again, and so there was nothing else that he could do but shape and fancy a pretty beast to suit his needs, and he thought upon her at all times.

Every man who has imagination, and who lives in the country, is sure to find out some day or other that he is a lover. For all that surrounds him and all that he sees informs him, in loving words, that beauty exists. He awakes in spring to see the rich meadows covered with yellow buttercups, while the most delicious scents fill the lanes. To live then oneself and to share such beauty with another is a proper desire. To be happy with another, in all the excitement and the glamour of spring, is the proper thing to do. Luke longed in his heart to commit, to rejoice in the committal of, all the most wanton excesses of love.

He imagined, and perhaps wisely, that a pretty beast would refuse him nothing. He watched the beasts and the birds, and discovered that he could get the nearest to them when they were the most amorously inclined. At that time, no doubt, they felt themselves to be very near to their God, and Luke longed to feel the same.

Midsummer came, the time when the earth's breasts heave with love and suckle the soft airs.

One evening, after feeding his robin—about the time when the first star showed itself above the hill— Luke wandered out into the Folly Down lanes in the hope that he might meet Mrs. Meek's old cat, that was called Toby. He wished to recommend it to give better heed to things temporal so that the cat might reach to things eternal.

Luke had walked quietly along the lane in the direction of the green, when suddenly he saw a struggle upon the bank, and something white—he could not tell exactly what it was in the dimness of the evening—fled from the rudeness of a man, who had caught his unsuspecting prey while she culled a rose. It darted like a swallow under the spreading leaves of the oak tree, threw itself upon the lowest bough, and began instantly to climb into the tree.

No one had been expected to pass that way, for all Folly Down had gone to Shelton that evening to a fête, where a brass band would be playing. The bird being flown, the man, who had been sure of his victim, swore so dreadfully at Luke that he found it hard to feel sorry that the man had no soul.

Luke Bird held his hands to his ears, and going in under the oak tree, he looked up. The creature that had fled from the bank was a female one. She was high up in the tree, but as soon as she saw Luke standing below she began to climb down.

He watched her. She was in his eyes an utterly new creature, a new beast of the fields. She threw things down at him, but he still watched her. He had first supposed her to belong to the monkeys—a tribe without souls to which man also belongs. But he soon saw she wasn't that, for though fear had sent her up the tree fast enough, she couldn't descend so easily.

She rested upon a bough and swung her legs. Luke Bird trembled, but yet he looked. She came down a little lower, and at last reached the lowest bough, by whose help she had climbed into the tree. As she was letting herself drop from that, a twig—and no lover could have been more naughtily inclined than this twig—caught her clothes. Luke Bird came near to her.

Luke had more than once thought that, while preaching to the creatures, he ought to have included country girls in his assemblage of living souls. Their manner, their games, and all their ways so exactly resembled pretty heifers, scampering fillies, and leaping ewe lambs, that Luke supposed that God might easily be persuaded to believe that all village girls were animals. Such creatures were entirely unlike the rude men. The girls allowed all things to be done to them without a complaint ; they performed the most servile and dolorous duties without one murmur. With only a very little stretching of God's imagination, He might see them as so many young geese or donkeys and present them with souls.

Luke's heart, as he lifted Jenny into his arms—for this pretty thing was no other than Jenny Bunce— appeared to swim in a great lake of love that had no bottom. He was sure she was no human ; her body was like a fallow doe's. Or else the touch of her reminded him of a lamb that he had once taken from a bush.

He held Jenny very close to himself, and some moments went by before he could release her from the bough. She never spoke one word, and so he knew what she was—a creature who wished to be saved.

XXIII

LUKE BIRD ASKS FOR JENNY

As a simple young man, Luke Bird's thoughts were more direct, and possibly more wise, than most people's are. He had discovered from his own experience that no man had ever listened when he spoke to him about his soul's welfare. That being so, Luke supposed, and we believe rightfully, that if a man really possessed a living soul nothing could prevent him from giving the first and best of his thought and the whole of his consideration—as a Christian should do—to this wonderful phenomenon that must rise from him and be born to glory or to shame when the man dies. Luke had more than once questioned himself—because he did not wish to take anything from man that really was his—in the following manner :

' Suppose,' he reasoned one evening, as he listened to the sound of the wind in the willow leaves, that achieved a more wonderful effect than any man-made instrument, ' suppose, for one moment, that such a thing as a soul existed in Mr. Grunter, why then, if this indeed were the case, the very knowledge of so wonderful a presence, within or about him, as mere ether even, or as an actual thing ; why, then the man's life would have to be different from what it is now, and he would, no doubt, at once cease to do those dreadful things to young women that Mrs.

Vosper informs the world of.   And if any man, other than Mr. Grunter, actually believed that so mysterious a personality as a soul existed as his own, all lives would be freed from care, no cruel deed could be done, no harsh word spoken, and all would regard the wonder within them as their real being and feel themselves as only the outward garment, the cover of this hidden mystery.

' But such divinity in man,' reasoned Luke, ' must be impossible, for man in almost every act of his life gives the lie direct to such an hypothesis.   By his own behaviour man has proved, beyond a doubt, that he has no soul.   But Mr. Mumby's bull is another matter.'

It was most plain to Luke that the very instant that he had named Christ to the bull the beast's soul was awakened.   The bull had at once lain down contentedly, and ever since that day it had fed quietly and never bellowed.   The bull had become an Ox— a wise and sober creature.

Though Luke gloried in this conversion—as wonderful as St. Paul's—Mr. Mumby, who often came to look at the bull, had other ideas.   Mr. Mumby spoke to his sons about the bull ; he complained about its easy and harmless manners ; he even called it a lazy beast, because it took so little notice now of the cows or young heifers.   He said it must be punished, and threatened to have the bull slaughtered.

In the field in which Mr. Mumby's herd generally fed, there was a little mound that in May was always covered with cowslips.   Luke would sometimes, after speaking to the herd, climb upon this mound, and view the village of a summer's evening, when the winds are warm. When he went to this mound he would carry in his pocket a little book, *A Serious Call to a Devout and Holy Life*, by William Law.

Mr. Mumby's herd of cows would feed about him, and sometimes a gentle beast would wander near to him and gaze at him with eyes of affection, and Luke would open his book and inform the creature what heaven was like, and read to it aloud a few pages in a mild manner.

Here indeed was a state of gentle delight, consistent with the indwelling of an immortal soul, guided by wise living through harmless matter to heaven, there to enjoy the large promises of a gracious Godhead.

But how different from such a scene were the village matters when Luke viewed them. He had often seen from the mound first one and then the other of the Kiddle maidens going in under the oak tree with a man whom he supposed, from all accounts, to be Mr. Grunter. From the mound it was possible to see all that happened upon the mossy bed, and Luke Bird, who liked that mound, became more sure than ever that girls, and especially the pretty Kiddles, were just creatures, and that, whatever else a man had, he certainly didn't possess a living soul.

' But do not be affected at these things,' he read in Law's *Call*—he was resting upon the mound one evening in September—' the world is a great dream, and few people are awake in it.'

Luke Bird lay out upon the grass and wished that the dream would bring him Jenny Bunce. He looked at the sweet blossoms of the white clover that bloomed again for the second time that year. Jenny was as fair as they, only she was warmer, and there was more of her, and Luke wished now that he had laid her in the mossy bed instead of allowing her to run away, laughing, when he had taken her down from the oak tree.

He looked to the cows to comfort him. These gentle beasts were all lying down. The bull was there, too, but he showed no signs of falling again into sin.

A splendid red Devon cow, watching him as she chewed the cud, appeared so placid and so holy that Luke felt how true is the Hindu belief which gives a divine being to such an animal.

Jenny Bunce had the same gentle eyes, that could trust as well as love—the holy eyes of a creature of God.

'How ill man might use them both,' thought Luke. ' The kind beast, if fattened, would be driven into a shed reeking with blood and filth, to be bludgeoned to death ; and Jenny, perhaps at that very moment, was being laid hold of by Mr. Grunter.'

Luke left the mound and wandered in the lanes of the village. His happiness was gone, and he found his new burden—love—hard to bear. He could never be glad again until Jenny came to him. He needed her rounded body entirely as his own.

Luke Bird lived curiously after that last visit of his to the mound. He never went there again, but he didn't tell the creatures any more of Jesus ; he began to tell them of love.

He went first to the bull—the cows had been driven into a new pasture—and told it about Jenny, and how much he wanted her. The bull, upon hearing this new tale, at once awoke from its lethargy and became very merry with the herd, leaping a high fence to reach them.

Luke spoke to the young mares about Jenny, and they whinnied with excitement.

All the beasts received this new gospel with even more joy than they had received the story of Jesus, and as soon as the autumn was really come, Mr. Bird felt that he must go to the inn and ask boldly for Jenny. He came to this conclusion the day before Mr. Weston arrived in the village.

The evening was very wet, and Luke vainly tried to button his coat against the wind that rushed down the lanes in angry gusts. The wind met him in the inn yard and nearly took him off his legs. After knocking two or three times at the inn door, which he should have opened at once, he waited in the rain.

He was like Mr. Fearing. 'There the poor man stood, shaking and shrinking. I dare say it would have pitied one's heart to have seen him ; nor would he go back again.' But at length he knocked loud enough to be heard, and was invited to enter.

He timidly opened the tavern door and went in. There were seated in the parlour, Mr. Kiddle, Land-lord Bunce, and Squire Mumby. These gentlemen sat in high state, like three kings, near to the fire, and Columbus knelt above them in his usual attitude of prayer.

Luke Bird stepped forward and spoke, but no one heeded him as he gave no order for beer. Besides, at the moment when he came in, a discussion was being proceeded with between the dealer and the farmer that was far too important to be interrupted by the talk of a lover.

The two were talking about horses—a subject that in all honest English homes takes precedence of all others. Mr. Kiddle had just given his opinion, sanctified by a suitable oath, that a horse could drink twelve gallons of water at one draught, while a cow could drink but eight.

Squire Mumby disagreed. He believed, he said, that his bull could drink as much as any b—— horse.

Now this was exactly what cunning Kiddle hoped he would say, and the dealer replied readily, wrinkling his spotted cheeks into a sort of smile, that he had a horse at home that could empty any pond—' and that is more than thee's bull can do '—that he could sell to Mr. Mumby the very next morning if the farmer would care to purchase such a wonder for thirty guineas.

The talk that Mr. Kiddle always brought round to the guineas usually stopped there, and so at that moment Luke came boldly forward and asked Mr. Bunce for his daughter Jenny.

Mr. Bunce smiled at the young man in a fatherly manner, for this was the first time that Luke had ever entered the inn, and the landlord wished to be polite to him.

' How much money 'ave 'ee saved ? ' asked Mr. Bunce, who, being a wise father, came to the point at once.

' Only a little,' replied Luke respectfully, looking in his nervous anxiety up at Columbus, and hastily wishing that the mariner might mention, along with his thanksgiving for getting to America, Luke Bird's love for Jenny. ' Only a little,' said Luke again, ' but that little shall all be Jenny's.'

The name stirred Luke's heart ; he pressed forward to Mr. Bunce.

' Jenny is not human,' he said ; ' she is much too beautiful to be without a soul. All of her, every little part, is adorable, the lobes of her ears are exquisite, and her little foot is made to be loved. I can give her no higher praise than to tell you, whom I long to call father, that she is a creature, a beast of the fields.'

' 'Tain't proper,' said Mr. Bunce, ' to call a landlord's daughter a brute beast.'

' I mean it as the highest praise that can be given,' said Luke eagerly, ' for beasts alone have souls. She shall share my money, we will eat butter and white bread, and we will drink from the well of pure water that is under a willow tree at the end of the lane.'

Mr. Bunce jumped up, oversetting his mug of beer. He was very angry.

' Horses, I do know,' he shouted, ' and some folks' great ugly bulls do drink thik, but then they know no better, though 'tain't proper nor lawful neither to name water as a drink for even a maiden in this house.'

Luke appeared abashed, but he said mildly :

' I know, Mr. Bunce, that Jenny will not be so well off with me as she is at the rectory, but I will give her all that I have to give. She is the maiden I love, and I must possess her.'

' First thee did name she a creature,' observed Mr. Kiddle, winking at the farmer, ' and now thee do call she a maiden, but how do 'ee know what she be ? '

' I don't like to say how I know,' answered Luke.

Mr. Bunce sat down. He leant back upon the settle and whistled softly. He looked like a sultan who has been asked to give away a slave girl to a nomad of the desert. He whistled no more ; he shook his head slowly ; he seemed to ponder deeply.

Luke waited patiently, with his heart in his mouth.

Mr. Bunce began to speak in stern words as though he were God.

' When such a time do come,' he said slowly, ' that thik bloody water well in lane, that be near to willow tree cottage, be filled wi' good wine, then Luke Bird may wed and bed our Jenny.'

Landlord Bunce solemnly held up his hand.

Luke turned away with a heavy sigh, but before he went out at the door he looked round at the picture of Columbus.

Columbus prayed, and why should not he ? Though Luke was weak in nature, he was bold in prayer, and he prayed that the very next day God, in His loving mercy, would fill his well with wine and bring Jenny Bunce to him to be his wife.

Luke Bird turned once more, bowed low to Mr Bunce, and withdrew.

XXIV

THE END OF A HARE

WHEN a young man is in love, that meek virgin,
nature, weeps and hopes, sighs and longs with him.
No movement of a tree stirred by the wind, no hurried
scuttle and rush of a rabbit in a hedge, no cloud in the
sky, but yearns with him and bids him hope. The
little gnats that court in the air tell him that the
sport is pleasant.

'Do not delay,' chirps the lecherous sparrow,
'take her at once ; every branch is a pretty bed,
enjoy her now.'

Even the cold toad from the marsh bids a lover
be happy under the moon.

The morning after his visit to the inn, Luke
wandered out into the Folly Down lanes. The willow trees and the ferns dropped moisture. Luke
had eaten his breakfast, his yellow butter and his
bread, with sighs. But out-of-doors, nature was
hopeful, and he felt that anything, even the fulfil-
ment of his love for Jenny, might come to pass.

The winter birds, the fieldfares, had come to Folly
Down, and a flock of them were feeding in one of
Mr. Mumby's fields. Luke liked these birds, and
it always pleased him to see them, for to them England was a friendly and lovable country, even in the
winter. Luke leaned over the gate of the field and
told the fieldfares how much he loved Jenny.

Luke's customary habit in the morning was to

gather firewood, and he chose a hedge to-day by which he hoped Jenny might pass if Tamar chanced to send her out to Mr. Meek's shop to buy linen buttons, tape, or boot-blacking. Luke carried a little axe in his hand, and with this axe he tried to cut out a piece of blackthorn from the hedge.

Though the stick he had chosen was dead, it was a stout piece of wood, and Luke's blows made no impression upon it. Sometimes a mere stick or stone has an adamantine resistance within it when attacked by a timid man.

This dead blackthorn root remained stubborn and firm, and though Luke showered many blows upon it, they were all in vain. Luke became more and more nervous.

To strike in this foolish manner at a little stick in the hedge would bring laughter upon him should any one see. He might far more easily have obtained his firewood from the willow bushes, a soft and kindly wood, that grew near to the cottage. But he had already gathered all the dead twigs from there, and he did not wish to tear down the gentle boughs that he knew would be covered with yellow blooms in the spring.

Luke was about to give up the attempt at getting out the root, when a merry laugh in the lane told him that Jenny Bunce had stopped, on her way to the shop, to watch him. She had seen him strike, and Luke, who did not wish to seem unmanly before her, struck again. This time he succeeded better, and tore the root out of the earth. Jenny smiled upon him.

Luke turned to her breathlessly.

' May I love you ? ' he asked.

Jenny bent her head low ; she hid her face in her hands and laughed.

'Oh, they t'others be always saying that,' she remarked as soon as she was able to speak, ' and Mrs. Vosper do say that I be got old enough now to know what love be.'

She moved her feet a little and tapped the mud coyly.

'Don't go, Jenny,' said Luke beseechingly, ' for you are the only girl in Folly Down who has a soul, and you ought to take care of it.'

'But haven't I a body too ? ' laughed Jenny. ' Now, just you see.'

Jenny unbuttoned her coat. Underneath her coat she was wearing a thin black servant's frock, with a low neck. She smiled upon him.

'Oh, Jenny ! ' exclaimed Luke Bird rapturously, for he was an ardent as well as a romantic lover. ' Oh, Jenny, if only I might ? '

'They doings bain't nothing,' said Jenny carelessly. ' 'Tis only what a young girl do like.'

Luke trembled ; he dropped his axe and went near to her. She looked at him gravely, puckered her forehead, turned quickly, and was gone in an instant.

Luke watched her running to the shop. A clod of earth thrown from behind the hedge struck his face. He looked over the hedge, but could see no one. Mr. Grunter worked sometimes in the fields ; Mrs. Vosper was always telling Luke Bird how Mr. Grunter used to amuse himself. Mr. Grunter must have been jealous, and so had thrown the dirt.

Luke Bird felt despondent. He had meant, as soon as ever Jenny had smiled upon him, to throw her upon the bank and to possess her. He had never expected that she could have been so cruel as to run away.

Luke turned down the lane. He left the stick that he had cut with so much difficulty in the ditch ; he was in no mood to care whether he had a fire or no that evening. He wished to meet some creature or other, some brute beast that he could whisper his troubles to. All creatures, he supposed, were better used than he. They could wanton as they chose, and no Mr. Grunter interfered.

Luke walked a little way outside the village and leaned over a gate. He had remained there for exactly one moment when a hare came near to him. Its black eyes expressed the dreadful terror from which it suffered. It was utterly worn out and could hardly move. Luke had never in his life seen a creature whose sufferings were more intense and real than this hare's. The poor beast looked fearfully at Luke, but it had no power to go farther.

Luke had only a moment to pity its lamentable condition, when a large greyhound sprang upon it. The hare gave one piteous scream, and the dog cast it to one side, dead. The dog had followed the hare for its own amusement, and now it loped contentedly towards the place from whence it came.

A thin mist was falling. Luke still leaned over the gate and looked down a grassy bank towards the Mumby's farm.

John and Martin Mumby were exercising their horses that they used for hunting, and were riding them at a little brook that trickled through the Folly Down valley. The horses turned and would not jump. The Mumbys lashed them with their whips. They turned them again into the meadow and rode once more at the brook. Both the horses jibbed. The Mumbys rose in their saddles and lashed them again. They rode furiously round the field, cursing and beating them. At length they came to the brook again, and the horses went over.

Luke Bird blushed. His own heart accused him. This second time in the space of five minutes he had wished to be as brutal as the Mumbys, and when he saw the fierce dog spring upon the tired hare, the dog had only done what he wished to do to Jenny Bunce.

He would have done worse than the dog. The greyhound had left the hare dead upon the grass, but Luke would have torn Jenny limb from limb in the excess of love. And then he saw the horses so cruelly beaten. But why was not Jenny a young filly that he could ride at the brook ? He would beat her worse than the Mumbys did their hunters. Why had he let her go so easily ? He might have stunned her with his axe and then have forced her to his will.

Luke's love became a fierce, despairing longing. In some way or other Jenny must be his.

He spent this November day in walking in the fields. He was always fancying that he saw the dog spring upon the hare, and the Mumbys lashing their timid beasts. The downs, the hills, the church tower, and even the dead thistles and brown bracken made him think of Jenny.

The earth had emptied itself of everything but her. It was a black, a gloomy land ; he wished himself wedded to her or else dead.

In all that Luke did now he only thought of, and saw, Jenny. What he ate was Jenny, when he cut the yellow butter it was her flesh that he divided, and he spread her flesh upon his bread. In his little room there was only himself and emptiness. Nothing, nothing upon earth could fill that emptiness but only Jenny.

He rose suddenly from his chair while he ate, ran hurriedly upstairs and threw himself upon his bed, thinking in the agony of his love that Jenny must be waiting for him there. He embraced the bedcover, supposing that he was kissing her body to death from her head to her toes. He shut his eyes in an ecstasy of desire, and believed that he still held Jenny, with all of her so near to him, as he had done when he lifted her down from the oak tree.

Luke wandered to the down where the old horse was pastured, that later in the day became so interested in Mr. Weston. By some lucky chance this horse, that had in its day been a well-bred hunter much petted by the ladies, was forgotten by Mr. Kiddle, who had offered it at a very small price to the knacker. So, instead of dying horribly in a cargo boat or French cattle truck, or the knacker's shed, it still remained in peace and quiet upon the downs, to be talked to by Luke—and noticed by Mr. Weston.

Luke went to the horse—who, a week later, died peacefully in its sleep in that very place—and told it about love.

' Only such a modest creature as you,' said Luke, patting its neck, ' is fit to hear me. I do not know much about love, but this I do know, that in all its ramifications, in all its manifold appearances, it should be used kindly. Love is the only thing in the world; all else is weariness and wormwood. In its wildest flights, in its most grotesque attitudes, love remains untainted. Unhappiness would fade and perish if love were always kind. All amusements that gather about this wonderful loadstone should be ever treated by all the committees of the world with tolerance and magnanimity. And the most strange abnormalities of love, its most distorted and fantastical expressions, should but be viewed by the magistrates as the rage of God.'

Luke patted the horse.

' All that I have in the world now,' he said, ' is my love for Jenny.'

Beside the willow copse, and sitting in his little cottage again, Luke Bird listened for the sound of Jenny's footsteps in the lane.

' But what is the use of listening for her,' he muttered sadly, ' when there is only water in the well ? '

XXV

LANDLORD WESTON

It is written in an old book that is still sometimes to be seen upon the front room table in a countryman's cottage, that the sun once stopped by request, as an express train will sometimes do at a wayside station. Except in one spot no notice was taken of the event, and the remainder of the people of the earth, other than those immediately concerned, pursued their vocations, their pleasures, and their pains without giving the least heed to the strange behaviour of the sun over a sandy desert.

And yet this story remains a true one, and why should it not be true ? A local occurrence of this nature, a divine juggling with time, can happen, so say our modern mathematicians as well as the more learned amongst our Doctors of Divinity, in any place upon the surface of our known world, or, indeed, throughout the whole universe, if God so wills it.

The proper unfolding of an idea in a novel is a far more important matter, and is seen so from heaven, too, than a mere battle between wandering tribes. But, as every one knows, the most important and far-reaching event is often passed by, unheeded, by nearly all of our fellow-creatures. And should Eternity arrive in truth, as here in fiction, you may take it from me that it will never be noticed.

Men would pursue their callings in just the same way that they do now ; they would rise in the same manner ; they would practise the same virtues, and they would never know that they were but the reflections of their former selves, and only seen in God's looking-glass. One never knows when one dies, and one never knows when everlasting life is begun.

When time stopped in Folly Down, nothing more came of it than a pleasant kind of holiday feeling and a joyful lengthening of an evening, wherein no sort of work need be done. A bull calf might be haggled over at the inn, or a question might be asked about Mr. Grunter, but the deal was never clinched nor the question answered ; and the only fact that was really noted at the inn was that the clock had stopped.

But from this recognised fact there may perhaps have crept into Mr. Vosper's mind, when he perceived that the evening hour of seven seemed likely to remain fixed and permanent, a happy thought that, thank goodness, the next working morning might never come. Mr. Vosper saw much wisdom in the new order.

' There need never be,' he felt, ' any more stooping down, when the white frost is still upon the leaves, to pull mangold in the nipping cold of an early morning, for now there would be only an everlasting —and he might be at the inn for ever now—lifting of a mug to his lips.'

' Time be truly stopped,' said Landlord Bunce, taking a last look at the grandfather clock before he set off to ask the question of the evening of Mr. Grobe.

' And real drinking be begun,' observed Mr. Vosper.

Mr. Thomas Bunce closed the inn gate gently, because the gate was his, and stepped cautiously into the

mud of the lane. He was muffled, as was his wont
when he went out in the winter, in a greatcoat of his
own and a shawl of his wife's that he valued as a warm
one. The air was very still, and the darkness thick
and heavy. Mr. Bunce carried no lantern. He had
so great a love of his own parlour light, and indeed of
any indoor light, that he preferred the darkness to be
real darkness out-of-doors.

Mr. Bunce, when once in the lane, stood still for a
moment. He wished to get accustomed to the
change from light to darkness, and he whistled a
merry tune. Thomas Bunce's mood was, even for
him, happier than usual. The arrival of any stranger
at the Angel Inn who took a friendly glass always
gave to Mr. Bunce a loving feeling to all mankind.
Mr. Weston had come in so genial a manner that Mr.
Bunce felt sure that even if Mr. Weston wasn't his
brother, he had at some time or other in his life been
the landlord of some thriving country inn.

'Landlord Weston,' murmured Mr. Bunce, looking into the thick darkness above him, 'Landlord
Weston.'

Mr. Bunce moved on. Near to the Folly Down
green he went by a Ford car that had a small light
inside it. Mr. Bunce very easily guessed that this
car was Mr. Weston's, and that, inside it, and hidden
by the curtain, some dozens of Mr. Weston's good
wine were stored.

The little light came from a small electric lamp,
fixed above the curtain, by the help of which a young
man, who, strangely enough, reminded Mr. Bunce of
the picture of an angel upon his own signboard, was
writing. The young man was employed—he held

his head rather near to the pages—in entering in a book the few orders that he had obtained from his visits to the more accessible cottages at Folly Down, while his principal, with the proper manners of a master, was taking his ease at his inn.

Landlord Bunce was no despiser of good things : his trade was drink, and he hoped he brought no one to harm by it. The world to honest Bunce was a very good place.

'Here,' Mr. Bunce had more than once said, looking up gravely at Columbus, and then slyly winking at Miss Mary, ' here, we are all churchmen.'

Mr. Bunce believed Mr. Weston. A clergyman, trained at college, should certainly be able to answer so simple a question as to who did the hurt to the Folly Down maidens. Bunce was an old believer ; to him the Church was infallible, and under the set seal of such an authority, Mr. Grobe must be infallible too.

Mr. Bunce viewed the world with a local eye, and that eye a deep one. He never, when he went from his house, forgot for one moment that he had a wife at home who loved to pickle onions, and if he could buy a sack of them anywhere he would always do so. When he went to church he always recollected the past doings of Jenny if Mr. Grobe chose the passage that read, ' Rend your hearts and not your garments,' because Jenny, as a small girl, had more often than not returned from playing with the boys with her clothes torn. When that had happened, Mr. Bunce had usually laughed as loudly as his wife had scolded, and he used to say, winking towards the parlour ceiling, ' That some great folks do want to know more than 'tis right they should about folks' little maidens.'

Because all things pleased Mr. Bunce, whenever he walked in the Folly Down lanes of an evening, if by any chance he met a girl, he would have a word with her, though merely in the way of amusement. He never exceeded a proper merriment, and, as he had more than once said, ' 'Tis best to mind they who be jealous.'

As a matter of fact, no man in Folly Down had a deeper and more loyal respect for anything that was dressed in petticoats than Mr. Bunce, and this was perhaps the reason why he could never believe that these soft ones could allow Mr. Grunter to touch them, ' while there be so good a lover on high.'

It is true that he laughed and joked with them all, hinting mildly of things that might happen if he and they were left alone on the green, but that was only his way of expressing his regard and admiration.

Mr. Bunce hadn't gone far ; he had paused in his walk to look at the young man in the car, and was still beside the green, when he was aware that some one was walking before him whom he took to be a woman. Mr. Bunce quickened his steps until he was sure that she could hear what he said.

' Can't 'ee find no woon about to cuddle and kiss 'ee ? ' called out Mr. Bunce, making use of the ordinary village convention that time upon time had been used before him at Folly Down in order to open a conversation. The reply that Mr. Bunce received was a sigh, as a man, and no woman, turned to him.

This new wanderer in the darkness was Luke Bird, who was searching for the gentleman who sold wine.

' While I sat sadly at my door,' explained Luke, ' wishing for Jenny, I overheard Mrs. Meek say that a man was walking about Folly Down who had wine to sell. Oh, Mr. Bunce, if the wine is cheap enough, I might fill my well, and then you must allow me to take Jenny and wed her.'

' If thee do fill thee's well wi' wine,' said Mr. Bunce, ' 'tis I who must drink first.'

' And so you shall,' replied Luke, ' but please tell me, have you seen Mr. Weston ? '

' 'Aven't 'e called upon 'ee yet ? ' asked Mr. Bunce, ' for I do believe 'is wine be as cheap as water.'

' No,' answered Luke sadly, ' he hasn't come to me yet, but if you think he is going to call I had better go home and wait for him.'

' 'Tis best thee should,' said Mr. Bunce, ' only do 'ee be careful, for thik Weston be a merry woon, and thee do look womanish. 'E be a Weston, and 'e hadn't been up at inn for five minutes before 'e went into kitchen and laid hold of poor Bess and did call 'imself she's brother. 'E don't trouble what 'tis, don't Mr. Weston.'

Mr. Bunce shook the sombre darkness with his laughter.

Luke turned away to go to his cottage, and Landlord Bunce continued his way to the rectory.

XXVI

A WONDERFUL GOOSE

ALTHOUGH the Reverend Nicholas Grobe had ceased for some time to believe in the living God, he had never for one moment forgotten, or ceased to care for, his wife who was dead.

Such a skittish young lady Alice Grobe had been, who could laugh as gaily as could be, and, with all her pretty ways, she had never grown tired of making fun of her husband.

She discovered his fears and made much of them. For as soon as the honeymoon was over, she began her merry tricks, quickly noticing that her husband had the utmost dread and terror for Mr. Mumby's geese. He would never approach the farm if they were near, and had once even climbed the oak tree upon the green to escape them, and had been unable to climb down again until the evening came and the maidens—and then Mr. Grobe modestly shut his eyes and coughed.

Mrs. Grobe heard this story, and at once purchased from Mrs. Mumby a goose and a gander for the rectory garden, on purpose to enjoy the entertainment of seeing Mr. Grobe, when he took a turn round the garden, run away from them.

Mr. Grobe was most regular in his habits, as a good clergyman should be, and every morning, at about half-past ten, before he began his usual reading, he used to take a walk in the garden, going first down a narrow path beside a rockery, and then returning, if the grass were not too wet, across the front lawn.

A goose is a very knowing bird, and these rectory geese never forgot the time when Mr. Grobe took his stroll, and they would lie in ambush near the narrow path, and rush out even more fiercely than they did later at Luke Bird upon the hillside.

Mr. Grobe could never learn to say ' boo ' to them. He used, directly they attacked him, to turn and flee away, hoping, with eager strides, to reach the front door before the angry birds caught him by the coat-tails.

Mrs. Grobe would watch from the window and clap her hands with delight.

But as soon as ever Mr. Grobe was safe in his study and had taken a favourite book into his arms, he at once forgot the geese and all his fears of them. Although he ran from the geese, Mr. Grobe was no coward, and one day, in walking down a lane to visit a dying woman, he was met by Mr. Mumby's bull, who was no Christian then, and who charged furiously upon Mr. Grobe. But the good man gently stepped aside, holding his Bible safe, and, reaching the cottage he was going to, he bid the woman die happy, for Jesus had died for her.

As any one may easily guess, Mr. Grobe's appearance was most quiet and staid, which was perhaps the reason, more than any other, that his pretty lady loved to play upon him so many a naughty prank. Even his modesty and bashful love-making amused her, for he would touch her so penitently, as though it were all his evil nature that prompted and directed such doings, and he would always say how sorry he was when he behaved the most lovingly.

' My dear,' he would beg of her, ' you must, you must forgive me, for all men are only nasty animals.'

She used to enjoy hearing him say that, and she would provoke him to go to any length at any hour of the day. She might perhaps be changing her frock in her bedroom, while he was looking into the Bible in his study, and trying to explain how the Saviour came to be born in two places at once—He said, that not in two places alone, but in every place He is born—and a naughty fit would possess her, and she would run downstairs and dance before him, wearing only her chemise. She would open his door so softly, and he, deep in his book, would hardly know what she was doing until she spoke to him.

' Now, look at me,' she would say, holding up the border of her chemise with both her hands as a dancer does, ' and you mustn't take your eyes off me for one moment. Now see what I can do, Nicholas.' She would make a mock bow.

' Perhaps you are not aware, Nicholas, that I am a young woman, perhaps you fancy me to be a young boy because my hair is cut short. Now look, Nicholas—and when I am gone you can read to yourself the conclusion to part II. of *Christabel*, that you are so fond of, and you will know what it all means when I 've done with you.'

Mr. Grobe almost looked afraid.

' I 'm not a goose, you know, and now I will put these ugly chairs to one side and dance to you.'

Alice Grobe danced with a lively grace and true movement. She would step so near to him that he

might have touched her, and display herself in so
wanton a manner that Mr. Grobe's heart would beat
with violence, and his hands would turn over the
pages of the holy Bible with hurried zeal.

When she was tired of dancing, she would throw
herself down upon the study sofa, her naughty eyes
even more naughtily inclined than ever her feet had
been upon the soft carpet.

Mr. Grobe would watch her for a moment, and
then he would leave the Bible and approach her
cautiously. He would kneel down beside her and
take her hand and kiss it.

' My dear,' he would say nervously, ' perhaps I
might—would you think me too horrible ?—but you
know how lovely you are.'

He would kiss her hand again and she would laugh.

' Oh, but I 'm not your daughter,' she would
whisper, ' I 'm your wife, you know,' and she would
draw his head nearer to her heated lips and force his
hands to fondle her.

This pretty lady ever renewed her wantonness.
There was always the person of her husband to draw
to her. There was always the danger, and she was
well aware of it, that Mr. Grobe might fall into the
arms of some old heathen in his bookcase, or else go
too near to God—and she certainly tried her best to
deliver him from such dangerous company.

She hardly ever appeared as the same person
before him. There was always some girlish fancy
that he had not seen in her that she could use to beguile him. She was able—a wayward beauty often
is—to gather ripe strawberries from under the forest
snow. Her smile or the look of her bare arm could

do that. All of her, at any time, would seem to peep slyly at her husband, mocking him and whispering :

'Ah, you are a grave, a sober personage, but I know what you are wishing to do to me. You have set up a fine thing in your grave mind to worship, that isn't always so hidden as it should be, and oh, heavens ! what naughtiness a cautious clergyman will stoop to do.'

In Lent her sportive manners sometimes went, her husband feared, a little too far, for she once ran down to him, after taking her bath one Sunday, while the church bells rang for Evensong, and tempted him to wanton with her. Mr. Grobe did then mildly hint that God might cease to love them if they did such things during that season.

'Oh, He won't mind,' she said gaily. 'You needn't be so afraid of Him ; He isn't a goose.'

'I fear He is a goose,' replied Mr. Grobe, innocently taking his wife into his arms and kissing her.

XXVII

MR. BUNCE VISITS THE RECTORY

Mr. Grobe stood beside his study fire.   He gently knocked out the ashes from his pipe and looked for a few moments at an enlarged photograph over his mantelpiece.   The photograph was that of a lady, more pretty certainly than any minister's wife should ever be.   The lady was holding under each arm a large goose.

Mr. Grobe filled his pipe again.   He lit it, and walking across the room he opened a cupboard from which he took out a bottle.   He feared the bottle might be empty, and it was empty.   Mr. Grobe drew the cork and tipped up the bottle into a glass, but no liquor fell.

Upon the little table near to his easy-chair, there was a large Bible.   Mr. Grobe placed the empty bottle beside the Bible and rang the bell.   He wished to ask Jenny to go to the Angel Inn and purchase another bottle.   No one answered his ring.   Mr. Grobe put the empty bottle away into the cupboard again. He was disappointed.   He supposed that he must have finished the bottle the evening before.

Upon other evenings, Mr. Grobe's melancholy had often been consoled by two things—the Holy Bible and the Holy Bottle.   If one had not eased his cares, the other sometimes did so.

Mr. Grobe fancied he took up the Bible.   He

seemed to move with it to the bookcase, placing it there, and yet when he looked again the Bible was upon the little table. He went to the fire. He knew he had not taken the Bible into his hands, and yet he was holding the book in his hands. He placed the Bible upon the little side-table. He sat down in his chair. He certainly had not lifted the book up, but the Bible was upon his lap.

Mr. Grobe looked curiously at the Bible. Had the book anything to tell him ? He placed it upon the table and looked at it. Was it telling him that a queer stranger was very near—was walking perchance at that very moment in the lanes of Folly Down.

It often happened that Tamar and Jenny both went out of an evening and left him alone. Jenny was supposed to lay the supper in the dining-room before she left the house, but she often forgot to, and Mr. Grobe, who wooed the long silent lamp-lit evening as one woos a fair bride, never took the trouble, if left to himself, to go to the dining-room to eat.

Mr. Grobe smiled at the Bible. The curious fancy that he had had about its having moved of itself now only amused him. He lay back in his chair ; the chair received him kindly into its arms. He felt a beatific stillness, a holy peace that follows the wind and the earthquake.

Mr. Grobe took a volume of poetry into his hands that he had been reading earlier in the evening. It was a book of poetry that he wished to have in his hands when he died. The author of these poems seemed to know all about his affairs, to know that all the gay and naughty notions of his wife had been at least safe with him. She had never harmed herself with him. She could dance as she liked, even with the lack of more than one garment of modesty, if she danced in his garden. She had at least been safe with him, and so long as his old-fashioned ways and fears continued to amuse her, she had never shown the least wish or desire to leave the rectory.

Mr. Grobe held the poetry book open in his hand. He came upon a passage marked years ago, and read it now :

> ' Well—one at least is safe. One shelter'd hare
> Has never heard the sanguinary yell
> Of cruel man, exulting in her woes.'

But was she so sheltered, for even though he, her husband, had always remembered to pull the curtains when his pretty wife wished to behave naughtily, her own child had been cruel to her, and had killed her.

With one moment, with the smallest alteration of time, God—and how could a loving God exist who would withhold His hand when He might save ?—surely if He had the power He would have allowed her to live a little longer.

Mr. Grobe closed the book of poetry written by an author to whom the title of 'the poet' has been unanimously given by the world. ' The poet Cowper '—none other, not even Shelley, has been universally called so.

Resting there in the silence, Mr. Grobe was conscious that a strange feeling, or more properly a strange presence, moved in the air that evening. Remembrance, more vivid and real than usual, brought his wife back to him. Even though the winter evenings were wont to comfort him, this par-

ticular evening, more than any other, vouchsafed to
heal his wound.

He forgave Tamar. She was out in the Folly
Down lanes now, in the darkness. It was like Tamar,
it was like her mother's child to fall in love with an
imaginary being who wore blue trousers.

No ordinary man would certainly do for Tamar.
She had all her mother's wildness, but a heart even
deeper than hers.

Suppose that Tamar did happen to discover her
angel under the oak tree ! Perhaps, out of such fair
lovers' doings, a fine rosy babe might be born—a
babe that would be sure to love a blue sky and
laughter, and be glad enough to make all the fun in
the world of its earthly grandfather.

' How silent everything is to-night,' thought Mr.
Grobe. ' Out of such a stillness a holy faith may
come. If this evening be but long enough, who can
tell what will not happen ? If the evening do but
last, then a bottle will be filled with wine ; then I
shall dare to name Him again.'

Mr. Grobe became so lost in his reverie that he
fancied his wife to be with him in the room. She had
always liked to be merry in his study, ' to make those
wicked old books ashamed of themselves for being so
dry—and now I want them to see what a nice girl is
made of,' and she would raise her frock, stand and
curtsey to Hooker's *Ecclesiastical Polity*.

' You old rascal ! ' she would say, taking out the
folio from the shelf, and looking at Hooker's portrait
in the first page. ' You old wretch ! You are wishing
yourself a shepherd so that you might play with the
maidens.'

' Ah, but he had a wife,' Mr. Grobe murmured.

' A shrew,' laughed Alice. ' I know she was a shrew and afraid of showing her own skin, I suppose.'

' And Hooker tended sheep too,' said Mr. Grobe.

' I wonder she let him,' laughed Alice, ' if they were ewe lambs.'

Mr. Grobe rose from his chair. The silence was broken ; there were sounds in the house. Tamar must have returned from her walk without her father hearing her. She must have answered the door too, and some one must have knocked. She was now bringing a visitor to the study. Mr. Grobe heard a rolling, unsteady step in the passage.

' Who is it ? ' he wondered.

Mr. Grobe looked at his watch. It was seven o'clock. He had not expected it to be so early : he thought he had been sitting there for some hours. Was he ill ? His asthma had been worse of late, but his breathing had been better this evening, and he felt no pain in his heart, that the asthma he was subject to left weakened. He felt better than he had been for years.

The rolling steps drew nearer. Mr. Grobe heard Tamar's voice talking to some one. Who could the visitor be ? Was it Tamar's angel that she was bringing with her to-night ? But an angel wouldn't walk clumsily ; he would come with a light step, as if he walked upon flowers.

Tamar opened the study door, and Mr. Grobe turned to her.

He was startled and surprised by her appearance. Her cheeks glowed like a bride's and her eyes shone, moist and loving. She wore a thin, white wedding frock, that Mr. Grobe knew was her mother's, and in Tamar's hair there were orange blossoms, revived by some magic means, that Alice Grobe had worn upon her wedding day.

Mr. Grobe was surprised, but he wasn't the kind of father to make much of such matters, and he only supposed that Tamar had dressed in such a manner in order to show Jenny Bunce what a fine bride she would be if her angel came to Folly Down that evening.

Tamar smiled. Her beauty was an awful thing to behold. It was a beauty, radiant and terrible—the triumphal loveliness of a bride who knows that the bridegroom is near.

' Mr. Bunce, father,' she said, ' wishes to speak to you.'

Mr. Bunce hadn't looked at Tamar. He was too wise a man to look at her in the dress she was wearing ; he preferred to stare at the hall lamp when he passed it.

Tamar admitted Mr. Bunce, and shortly afterwards the front door of the rectory opened and shut. Tamar was gone out to look for her angel.

Mr. Grobe welcomed his visitor good-humouredly. He motioned Mr. Bunce to a chair, and the landlord sat down.

Landlord Bunce appeared well pleased to be there. Tamar had met him in the garden and had led him in. The first thing good Bunce did when he was seated was to nod at the fire, the second to look above the mantelpiece, in the fond hope of seeing another Columbus there.

It was like Bunce to expect to see Columbus everywhere, for he could never believe that any home would be complete without this praying figure. His clock was different ; that had a story, a history, and a worshipper. Columbus was a person that should be everywhere. But even if there were no Columbus over the mantelpiece, there was a picture of a pretty lady. Mr. Bunce smiled at her.

What Mr. Bunce had come for, Mr. Grobe did not know, neither was it easy for him to discover at once what it was that had brought him. It appeared necessary for Mr. Bunce to get used to his chair before he communicated his business. He had sat in the easy-chair as gently as if he supposed the cushion to be the lap of a young woman, but at last, after everything had been mentioned that could be mentioned about Folly Down, Mr. Bunce suddenly said :

' I be come, for 'tis a long evening we be got into, to ask a question of 'ee.'

After this sally Mr. Bunce became utterly silent. He could only gaze round the room, for he wished to obtain the help and countenance of the chairs and table in his enquiry. At length he proceeded.

' I have been advised,' he said, ' to seek thee out, who be a man learned enough to bury or to marry any woon in Folly Down.'

Mr. Grobe bowed. Mr. Bunce's words were evidently intended to convey the highest praise. He wished he had a glass of spirits to offer to him, but, alas ! his bottle was empty.

Having once really begun, Mr. Bunce looked around the clergyman's study for further inspiration. He noticed the bookcase.

' Learning,' he said, ' be shut up in all they large

books, and Mr. Grobe be the woon to know our little village.'

Mr. Grobe looked down modestly. Mr. Bunce rolled in his chair.

'Thee do know all things,' he exclaimed excitedly. 'Thee do walk in the fields in primrose time, thee do climb Folly Down hill, where they little yellow flowers do breed in June, and thee do go down beside green, for to spy what they maids be doing when they be out. But all that do happen outside ; bain't nothing to what be written down in they wide books. All wonders be written there, all they women's doings. They large pages,' reflected Mr. Bunce, waving his hand in the direction of the bookcase, 'be filled wi' the superfluity of naughtiness ; all the learned ways of wickedness are writ there. How indeed could a poor man, same as Grunter be, know what to do for the worst wi' a maid, when all they holy matters be only for the wise and the learned.'

Mr. Bunce paused. He looked from the books to Mr. Grobe.

'A minister of the Gospel,' he said respectfully, 'do know all that they books do tell.'

Mr. Grobe bowed.

Mr. Bunce moved his chair very near to the minister's. He put his finger to his lips, he looked suspiciously round the room, he leaned forward and whispered in Mr. Grobe's ear.

'Did 'ee ever,' he asked, 'on woon of they sad summer evenings, when a poor landlord do fear that no lamp mid ever be lit again, and when up in silly sky they foolish birds be still singing, did 'ee ever peep in under oak-tree leaves and see what they books

do tell of—woon or t'other of they Kiddle maids
a-doing something that be curious to look at ? '

' Very curious indeed,' replied Mr. Grobe reflectively ; ' but I fear you give my poor books the credit
of an exact knowledge of human happenings that,
alas ! they often lack. There are some classical
examples of amorous dealings, but few others,
though you know, Mr. Bunce, that in the old days
the gods' doings were spoken of very freely.'

Mr. Bunce slapped his knee.

' There be only woon now,' he said.

Mr. Grobe sadly shook his head.

' I don't say,' remarked Mr. Bunce, ' that 'tis 'E
who be always under oak tree wi' a maid, but what I
do say be this, that 'twas 'E who first started they
funny practices.'

' I fear not,' said Mr. Grobe. ' But what is your
question, Mr. Bunce, for if you will be so kind as to
tell me what it is, I will answer you as best I can ? '

' 'Tis this,' cried out Mr. Bunce, sitting upright in
his chair, and speaking in a loud tone : ' be 'en wold
Grunter or God Almighty who do all the mischief
in Folly Down ? '

This question, so suddenly delivered by Mr.
Bunce, so surprised Mr. Grobe, that for some
moments he was entirely silent, and could only
regard, in an astonished manner, the landlord of the
Angel Inn.

Mr. Bunce appeared to be sober, and he evidently
expected a reply.

Mr. Grobe leaned back in his chair and made a
slight sound with his lips—a surprised ' Whew ! '

He leaned near to Mr. Bunce. He placed his

hand lightly upon the landlord's shoulder, so that had there been a fly there he would not have harmed it.

' There may be some,' said Mr. Grobe very gently, ' though perhaps amongst them you would find no dean or bishop, who would have preferred that you put God's name before Grunter's.'

Mr. Bunce gazed at the pastor. He was aware of his error, but still he knew, whichever name he had placed first, he had given his minister a hard question to answer.

Mr. Grobe bent his head low, he was evidently considering the matter very gravely, and he looked as though he felt very sad.

Mr. Bunce was sorry for him, and hoped that by a hint or two he might enlighten him a little about one of the parties alluded to.

' We do all know wold Grunter,' he said encouragingly. ' In times past 'e did trap rabbits and cut nettles, and now 'e be the clerk to the church who do call out Amen. But though they doings be something, they bain't all that Grunter do do, for Folly Down folk do say that Mr. Grunter have another profession. Now God be different to Grunter, for 'E bain't to be seen.'

' God is indeed different from Mr. Grunter,' said Mr. Grobe sorrowfully, ' for He doesn't exist.'

It was now Mr. Bunce's turn to be astonished, and we may certainly forgive him for being so. To a good churchman, as our landlord was, Mr. Grobe's remark that there was no God sounded like the word of a fool. Had any one else in the village other than Mr. Grobe committed himself to this strange and unforeseen announcement, Mr. Bunce would cer-

tainly have contradicted it at once, for with such un-
belief as that going about the world, what value would
any one have for Mr. Bunce's opinions ?

Mr. Grobe saw his embarrassment and wished to
comfort him.

' Do not be disturbed, Mr. Bunce,' he said, ' for
as God is so little heeded amongst men, He is not
likely to be very much missed.'

' I shall miss Him,' said the landlord, ' very much
indeed, for who are we to blame now for all the
wickedness of the world ? '

' We must blame ourselves,' said Mr. Grobe
readily.

' 'Tis more likely we should blame each other,'
observed the landlord, laughing. ' But, no, no.
Thik fancy tale won't do for I. I bain't going to be
blamed for nothing by me neighbours, and maybe
'tis too much learning that 'ave made 'e say there
bain't nor God.'

' I hope you are right, landlord,' replied Mr. Grobe.

XXVIII

MR. BUNCE IS INSULTED

Nothing so far that evening had caused Mr. Grobe to have the least suspicion that time was behaving in any way out of the common, though perhaps he did fancy that the evening was going a little slowly.

Mr. Bunce seemed to be in no hurry to rise and go. That was a little curious, but then Mr. Grobe knew how the good landlord loved a comfortable room and enjoyed the lamplight, more than any daytime environment.

Mr. Grobe now wondered a little. What if the minutes that moved so slowly stopped altogether? Perhaps all that would happen would be that the lamp would go out and Mr. Bunce would depart. The fire might go out too, and perhaps darkness might come to others than the lamp and the fire ; perhaps a long dark night might come to him. He was as ready for it, he hoped, as ready as any man could be. Of course there would be Tamar to be left behind, but if Tamar found her angel all must be well with her. And what mattered it how long and how dark the night was, for if God didn't exist, what need was there for Nicholas Grobe to exist either ?

Mr. Grobe was a sincere, an honest man. Whenever any one asked a question of him, he always made it his business to answer as truthfully as he knew how.

He had answered Mr. Bunce, but he did not wish that his answer should lie too hard upon the church clerk and sexton, Mr. Grunter. He did not wish, because he doubted the existence of one of the competitors, to lay all the blame, as must needs be, upon the other.

Mr. Grobe stood up. He leaned against the mantelpiece ; he held his pipe in his hand, and he filled it slowly. The room was warm and pleasant ; the lamplight gave a lively being to everything there ; the fire and the cushioned chairs, if they could have spoken, would have consoled their master, telling him that true love can gather force in remembrance, and that sorrow, if one sorrow long enough, can become a thing of beauty in the heart of a man.

Mr. Grobe lit his pipe. He turned and looked kindly upon Mr. Bunce.

' Although I am afraid,' he said, ' and I wish to be honest with you, that I must put God out of the question, because I cannot believe in any Holy One who, having all the whole power to save in His hands alone, could allow a horrid train to crush a lovely woman to death '—Mr. Grobe paused to lay his hand reposefully upon the Bible—' it is best to be honest,' he said, ' and, if God Himself came into this very room this evening, He would be honest too, and He would no doubt say, as I of Him, dismissing me from His thought with a nod, and so from existence, that He didn't believe in Nicholas Grobe. That would be only just and proper that while I, and many another, say that of Him, He should say the same of us. We should only receive our lawful due at His hands. Even when I used to believe in Him, I would sometimes say, in my poor and indifferent sermons, that God Almighty has the right to do what He will with

His own. Even if He makes a good thing, He has a right, the lawful right of a creator, to destroy it, to stamp it out everlastingly, to say to the man, "Thou shalt never be through all Time and Eternity a living soul again." Why, indeed, should He make any fine pother over us, when He can create or destroy when He will the vastness of the firmament or the minutest atom?

'Alas! that is how I used to talk, but how can such dreadful powers be called love? No, no, Bunce, there is no God.'

Mr. Grobe leant over the landlord's chair. Mr. Bunce was sadly depressed.

'But even with God gone,' Mr. Grobe said more cheerfully, 'as I fear He is, from our world, there is no need for us, or rather the folk of Folly Down, to lay all the blame of all the fleshly folly upon Mr. Grunter, because we may easily suppose that there may be others in the village who are quite as able and quite as willing to make love to the maidens under the oak tree as the good clerk—you yourself, Mr. Bunce, are a man!'

Mr. Bunce rose angrily; he shook his fist in the face of the pastor; he appeared to be much annoyed at this mild suggestion. He held up his hand in imitation of his former master, the Dean, who would do so when he corrected any error that a servant committed. Mr. Bunce was shouting.

'If God 'Imself did ring front door bell,' he exclaimed, 'and were brought by Miss Tamar or our own Jenny into this room, I would say out as loud as I be now talking that 'tis 'E and not Grunter who do cuddle they naughty maids.'

Mr. Bunce was not the man to miss the chance, though he was angry, of saying the right thing to a neighbour. And, although a knock at a door isn't a ring, Mr. Bunce had most properly said ' the front door bell,' as a nice compliment to a gentleman's house, where a bell should be the correct means of conveying the intelligence that some one has called, even though a knocking at the door does imply the same wish to enter as the pealing of a bell.

Mr. Bunce had hardly spoken when a modest rapping was heard at the rectory front door. Mr. Bunce remained standing. He looked at Mr. Grobe, and his eyes grew larger and rounder.

' There be some one outside, Bunce,' he said, speaking to himself as he sometimes did when any-thing unforeseen might be going to happen. ' Do 'ee know that some one be waiting outside, Thomas Bunce, and though 'tis thee's habit to name some folk at home, yet maybe 'tis best to be silent when thee be visiting. Thee bain't afraid, Thomas, no, no, thee bain't afraid, for 'tis a nice handsome thing to say of a holy king, that 'e do fancy a fine pretty maid. 'Tis a word of praise and worship to say who be the merry woon, Mr. Bunce.'

Another tap was heard.

Mr. Grobe waited, with his hand upon the Bible. He listened to hear if any one answered the knocking. But no step was heard in the passage, for neither Tamar nor Jenny was in the house.

Mr. Grobe's thoughts had been solemn : he had not heeded what Mr. Bunce was saying, but now he spoke to him.

' Please be seated, Mr. Bunce,' he said, ' and I will go and see who this evening caller is.'

Never in all his life did Mr. Bunce think that he had waited for so long a time as he waited now, expecting Mr. Grobe's return. He thought he sat there for years. But at last Mr. Grobe opened the door and admitted the visitor, who was Mr. Weston, and whom Mr. Bunce was very glad to see, for he feared that, had it been the Other, something might have been said about his words of praise.

' 'Tis well 'tis you and not t'other,' said Mr. Bunce, ' for us two be friends.'

Mr. Weston shook Mr. Bunce heartily by the hand.

' 'Tis a strong grip thee have,' said Mr. Bunce, glad to be relieved from so crushing a handshake.

' Oh, we are friends,' said Mr. Weston.

Mr. Grobe placed a chair near to the fire for the stranger, whom he had already suspected of having something to sell. It was by no means an unusual thing that a gentleman connected with trade should call at the Folly Down rectory, and though this time it happened in the evening, such a call had nothing extraordinary about it.

Indeed, only a week before, a very polite and genteel young man, with kind eyes, who represented a firm that sold portable glass-houses and garden chairs, had called a little late in the day, having had a mishap upon the road. He had been very kindly welcomed by Mr. Grobe, who received the price list of his goods gratefully, promising to consider, when the summer came, the purchase of a chair.

A lonely man like Mr. Grobe was glad to admit

any genuine trader, though he deplored the fact that so many cheats visit the villages who, dressed as gentlemen, find it a very easy matter to rob the poor of their money. But on the whole, when Mr. Grobe considered the matter, fewer impostors visited Folly Down than might very well have come, when every village person is so easy to gull by a plausible man.

Mr. Weston was by no means the sort of trader to keep any one in suspense as to what he had to sell.

'I am a wine merchant,' he said, as soon as he was seated. 'I am able to supply a very good wine at a low price. I give ten per cent. discount for ready money. My wine is new.'

'But I am afraid,' replied Mr. Grobe, 'that I prefer old wine.'

'My firm,' said Mr. Weston, 'has been established a long time, and when I describe the wine that I am offering you as new, I do so but to contrast this vintage with our oldest and strongest wine, many pipes of which we always store in bond, but only deliver when a very special request is made.'

'A dark wine of a high price, I suppose ?' said Mr. Grobe.

'Yes, a deadly wine,' replied Mr. Weston in a low tone. 'And by no means to the taste of Landlord Bunce,' he added, smiling.

'No, no,' said Mr. Weston, looking curiously at Mr. Grobe, 'the wine that I like best to offer to the public—for, though I hate nothing that I have made, I prefer to sell this lighter kind—compared to our oldest is very new, and this new wine can be drunk at all times without the chance of a headache.'

'Do not, I pray you, think my question a strange one, Mr. Weston,' said Mr. Grobe, 'but do you yourself ever drink that deadly wine that you speak of?'

'The day will come when I hope to drink of it,' replied Mr. Weston gravely, 'but when I drink my own deadly wine the firm will end.'

'And your customers?' asked Mr. Grobe.

'Will all drink of it too,' said Mr. Weston.

'Ah,' observed Mr. Grobe, 'it would be better, I think, to begin with your milder wine.'

'Mr. Grobe be right enough there,' laughed Mr. Bunce, 'for most like, thik dark wine Mr. Weston do name would make a man so dead drunk that 'e wouldn't know nothing no more.'

'You never spoke a truer word in your life, landlord,' said Mr. Weston.

Mr. Weston turned to Mr. Bunce. Evidently the wine merchant wished to allow Mr. Grobe a few moments to decide whether he wished to give an order or no, for, in all his trading, Mr. Weston has always granted time to those who may wish to buy of him.

'I fear,' said Mr. Weston, smiling at Mr. Bunce, 'that even all the learning of the church, accumulated during nearly two thousand years, has been unable to answer your question.'

'No, 'e haven't answered,' replied Mr. Bunce brusquely, for he still felt aggrieved that Mr. Grobe had suggested that he, being a man, might be a sinner too, 'and 'e do say 'tis any of we men have been a-playing wi' petticoats, maybe 'tis thee or I, Mr. Weston.'

Mr. Bunce spoke to Mr. Weston in a far more familiar manner than he addressed Mr. Grobe, for, having made up his mind that Mr. Weston had once been a landlord, he fancied himself more drawn to him than if he had been his lost brother.

' But thik bain't the worst,' said Mr. Bunce, giving Mr. Weston a sly dig in the ribs, ' 'e did tell I that there bain't nor God.'

Mr. Weston coughed. He appeared to take a sudden interest in the portrait of the young lady who held the geese. Mr. Grobe was looking at her too, but he hadn't only been looking at Alice, he had been thinking about Mr. Weston's Good Wine.

His thoughts had taken him far, though soon he spoke quite amiably.

' I should very much like,' he said, ' if you have no objection, to take a glass of your lighter wine before I order a bottle of the other. I should like to taste it now, for this evening I have nothing to drink.'

' Those that ask of me, sir,' said Mr. Weston, ' receive what they ask for. I have already anticipated your wish, and have brought you a sample bottle.'

Mr. Weston rose from his chair.

' Kindly excuse me,' he said, ' for I have a few more calls to make, but you may be sure I will return to you again before I leave Folly Down, to receive your orders.'

Mr. Grobe rose too, but Mr. Weston gently restrained him.

' Do not trouble to conduct me,' he said. ' Strange though it may sound, your door has been open to me too long for me to forget the way into your house.'

Mr. Weston bowed, opened the study door, and was gone.

XXIX

WOMEN AT THEIR DOORS

ALL Folly Down knew that Miss Tamar Grobe expected one evening to find an angel waiting for her under the oak tree. Even when Tamar was a child and little thought that any one was looking, she had often been seen by prying eyes to stand and look up with admiration at Mr. Bunce's signboard.

In those early days Mrs. Grunter, who loved to stand in her open doorway—just as Mrs. Meek loved to stand in hers—and they were neighbours—remarked one evening, 'Little maid Tamar be for ever expecting signboard angel to come down from 'is post to tickle and tumble she.'

Growing older, Tamar's beauty had the fine distinction of being noticed by Mr. Kiddle, who said, one Sunday evening at the inn, after church was over:

' Miss Tamar be a pretty-mannered heifer to go to grass in glebe meadow, and 'tis to be hoped they young bulls won't break fence after she.'

People wondered if Tamar would, having been sent to no young ladies' boarding-school where, it is said, all things may happen, receive any young man to court her at home.

But though Mrs. Vosper—and indeed all the other women—watched day by day all the approaches to the rectory, no young gentleman came. And Miss Pettifer of Madder, who kept a live servant in cap and apron to answer her door, used often to say, and in by no means a gentle tone of voice, that poor Tamar Grobe—' and what a sinful name to give a child ! '—was monstrously neglected by the fool who was her father.

But the gossips of Folly Down, the common people, were wont to look at Tamar and at Mr. Grobe, too, in quite another manner than Miss Pettifer. What was quite unbelievable to a lady who received dividends by post was believable enough to them. The people of Folly Down knew well enough that no artist, how-ever gifted, can paint the picture of an angel—or of a devil either, for that matter—without first having seen a vision of one. So many simple people have seen in their hearts something that they could paint, had they but the colour and the brush, that none ever doubted the reality of another's picture. Mrs. Vosper believed that, had she been to Lord Bullman's school and learnt a little, she would have made a fine picture of the Emperor of China, whom she had once dreamt of. No one in Folly Down had ever doubted that the original of the picture upon the Angel Inn signboard must be somewhere, and so they supposed it was by no means impossible that such an appearance in human form might one day come to Tamar. He would fly down, change his wings into a Sunday coat, go in under the oak tree, and wait for his young girl.

Mr. Grunter had been one of the first to believe in the angel, and he once said to Mrs. Vosper, when she chid him for not being more courteous to the young lady, that Miss Tamar wasn't the sort of party he ever wished it to be said he meddled with.

'Because,' Mr. Grunter remarked, knowingly enough, ' they angels bain't over particular who they do strike dead wi' their swords and spears. And though I be famous meself,' said Mr. Grunter, in a very lofty tone, ' I bain't woon who do want to stand in the way of other folks' doings. I bain't nor king of England to say that nor angel be allowed in 's kingdom, and no policeman neither to catch folk under trees who be happy.'

' She be a crazed young thing, though she be pretty, and if any maid be like to see what bain't there, 'tis Miss Tamar,' Dealer Kiddle remarked to Farmer Pardy at market.

' True, dealer,' said Farmer Pardy with a chuckle, ' 'tain't what they maids do see that they be looking for.'

When a young girl feels the hot sap of love rush to her heart and turn to dance furiously in her veins, because she knows that the consummation of all her most secret thoughts and desires is at hand, she isn't likely to go quietly to her home to join her father at supper. She prefers the darkness of the night that may ease perhaps the agony of her suspense. The deepest darkness she transforms in a moment, for her light shines like a glow-worm's, and the night air is bewitched with wonder.

But even in the most exciting anticipation there is often a doubt, and in Tamar's case this doubt was certainly excusable. She stood near to the green, but she dared not approach the oak tree, because she feared that her angel might not be there.

She hadn't waited long, dressed in her wedding garment, before she heard the voices of women. Mrs. Grunter and Mrs. Meek were out as usual at their doors. It was a common thing, when all the

rest of Folly Down was silent, to hear these two
women talking.

Tamar stood patiently. She knew very well what
they always talked about, and she thought she might
learn a little. . . .

There was one mystery that Mrs. Grunter could
never understand. She was as proud of the acknow-
ledged accomplishments of her husband as he was
himself, and she was never tired of spending hours in
her bedroom of a moonlit evening, pressing her face
against the tiny panes of glass in the dormer window,
always expecting to see her husband lead a girl to the
mossy bed.

Alas for Mrs. Grunter ! Though she had watched
so often and so long she had never seen him go there,
though the excitement of expectation made her life a
happy one—so strangely does happiness approach us
here upon earth.

Mrs. Grunter watched and wondered ; she wondered how it could possibly be true that any living
man could be as interested in young women as her
husband was. She very naturally supposed that all
women, both young and old, were made and
fashioned like herself ; ' and what be we ? ' she
would say to Mrs. Meek ; ' we be only women.'

And Mrs. Meek had her mystery too. She was
sure that there must be something very strange and
peculiar, an odd secret connected with the sex, that
Mr. Meek, although she had borne him six children,
who were all married or dead, knew all about, though
he would never tell her.

' All talk,' Mrs. Meek used to say, ' do begin at
Angel Inn.'

There the men, Mrs. Meek believed, leaned their heads together like conspirators, and whispered to one another tales of mystery about the women that no woman knew of. She believed that Mr. Meek, though he didn't talk at the inn himself, listened to all that was said, and she gave him the credit for being in possession of the most untoward and awe-inspiring facts, culled from that Holy of Holies, Mr. Bunce's parlour, though he did nothing but warm himself at the fire, like St. Peter, and listen to what went on. . . .

Tamar stood, with a beating heart, in the stillness of the evening. Perhaps the women, like the shepherds in the poem, would speak of their loves. Tamar wished to hear more, for, whenever she had met Miss Pettifer of late, that lady had remarked :

' You will never know anything, Tamar, and your husband, if you ever get one, will spurn you from him because, in the most simple matters of married life, you will show your ugly ignorance.'

Tamar remembered Miss Pettifer's words and listened.

' Wold Grunter,' Mrs. Grunter was saying, ' did go out to-night as 'e always do after tea-time. These be 'is ways : 'e do eat what 'e be minded, and then do push a chair to fire, and do watch they fire's flames. 'E do bide and sit, 'e do watch the fire and nod to the flames. But 'e don't bide long. Soon 'e do shift 'isself from chair, find 'is hat and put it on 's head, open door and go out, telling I to mind the cat don't get the butter. 'Tis peace for we when they men do go, and I did take up shirt to hem, but 'tweren't long before door did open and 'is head did say—" Thik there sky be on fire, mother, and God

Almighty be doing dictation." 'Twas little Tommy who did teach 'im thik word. "If there be writing on sky," I did say, "'tis a sign that 'twill rain tomorrow.'"

'I do hope that 'tweren't nothing about we that was writ,' remarked Mrs. Meek suspiciously, 'for I be sure that there be things said about us that we don't hear of.'

''Tis strange how they do talk,' said Mrs. Grunter. 'And what be we, whether young or old, rich or poor, to make a man, same as me husband be, to wonder or search? We bain't nor gold mine for a man to seek guineas out of, and, come to that, we bain't nowhere so interesting as a man be.'

Tamar moved a little, but still she waited.

'There mid be something,' said Mrs. Meek, in a mysterious tone, 'that men be always telling about we; 'tis something we know nothing of that be very secret.'

'No, no, there bain't nothing,' observed Mrs. Grunter; 'and what could there be, for 'tis plainly seen by the clothes that we do wear that we be women.'

'Maybe that 'tis from our clothes that all men's talk do come,' remarked Mrs. Meek thoughtfully.

'Then 'tain't small stitches they do look to,' laughed Mrs. Grunter, 'for I did never sew small woons.'

'No, 'tis we women that do interest they,' persisted Mrs. Meek.

'Then 'tis all said to please,' said Mrs. Grunter, with a sigh, 'for we bain't nothing to interest, and that all men do know.'

'Though men do talk,' remarked Mrs. Meek sadly, ' nothing don't happen.'

' But what do 'ee want to happen ? ' asked Mrs. Grunter, ' for bain't deaths, births, and marriages enough to amuse ? '

Mrs. Meek shook her head.

' Then what do 'ee want ? ' inquired Mrs. Grunter.

' A miracle,' replied Mrs. Meek.

' Then 'tis best I finish Grunter's shirt,' said Mrs. Meek's neighbour.

The two cottage doors shut.

TAMAR IS OFFERED WINE

Out of the far-reaching darkness the footsteps of a man drew near to Tamar. She expected that whoever he was, he would turn aside when he saw her, for any resident in Folly Down, and Mr. Grunter more than any, would certainly never dare to approach a lonely figure dressed as she was, in white. Even Mr. Bunce, had he been returning from her father's, would have shut his eyes as he went by her, blaming God for allowing white-clad Folly Down ghosts out of their graves.

But the steps were not the landlord's, nor was the voice that spoke his either.

' I have hopes,' a voice said quite near to Tamar, ' that you and I may do some business together, young lady.'

Tamar wasn't alarmed ; the tone of the voice reassured her. She fancied she knew it. A few days before a grey-headed and bearded man had visited Folly Down, selling twopenny tracts, and having also with him a few religious books that he tried to sell too. Tamar remembered that this old man had said that he hoped to return in a week or two bringing with him a larger stock of books that would, he knew, please those who purchased them.

Tamar had done a rather foolish thing, for one never knows how a stranger will behave in a house —she had invited the old man into the rectory kitchen.

He looked keenly at her when he was come in, though he appeared well enough behaved, for he wiped his boots carefully upon the mat before he entered.

The man who now spoke to her in the darkness Tamar believed to be the colporteur returned with a new selection of books, who had recognised her even in that dark lane and in her wedding clothes as one of his late customers.

When a maiden awaits her bridegroom, but instead is met by an old pedlar, one can easily imagine that the pedlar would not be welcomed very gratefully.

Tamar was more annoyed than surprised.

' I do not require any more books of yours,' she said, ' and I must tell you that the book you sold me for two shillings was extremely dull and dry. There was nothing in it, no love at all from beginning to end ; it was all about God.'

' But surely,' replied the supposed colporteur, ' that is no reason why the book should be dull, for the life God lived when He came down amongst men was an extremely exciting one.'

' I simply don't agree with you,' said Tamar, ' for He never made love to any one.'

' You mean,' said the other, ' that He made love to all.'

' I mean what I say,' said Tamar.

Her companion sighed softly.

' I fear,' he said, partly to himself and partly to Tamar, ' that when one tries to conform to a capricious and ignorant public—to do which is always a sin against true art—and is compelled to leave out so much of the truth, a poor author, however high he be placed, should be pitied rather than blamed.'

'Who are you?' asked Tamar suddenly.

'I am no colporteur,' replied Tamar's companion.
'I am Mr. Weston, the wine merchant, and I hope,
Miss Tamar, for you appear to be dressed for a
festival, that you will be good enough to taste my
good wine.'

'You had better call at the rectory,' said Tamar.

'I have already been there,' replied Mr. Weston,
'and your honoured father, whom I have known for
a long time, welcomed me very kindly. But my wine
is as fit for a lady's drinking as for a gentleman's, and
I am sure you will like it.'

'The colporteur carried his books upon his back,'
said Tamar thoughtfully, 'but where is your wine,
Mr. Weston?'

'My wine is everywhere,' replied Mr. Weston.
'At least, when I say that it is everywhere, I mean
that my sales are so large that my wine is often found
in the most unlikely places. Only a moment ago I
was asked to leave a bottle under the oak tree, where
a very tall and beautiful young man is resting himself.
I have been bold enough to tell this young man that
you will join him there; he sends you his compli-
ments and hopes you will drink with him.'

'You don't mean Mr. Grunter?' cried Tamar.

'No,' said Mr. Weston, 'the young man isn't Mr.
Grunter; he is no one from Folly Down.'

'He is my angel,' said Tamar.

Mr. Weston did not contradict her. He raised
his hat and bowed to her in the darkness, and walked
away.

Though Tamar longed to go to the oak tree, she
still loitered. Not that she disbelieved Mr. Weston,

who was evidently only a tradesman like Mr. Fairholt of the stores at Weyminster. She had never, as far as she could remember, met a wine merchant before, but most people who have anything to sell are usually polite, as indeed they have to be if they wish to succeed in trade.

Often a very important message is entrusted to the hands of quite a common man, and Tamar was sure now that something wonderful was going to happen to her. She believed that the hour was near when she should be completely happy.

She remembered the light in the sky. She recollected the conversation that she had overheard at Mrs. Vosper's. She hadn't forgotten that Mrs. Meek, before she closed her cottage door, was eager for a miracle.

Tamar supposed the time to be evening, but the hours seemed already to have gone far into the night. A sudden fear came to her. She had once dreamt that she was a white lily in a garden and had wakened up, crying out that her angel couldn't wed her unless he were a lily too. Tamar kissed her bare arm, she bit her hand, she was certainly a girl still and no white flower. Tamar now felt those tremblings come upon her that arrive before the consummation of a long-wished-for embrace.

Though the November night was so silent, Tamar now heard in the upper boughs of the oak tree a rushing and a mighty wind. She listened fearfully, the sounds died away, and she only heard her own heart beating.

The wonderful anguish of desire created an atmosphere of fire about her. She heard a sound again.

The damp wind had risen and was soughing in the boughs of the great tree.

Tamar felt a delicious change come over her ; she was become a thing of sweet willingness, an abandoned creature, a gracious sinner. Nothing now in earth or heaven would keep her from her mate, who must soon take away her reproach and awake a happy infant in her womb. She yearned mightily for the salvation of love.

The November darkness is a cold thing to touch, and to go to a leafless tree, where all that she was likely to find as a lover was a mossy root, showed a faith in Tamar in a tradesman's promise that is not often found in a young woman.

Tamar was a white thing in the darkness ; she stepped upon the grass exultingly ; she believed in Mr. Weston's Good Wine.

The wind rose again and blew coldly about her. She stopped for a moment in doubt, ' for after all,' she thought, ' the man might only be Mr. Grunter.'

She saw a dim light in the lane, the light of a Ford car that had been left by the green.

Tamar hesitated no more. She went in under the oak tree and into the arms of a man. The arms were strong and eager, and Tamar felt her lips kissed with all the fierce passion she had dreamed of but had never known.

' Who are you ? ' she asked breathlessly.

' I give you three guesses,' replied her lover, kissing her again.

' Are you Mr. Grunter ? '

' No.'

' John or Martin Mumby ? '

'Wrong again.'

'Oh, but you shouldn't kiss me like this if I don't know who you are!'

'But you do know me,' said he. 'You asked me to come down from Mr. Bunce's signboard once.'

'You are my angel,' Tamar whispered.

'Yes, I am Michael,' was the reply.

'May I taste Mr. Weston's Good Wine?' asked Tamar. 'He told me I might drink some under this tree.'

'You must drink all of it,' replied Michael, taking Tamar into his arms, 'for this is your wedding night.'

Although Tamar had seen things happen there, and had always supposed that the mossy bed between the great roots of the oak tree must have been a soft one to so content and please the Kiddle maidens, yet she had never imagined, even in her most wanton and abandoned thoughts, the delight that she was this night to know. She smiled at Michael, and fancied herself a child again, looking up at the signboard.

She had always admired the blue trousers, and soon her angel would be married to her at the church, and then they would return together to the oak-tree bed.

XXXI

A GOOD EXCHANGE

Mr. Thomas Bunce did not remain long at the Folly
Down rectory after the departure of Mr. Weston.
His most tender feelings had been deeply hurt by
Mr. Grobe's suggestion that, because he was a man,
he might at any moment during any day, or even
during a very long evening, behave like one.

Neither was that all, for no one likes to leave his
own fireside, where he knows the look of the pictures,
to go to another's, in the hope of having an important
question answered, and to be obliged to return as
wise as he went.

Mr. Bunce sat in a gloomy silence. Now and
again he looked at the Reverend Nicholas Grobe as
if he expected him to say to him, as the Dean used to
do when he filled his fourth glass of port after dinner,
' You may go, Bunce.'

But Mr. Grobe did not speak, and the landlord
believed that his host had entirely forgotten him.
Mr. Grobe was leaning with his head in his hand and
his elbow upon the arm of his chair, in deep thought.

Mr. Bunce eyed him crossly. He might have forgiven him for saying that any man could be wicked,
he could forgive him for saying there was no God and
for not answering his question, but to forget him
altogether was most insulting.

But Mr. Bunce was never angry for long, and he
wasn't the sort of man to be troubled by a disappoint-

ment. No sooner did he know that he had got nothing out of the journey than he decided, in order to bring more light upon the subject, so that he might prove to Folly Down the error of its imaginings, to return at once to the Angel Inn and enquire directly of Mr. Grunter, the Folly Down clerk and grave-digger, whether he was or wasn't the man who harmed the maids.

Mr. Bunce came to this decision for a very wise reason. Up to a few days before Mr. Weston's arrival Mr. Grunter had been very regular in paying for the beer that he drank at the inn. But one market day, going to buy a new spade, he happened to encounter Mr. Morsey in the Maidenbridge High Street, who was both clerk and sexton to a village called Norbury. Mr. Morsey was shocked to learn that his fellow in the same mystery ever paid his score at an inn.

' 'Twill bring 'ee bad luck,' he said.

' And what kind of bad luck shall I have if I pay for my beer ? ' asked Mr. Grunter.

' Thee 'll be told to dig up a dead corpsey,' replied the Norbury sexton mysteriously.

After that meeting Mr. Grunter casually informed Landlord Bunce that to pay for the beer he drank was against his principles as a sexton. Mr. Bunce gave no heed to him, and merely wrote his bill upon a slate. But as no money came, Mr. Bunce now decided that the loss of Mr. Grunter in his parlour would be no loss to him, and so why should he not ask Mr. Grunter the plain question and have the matter settled for ever ?

With this wise resolve, Mr. Bunce left Mr. Grobe.

As soon as he was gone—and Mr. Grobe did rise to open the door to him—the atmosphere of thoughtful quiet again took possession of the rectory study.

With the room his own again, Mr. Grobe feared that the gentle hours of the long evening might—and he loved them so—have been shortened by his late visitors. But he soon felt convinced that both Mr. Bunce and Mr. Weston could only have stayed for a very short while, for the fire still burned brightly, and it was certainly before Mr. Weston arrived, if not before Mr. Bunce, that he had replenished it with fuel.

He was again pleasantly aware by looking at it that his watch was still stopped at his favourite evening hour, and from his own feelings respecting the duration that filled the interval between tea and bedtime, time, if it had moved at all, had certainly not hurried. But, whatever time was doing, that very moment was a proper one, as the present moment always is to an honest man, to take a drink from his bottle.

Mr. Grobe started from his chair, but only to remember that his gin bottle was empty. And yet he smiled at the fire, for hadn't that gentleman, Mr. Weston the wine merchant, spoken of leaving behind him a sample of his good wine? He had said so, and the gentleman hadn't looked the kind of man to promise what he couldn't perform. Indeed, Mr. Grobe knew, as soon as ever he entered his doors, that Mr. Weston was a man of his word.

Mr. Grobe had not noticed any small bottle left about in the room when he opened the door for Landlord Bunce. But before he looked for it, he thought he would open his Bible and find a text for his next Sunday's sermon. Mr. Grobe now turned to the side-table, where he knew the Bible was.

The book was not there, but in its stead there was a great flagon of red wine.

Mr. Grobe was a melancholy man. His sorrow never left him, and it was a double sorrow. First, it had been for the loss of his wife, a young woman, a happy and a naughty one, now laid away in a cold clay bed. Then in his heart he had buried God too —an awful burial.

Mr. Grobe lifted the flagon. It was already un-corked. He forgot to wonder where his Bible had gone to, but suddenly he thought of it.

'Perhaps,' he said, speaking aloud, 'Mr. Weston has taken my Bible and left his wine—a very good exchange!'

Mr. Grobe took a wineglass out of his cupboard. This glass he dusted carefully, for he had no wish to let any dust mingle with Mr. Weston's Good Wine. Although London gin was Mr. Grobe's favourite drink, he was certainly no despiser of wine. He had indeed often mentioned wine in his sermons, long after he had ceased to mention God.

The juice of the grape was a favourite subject of his to take in the pulpit, and it did the hearts of his hearers good to hear him upon it. The very word 'wine' pleased the people and awoke the church-wardens, Mr. Bunce and Squire Mumby, from their slumbers, as often as they heard it spoken. Mr. Grobe would extol in moving terms the delights of the grape, and bless the vine for yielding so good a gift to man.

He had often taken the trouble to explain how,

from the very earliest days, the vine, the richest and the most valued of all the plants of the field, had been cultivated by man. From the first page to the last of the Bible, the juice of the grape was drunk most heartily, ' and, indeed,' Mr. Grobe would say, with a sigh, ' sometimes, as was the case with Noah and Lot, a little too well.'

Mr. Grobe would tell his hearers how the Son of Man, from the beginning to the end of His short stay upon the earth, had praised this good liquor, and was called a drunkard for delighting in it. He told them how Jesus could distinguish between a good and a bad vintage, and that the wine He gave so freely to the company at Cana must have been Tokay.

' Our blessed Saviour,' he said, ' was no niggard, no crafty one in His giving. He gave lavishly, and it is perhaps well that the gospel does not inform us how the guests of that evening reached their homes.'

Mr. Grobe held out the flagon and poured out a glass. A rich odour, pleasant and vinous, filled his room. He raised the glass and held it level with the globe of the lamp. The deep colour of the wine was wonderful and rare : he leant over the wine, and the scent of it was ravishing.

' How beautiful,' he thought, ' must have been the fair hillside where the grape from which the wine had been pressed was grown. Was it Spanish wine or Burgundy ? Or wine from Gascony that so pleased Michael de Montaigne in his tower ? Was it Italian wine, so fine and so heady, that makes all men polite ? '

Mr. Grobe went to the window ; he opened it widely. All was silent, but as he looked into the darkness the wind rose suddenly, whirling the leaves in the Folly Down lanes, and then again there was silence.

Mr. Grobe closed the window and returned to his chair. He looked from Mr. Weston's Good Wine to his bookcase.

Good wine was there too ; there the thoughts of wise men of all ages and countries were gathered. Good wine that had never yet failed him. Good wine that had ever given a deep drink of the proper colour and taste to the gentle reader.

Mr. Grobe looked lovingly at his books, more lovingly than he had ever looked at them before. They had wept and mourned with him, they had sorrowed with him, they had often tried to comfort him, they had reasoned with him about his sorrow and about the loss of his God.

Mr. Grobe stretched out his hand. He raised the wineglass to his lips and tasted the wine. He drank the glass slowly. He emptied it, and placing the glass beside the flagon he filled it again.

He remembered his wife who lay at rest and at peace in the Folly Down clay. What harm could come to her there ? Something there is, he felt, that at least protects the dead from harm. Outrage them, destroy them, cut them with knives, and they take no hurt. Cast a corpse from the highest cliff into the deepest sea, and the fall will not trouble it. What tyrant, what trouble, what sorrow, can harm the dead? They rest from their labours, they have drunk the best wine.

Mr. Grobe drank the second glass and filled again. A deep peace came into his heart.

' Should Alice come now,' he said, ' or should I go

to her, we will share this new joy—a joy that makes those lighter follies that we used to play at but the happy pranks of children.'

Mr. Grobe drank another glass. He lay back in his chair. Mr. Weston's wine was showing him the truth of the world.

'The living should be happy,' he thought, 'though nothing lasts for them long. They fret and pine, but why should they fret and pine, with Mr. Weston's good wine to be bought so cheap? But the poor and simple know him. The secret is out. For how else could they labour so contentedly, how else could they bear all the toil of their lives? The people buy their wine of Mr. Weston.'

Mr. Grobe drank another glass.

The wine filled him with a gentle melancholy—a mood in which one could live graciously, in which one could die contentedly. His was the mood now, the mood of illusion, in which most of the children of the earth live and have their being.

Mr. Grobe drank again.

'All the shifting texture of the world,' thought Mr. Grobe, 'leads to the only lasting way of life, the way of sorrow.'

Mr. Grobe drank another glass—he believed in God. He had but buried Him, a little too deeply perhaps, but in a very good and suitable grave—the heart of a man.

Mr. Grobe was content. How long he had been drinking the wine he did not know. He held up the bottle to the light. The bottle was as full as when he had first begun to pour from it.

Mr. Grobe filled and drank again.

XXXII

MR. GRUNTER STEALS A SHILLING

Besides the choice employment vouchsafed to him by so many Folly Down tongues, Mr. Grunter had also his other and less secular labour to perform in connection with the Folly Down church, to which he was clerk.

Mr. Grunter's two present vocations in life had been pressed upon him almost at the same time, for upon the same day when he was seen alone in a field with a maiden, he was invited by Mr. Grobe to take the post of clerk and gravedigger to the church.

The invitation came to Mr. Grunter because the former clerk and sexton, Eli Barker, happened to die. Mr. Barker's death compelled Mr. Grobe to find a new church servant. Such a servant he believed he saw in Mr. Grunter, whose face was large and silent, with a sort of dull and final expression upon it that would suit a funeral, though he could, no doubt, by the application of a glass, be made to smile at a wedding.

' The face, the look of a man,' thought Mr. Grobe, ' should point out his labours, and if ever a man had the proper formalities of gesture and gait suited to the convenient following of a corpse or a bride, that man was Mr. Grunter.'

' You can say " Amen " and ring the church bell, I suppose ? ' said Mr. Grobe when he called at Mr. Grunter's cottage.

' Mrs. Vosper do go about telling folk I can do more than thik,' replied the prospective clerk proudly.

' And you understand the order of weddings ? '

' I know their beginnings,' replied Mr. Grunter, with conviction.

' Our churchyard is rather overcrowded,' said Mr. Grobe, ' and Eli Barker used to tell me that more than once, when he was got down some distance, he used to strike wood.'

' 'Tis most likely 'e did,' replied Mr. Grunter unconcernedly ; ' but had 'e known what I do about some living folk, he would never have feared a dead woon.'

' Thank you, Grunter,' said Mr. Grobe, ' you are appointed from to-day.'

Mr. Grunter had once heard it said, when he was a very little boy, that the King of England always carries the sceptre of the realm in his pocket when he walks about the royal park, or enters the tavern at Windsor by a private door.

Mr. Grunter had always felt a kinship with royalty, and he had heard it said by a woman—a cousin of Mrs. Vosper's, who lived in London, and so knew all —that princes and kings were as merry in the matter of certain plump and smiling maidens as ever was a poor retired rabbit-catcher of Folly Down.

In every respect, as far as possible, Mr. Grunter, being a good subject, wished to act like one of the royal brood, and so he always carried the church key, that was nearly as large as a sceptre, in his trousers' pocket, to show his authority.

Mr. Grunter had taken the key to the inn. The fact that he himself had noticed that time was done

with, at least for a little while, and that Eternity had
shown itself, had made little or no difference in Mr.
Grunter's demeanour. He was the same whatever
others might be. But something had interested him
this evening—the adventures of a shilling.

The shilling belonged to Squire Mumby. He
had received it in exchange for a note, but, in leaning
forward to point out the more convincingly to Dealer
Kiddle how cheaply calves were sold at the last
Maidenbridge Fair, Mr. Mumby chanced to brush
this shilling off the table into Mr. Grunter's lap.

Mr. Grunter allowed the shilling to remain where
it was, until he was sure that Mr. Mumby had forgotten it. And then he remarked :

' Even if 'tain't nor maiden, 'tis something.'

Besides being a rabbit-catcher, Mr. Grunter had
once been a shepherd too. And at night time, during
the lambing season, he had, out of mere curiosity,
sometimes looked up at the stars and discovered that
they moved.

Though the evening had been so misty, now and
again the clouds had divided, and as Mr. Grunter
was on his way to the inn he thought he saw a star
exactly above the Folly Down church tower. With
the silver shilling in his possession—that, being
newly coined, had looked to him a little like a star,
Mr. Grunter had a desire to see if the one over the
church tower had moved. The stolen shilling had
reminded him of it.

He went out to the door. The night had cleared
somewhat. The church tower was plain to be seen,
and the star was above it. Mr. Grunter wasn't
surprised. A star, he supposed, had a right to do

as it chose, and if one wished to stay about in the sky for ever or for an hour, it was its own affair and not his.

But what did surprise him more than the coming of Eternity and the standing still of a star, was that there were lights burning in the church.

Mr. Grunter leaned against the doorpost. He tapped his pocket. The church key rattled against Mr. Mumby's shilling.

Mr. Grunter stared at the church and exclaimed ' Robbers ! '

Although the Folly Down clerk was well aware that there were ways and means of getting into the church other than by the great door, yet of one thing he was sure, that no service could ever go on there without him, and so he supposed that thieves must have broken into his holy charge.

Time and the stars might stop when they chose, that same still November evening might last through all Eternity, the sun might never shine again in the sky, but, however strangely such simple matters as these chose to behave, Mr. Grunter did not intend that robbers should do what they chose with the pennies in the poor-box, nor continue to burn the church oil and candles in the extravagant manner they seemed to be doing.

' But who,' exclaimed Mr. Grunter, ' can be there ? Who in Folly Down were the most likely to steal ? '

A fond feeling for virtue rose in Mr. Grunter's heart. He excitedly declaimed against the sin of theft, addressing himself to an imaginary audience in the inn yard.

' There bain't no one,' cried out Mr. Grunter,

' who will let anything alone. Folk do take what they do see, and now a thief has lit up church only to see what be worth taking.'

Mr. Grunter walked out of the inn yard in righteous anger. He went by Mrs. Vosper's cottage, and a girl, one of the Kiddles, who stood in the doorway, called to him to come in, but Mr. Grunter, heedless of his reputation, never once paused to look at her. When he reached the churchyard, Mr. Grunter expressed his surprise in a loud gasp.

A bride and bridegroom were coming down the path.

Mr. Grunter stepped aside amongst the graves. He watched them go by. The pair went down the lane and, crossing the green, went to the oak tree.

Mr. Grunter stepped again into the churchyard path.

Folly Down church was fully lit. The great door, studded with nails, was wide open. Through the open door the light streamed and showed a number of little spots of bright-coloured paper that were spread about, and rice that lay in the path, like small hailstones.

Mr. Grunter paused in anger. Such a scene as this occurring, as it should properly have done with him there, had been wont to put certain coins into his hands, that he had been vastly glad of.

Grains of rice, these tiny spots of coloured paper, were the signs that meant to Mr. Grunter a time of personal jollity, and never did he hear those words read by Mr. Grobe from the Form of Solemnisation of Matrimony that ' It was ordained for a remedy against sin and to avoid fornication,' without thinking of the cold ham and sherry wine that a wedding gave, of which being clerk he always took his share.

Mr. Grunter entered the church in a rage. At first, when he stood in the aisle, he supposed the church to be empty, but a little later he saw that this was not the case, for a gentleman was standing at the lectern and reading in the great Bible. Now and again this gentleman would smile when he came upon a good sentence, and again he would shake his head disappointedly.

Directly he saw the gentleman Mr. Grunter knew him. He was the very same Mr. Weston who had visited the inn.

Mr. Weston closed the book with a proud sigh when Mr. Grunter stepped up to him. The clerk could only scowl, and Mr. Weston was the first to speak.

' I am very much surprised,' he said, ' that you, Mr. Grunter, who, from all accounts, know so much about weddings, in fields as well as in churches, should have been late for this one. I fear that your reason for being away is that, instead of accepting the opinions of Folly Down about your own free and merry doings, you have been won over to the way of thinking of Landlord Bunce, who believes that all the follies of Folly Down are due to one immodest act. The act that occurred when, instead of leaving life as a simple jelly, Some One whom I will not name '— Mr. Weston blushed—' must needs amuse Himself by taking something that belongs to a man—a very fine rib we will call it, by which he created a woman. That rib is the cause of every one's sorrow, because it is the cause of all life. An author must——'

But Mr. Grunter interrupted him.

' And what the hell be thee doing here ? ' the clerk, who had now found his voice, asked.

Mr. Weston frowned. He evidently deprecated the rude and vulgar tone in which Mr. Grunter had addressed him.

' An honest tradesman, Mr. Grunter,' he said, ' must, in bad times like these, sell his wares where he can. You must know that in one of the church sacraments wine is used. You yourself have complained to the churchwardens, Mr. Bunce and Mr. Mumby, that the brand they administer here is the very cheapest and the worst.'

Here Mr. Weston, evidently wishing to refresh his memory on some point or other, opened the Bible again.

' What be thee reading for here ? ' asked Mr. Grunter, who very naturally wondered that any one should wish to look at a church book out of service time.

' Oh, only my book,' replied Mr. Weston carelessly.

' 'Tain't thee's name that be at the beginning,' said Grunter, with a laugh.

Mr. Weston didn't reply. He closed the great Bible and stepped down from the lectern. He walked slowly down the aisle, looking in an interested manner about the church, as a man might do who was viewing the interior of a rather peculiar building for the first time.

' This is the only church I have ever been into,' Mr. Weston remarked, turning to Mr. Grunter, who followed him closely.

'Thee bain't nor heathen, I hope,' said Mr. Grunter, to whom the church stood for all that was respectable in human life, ' and I trust thee bain't no dissenter same as Luke Bird, who do tell snared and trapped rabbits about St. Peter's crucifixion.'

'No,' replied Mr. Weston, ' I am neither a dissenter nor a heathen. I am only a wine merchant.'

Mr. Weston entered the vestry. The book wherein the marriage lines of Tamar Grobe and Michael were written was still upon the table.

Mr. Grunter looked suspiciously at the handwriting and muttered in a low tone, ' The devil never went to school at Folly Down, and that I do know.'

Mr. Grunter had from the beginning of his entering the church watched Mr. Weston very curiously. In the aisle he had begun to ask him something, but had stopped abruptly, as if he feared to proceed in his enquiry.

Mr. Weston now turned to look at the photograph of the last rector, who was a very good man, while the clerk, according to custom, placed the marriage register away in the safe, and he became bolder.

' 'Tain't legal in this country to be married at night time,' he said.

' But how do you know,' enquired Mr. Weston, ' that it is night time, for all the clocks in Folly Down stopped at seven ? '

' 'Tis night time,' said Mr. Grunter, ' because sun bain't shining and small singing-birds be hidden.'

' People say of you, Mr. Grunter,' remarked the wine merchant, with a smile, ' that you know a great deal too much about what is hidden, where a maid is concerned.'

257

Mr. Grunter's look broadened ; he became happier. He liked such praise.

'Who be going to sell wine to next ? ' he asked rudely.

'Give me your advice,' replied Mr. Weston.

'There be Mrs. Meek,' said the clerk, ' who do like a drop now and again, but do 'ee mind thee's money, for all the folk in Folly Down be bad payers.'

'I am sorry to hear that,' said Mr. Weston.

'And I am sorry to say it,' echoed the clerk. 'An' 'tis a pity that a small village should be so wicked. But if it so happen that thee 've brought more wine with 'ee than thee 's likely to get cash for, 'tis best thee visit no more houses, but let I mind they bottles till thee come again.'

'I have not yet visited Mr. Bird,' observed the merchant.

''E be only a silly preacher,' said the clerk, ' and 'e bain't no buyer of wine.'

Mr. Weston moved his hand suavely.

'A good soldier,' he said, ' never believes that he can be worsted in a battle, and a good tradesman never for one moment thinks that his goods will not sell. You have only to believe in them yourself and your goods will go.'

Mr. Grunter was alarmed. He moved to the further side of the vestry table.

'Thee haven't never been a clergyman, 'ave 'ee?' he asked nervously.

'No,' replied Mr. Weston sternly, ' I have never been a clergyman, and what is more, I never want to be one.'

Mr. Grunter was silenced.

'But I must not speak too strongly,' remarked Mr. Weston to himself, 'for I do not wish this honest man to be afraid of me.—Though I have never been a preacher,' he said, blushing, 'I have written a little.'

'Advertisements and bills, I suppose,' suggested Mr. Grunter.

'Oh, no,' said Mr. Weston proudly, 'a printed book all about myself.'

Mr. Grunter laughed loudly. But Mr. Weston was in no way abashed.

'I could read a chapter to you, Mr. Grunter,' he said.

Mr. Grunter considered for a moment. He pressed his hands to his ears.

'I be gone stone deaf,' he said. ''Tis how I be taken at times,' he explained, 'so 'tis best we do talk of what I can hear.'

Mr. Weston looked at Mr. Grunter in deep disappointment.

'My book must indeed be out of fashion,' he said sadly, 'for even Mr. Grunter will not hear it read.'

'I can hear anything that be said about women or drink,' said Mr. Grunter, who felt a little sorry for Mr. Weston's sad looks.

'I am glad you are not deaf to those subjects,' observed Mr. Weston. 'But tell me, Mr. Grunter, when I have seen Mr. Bird, is there no one else—for time is of no moment to me—whom I ought to trade with in Folly Down ?'

Mr. Grunter tried his best to remember.

'Squire Mumby be at Angel Inn still,' he said, 'as no time haven't been called, but there be two sons of his who be at farm, though they two don't never drink nothing unless 'tis give to them.'

And now, for the first time since Mr. Weston had been in Folly Down, his look became ominous and dark.

He was standing with Mr. Grunter in the church, where the clerk had been employing himself in putting out the lights. Only one light was left lit, under which Mr. Grunter and Mr. Weston stood.

Mr. Weston's brow cleared a little when he saw the scared round face of Mr. Grunter, who was as fearful now of staying where he was, as of going away.

'Tell me about these young gentlemen,' Mr. Weston asked. 'Do they drink wine? Are they fond of a rare and rich vintage?'

'If thik rare vintage,' replied the clerk, 'do mean a pretty an' plump maiden wi' buttons to unfasten, they be very fond indeed.'

'That is exactly what a rich vintage does mean,' said Mr. Weston, rubbing his hands joyfully.

'Then,' said Mr. Grunter, 'if thee do call all Folly Down folk to drink of thik vintage, me time of glory be over. For only three years have I been noticed by any one, and afore that I mid 'ave been a piece of dung, for no woon heeded I. No woon didn't notice poor Grunter till 'e were named a sinner, being caught by wold mother Vosper in the same field wi' Ada. Then 'twere all out about I.'

'What was out?' asked Mr. Weston, who had been partly heeding the clerk and partly heeding his own thoughts.

'That wold Grunter be the woon for a green-grass

wedding, and since thik fine day all such doings 'ave been put upon I.'

' I heartily congratulate you, Mr. Grunter,' said Mr. Weston.

' Yes,' cried the clerk gladly, ' so long as there be woon maid left in Folly Down I mean to be famous, and if time be now ended, as folk do say, I mean to be famous for ever.'

' You are as ambitious as a pope,' observed Mr. Weston.

' 'Twas Mrs. Vosper who did make me so,' affirmed the honest clerk, ' for when any of they t'others do take a maid under oak tree, they do hang me wold boot on bough to show who 'tis who be there, for folk do know I do take they off when me feet do pain.'

' A good way to begin,' said Mr. Weston. ' And so, if I am not mistaken, you only live to be talked about.'

' No woon about here do want to die,' remarked the clerk, ' an' what else be life for but to make talk? And I be always sorry for the poor beasts that Bird do preach to who have nothing to say. But one thing I be sure of.'

' And what is that ? ' asked Mr. Weston.

' That 'tis a mortal pity,' replied the clerk, ' that any woon should try to lead a good life, for when a man do do good, there bain't nothing more to be said.'

' But when he does evil there is much,' suggested Mr. Weston.

' Yes,' said Mr. Grunter. ' 'Tis a good loving act to be a sinner, for a sinner be the true saviour of mankind.'

261

' Ha ! ' exclaimed Mr. Weston, taking out his note-book and writing down Mr. Grunter's words. ' I never thought of that ; but it 's always so, when one has finished a book, and it is printed, a new idea comes that would have made it all so much more interesting.'

For some reason or other at this moment Mr. Grunter wished Mr. Weston to go.

' If thee do mean to get Luke Bird to buy off 'ee,' he said, ' 'tis best thee take and go to 'is cottage, for Bird bain't nor tavern roisterer, and 'tis best for I to put out thik light.'

Mr. Grunter edged himself away. Ever since Mr. Weston had called himself a writer, he had regarded him with suspicion, and he now wished himself out of his company.

' A poor man,' he grumbled, ' mid have to get 'is own living in Eternity as well as in time, and even if this evening do last for ever, me wold 'oman will mind when supper time do come.'

Mr. Grunter stepped back, but the wine merchant touched his arm.

' I have work for you to do, John Grunter,' he said.

' And who be thee to command folk ? ' asked the clerk.

Mr. Weston uncovered his head and looked at him. Until that moment he had kept on his hat.

' Who be thee ? ' asked Mr. Grunter, in a lower tone. . . .

' I know thee now,' said Mr. Grunter.

' Then tell no man,' said Mr. Weston.

Mr. Grunter looked happy ; he even grinned.

' I did fancy at first,' he said in a familiar tone,

'that thee was the devil, and so I did walk down church aisle behind 'ee to see if thee's tail did show.'

Mr. Weston told the clerk what he wished him to do.

Grunter started back in a fright.

'But she drank of my best wine,' said Mr. Weston.

'Don't 'ee waste none of thik wine upon I,' cried Mr. Grunter, shrinking away, ' for thik wine be too strong for a poor man who bain't used to drinking.'

Mr. Weston smiled. The clerk looked at him gloomily.

'All they t'other dead bain't got to rise to-night?' he enquired, ' for wold grandfather did promise to beat I wi' 'is Sunday walking-stick if ever he got me hold in heaven, and what if Potten who be buried under elm tree do begin to talk?'

'No,' said Mr. Weston, ' you must only open one grave to-night, Grunter.'

XXXIII

OLD TALES

When Mr. Bunce advised Luke Bird to go home to his cottage and wait for Mr. Weston, he went immediately.

Mr. Bird had once been a temperance reformer, but the kingly power of love had wrought a difference in his former zeal. His opinions were now changed, and he longed, with all his heart and soul, for his well by the willow copse to be filled with wine.

In other ways Luke was changed too. The gentle willows whose leaves in summer time, when the wind blows, shine like silver, had told him that if he wished to know what heaven was he must discover it in Jenny Bunce. He knew that if she came to him, he would preach no more. He would leave all creatures to their own ways, so long as he might listen to the wind in the willows and hold Jenny in his arms.

Luke supposed that it might be the manager of the Maidenbridge brewery where he used to work as a clerk who had come to Folly Down. He knew the firm of Hop and Co. sold wine as well as beer.

Luke Bird well remembered the last manager, a great boisterous fellow, with a huge beard, who was wont to boast how he drank port with Lord Bullman in the old-fashioned manner, until both the merry gentlemen rolled off their chairs under the table. Though Weston hadn't been that man's name, it was more than likely that Mr. Burleigh had drunk himself to death, and the visitor to Folly Down might be the new manager of the sales department at the brewery.

No spot in the world can be more silent and coy, and no home more ready for love, than a tiny thatched cottage near to a damp copse of willows. And no place in the world could have been found more suited to a young man whose heart was all excitement and sighs, and whose desires went all to a young woman, than Luke's cottage.

Mr. Bird had left his door open when he went out, and lighting a candle when he returned, he saw that a little owl had flown in—one of the tribe that has only of late years become common in the west of England.

The owl had perched upon the bookcase. Had his present thoughts been different, Luke Bird would have told the owl about Jesus, but now, instead of that story, he told the little owl about Jenny, and the Lord of Heaven, knowing that Luke was a lover, praised him for doing so. The owl listened with attention, winked knowingly, and flew away.

Luke Bird sat beside his bare table ; his feet were upon the damp stones that were heaving with moisture. He looked out into the night that had cleared a little.

Luke had contemplated so often the carnal act of love that his mind had been somewhat infected with the cruelty of nature. But now it was the longer and more lasting consequence of the act that he dwelt upon, that mild time of joyance when all is well.

Folly Down, its pretty ways, the meadows, its downs and its running brooks, the blue and brown butterflies of summer—all the world would be his if he wedded its fairest maiden. And she, so simple and so kind, would take his hand and guide him through all the thorny places if they met any. He would listen to her silly talk, and discover in it a wonderful salvation through faith in believing. He would live so, and die with his hand in hers.

As he was coming to the cottage, he had passed his well and peeped in. The well was a shallow one, fed by surface water, and though it was full now to the brim, Luke didn't suppose that it held more than thirty gallons, and that quantity of wine would certainly fill it to the brim.

Luke Bird, sitting beside his table, pressed his hands against his forehead and considered. He bethought him of all the tasks set by cruel fathers in past times to the young gentlemen who sought their fair daughters in marriage.

Luke Bird had never been a practical young man, but love made him so now. He supposed that Mr. Weston, having come into the village, would be sure —Luke knew the customs of the brewery—to visit Folly Down once a fortnight. He decided that if he bought a gallon of wine each time Mr. Weston came, in little more than a year his well ought to be full, and Mr. Bunce couldn't then refuse him Jenny.

Luke wished to be prepared for any unforeseen turn that affairs might take. Suppose that Mr. Weston carried his wine in a barrel ? If so, he must find something in which to pour the wine he hoped to buy when it came. Luke Bird hunted in his cottage room, and was soon lucky enough to discover two earthenware pitchers that he had bought of a gipsy. These he set ready upon the table.

The next thing he did was to go to his money-box and take out every coin that he found there. They amounted to about two pounds, all in silver. This money he placed upon the table near to the jars.

Luke then drew his chair to the open door and listened. A little soft breath of evening air came in, and the candle flickered. Luke opened Law's *Serious Call* and shielded the candle with the book. Had that happened in former days, before he thought of Jenny, he would have made a fine sermon for Mr. Mumby's bull, on how the spirit of light was kept burning by true religion.

But now his only wish was that the candle should not go out, so that the wine merchant might see the light in the cottage as he went by and pay a call. He was sure that Mr. Weston would come. He had only to wait and the tradesman would appear. Folly Down is so small a village that though Luke lived a little way down a lane, he could hear any voices that were speaking beside the green.

It chanced that as Luke was waiting for Mr. Weston, Mrs. Meek finished her ironing and opened her door again. And a moment later Mrs. Grunter, hearing her neighbour's movement, opened hers too.

Luke had listened before to these two talking. And now, hearing them, Luke thought again how fine a sermon, had he not been converted to the new religion of love, he might have preached to Mr. Mumby's bull. Such a sermon about the village voices that croon for ever, voices that may be heard in any lowly doorway throughout the world. All the straws, all the torn and blown pieces of paper, come to the gossips to make pretty tales for a sultry evening. Everything must be told, nothing can be hidden, and even an old and forgotten whisper becomes a true story in time. As he waited for Mr. Weston, Luke listened to what was being said.

' 'Tis a long evening,' remarked Mrs. Meek.

' An' 'tis a funny woon too,' replied her neighbour, ' for me husband John be gone mad in 'en and 'ave just been in to fetch out 'is pick and shovel.'

' 'E bain't drunk, be 'e ? ' asked Mrs. Meek, ' for a drunken man do act funny, for me woon husband did come home last Christmas time wi' both his hands burnt.'

' A sad accident, I suppose ? ' questioned Mrs. Grunter.

' Yes, and 'tis well we do keep olive oil in shop, but 'twere all because 'e did want to steal a flame or two to warm 'imself wi' at home, you know. 'Twas Kiddle who did treat 'im, and the more Meek did drink the nearer 'e did go to they blazing coals, and at last, when time were called, 'e did thrust both his hands into fire. But what were 'en John did take out 'is pick to do at this time o' night ? '

' 'E didn't tell I much,' replied Mrs. Grunter. ' Only there were the boot he did once bury wi' Ada Kiddle, and he mid be going to dig en' up again.'

' Folk do want their own,' observed Mrs. Meek.

' So they do,' replied her neighbour, ' and Grunter bain't the man to allow any of 'is own property to rest in peace as 'tis said on stone, if so be 'is pick and spade will find 'en.'

' 'Tain't no madness that do want one's own,' remarked Mrs. Meek.

'But 'tis madness,' replied Mrs. Grunter, 'that do tell a plain Christian woman that God Almighty be in Folly Down, and that two bloody suns be shining in sky.'

' And what else did he say ? ' asked Mrs. Meek.

' Only this,' replied her neighbour, ' that I needn't hurry me frying of they kippers, for 'tis everlasting life that be come, and they fish mid cook for a thousand years before they be eaten.'

' He 'll tell a different story when supper time be near,' remarked Mrs. Meek, ' but how came it that Mr. Grunter did never mind 'is own boot before ? '

' It do take years for 'e to mind anything but women,' answered Mrs. Grunter, ' though 'e did limp home thik day, swearing at the stones.'

Silence came, but again Mrs. Meek spoke.

' Time be slow and stubborn,' she said, ' in a small village where there bain't much news to be told. Time be a slow-going wold cow wi' we, and Ford car by green do stay still as though 'twere fixed in road.'

' Little Tommy Barker did peep into van and did say there be something asleep in 'en that bain't no bottle,' remarked Mrs. Grunter.

' 'Tain't no ugly thing, I do hope,' said Mrs. Meek nervously.

' No, no,' replied the other. ' Tommy did say 'tweren't nothing nasty, and maybe 'tis to be sold, for anything that folk will buy a tradesman will sell.'

Mrs. Meek grew thoughtful.

' 'Twas a sad silent evening,' she said, ' same as this be, when Ada Kiddle were found dead, and I do mind how me corns did hurt, and something be always going to happen when they do pain.'

' I do mind Ada's drowning too,' observed Mrs. Grunter, ' and only the day before she did it, she did ask I what ways there were to put an end to a poor maid.'

'And what did thee tell she to do?' asked Mrs. Meek.

'I did tell Ada,' replied Mrs. Grunter, 'that Dodderdown were the village for hanging, Madder the place to cut a wold throat, and that the folk of Folly Down do like drowning best.'

'Thee never mentioned Squire Mumby's pond, did 'ee?' enquired Mrs. Meek.

'Oh, yes, I did,' answered Mrs. Grunter. 'I did say that there weren't no vipers in 'en, as folk do say, but only a few large toads.'

'Ada did look nice in a coffin,' said Mrs. Meek.

'Not so nice as Jenny Bunce mid look in oak-tree bed,' remarked Mrs. Grunter.

Luke Bird sighed. He was a lover, and he listened.

The two voices continued. They appeared to be telling of a feast where every dish was good meat. They ate of these dishes with glee. They told old tales. They told how Mrs. Vosper, who was once gathering sticks in the rectory hedge, happened to peep through a hole in Mr. Grobe's summer house. And there was Alice Grobe playing her merry pranks with her husband, and to her sport Mr. Grobe both mildly and righteously assisted, employing those simple and discreet manners, that a plain man has used, since the beginning of the world, to quiet a wanton girl.

When this tale was over, Mrs. Grunter said:

'Some one be starting thik car, and 'tis best for we women to bide indoors to-night, if Landlord Bunce be a true talker.'

And, in order to appear more chaste than her neighbour, Mrs. Grunter went indoors first.

XXXIV

MR. WESTON READS A
CHAPTER

LUKE BIRD watched the darkness outside his door,
and now and again he looked, as King Alfred was
wont to do, at the candle.

He looked at the candle anxiously. He had no
oil in the house for the lamp, and the candle was his
last one. If this candle went out, Mr. Weston would
see no light and go by ; there would be no wine
bought, and no chance of Jenny. And if no Jenny
came to him, what should he do ?

He might preach to the worms ; perhaps they, and
not the beasts, were entitled, by their enormous in-
dustry—for they make and mar mountains—to salvation. No, his preaching was done with for ever.
He could not, after losing Jenny, even preach to a
worm.

Then he must take the same road as Ada Kiddle.
If his candle went out, he would go in the darkness
to the Folly Down pond.

The candle had one inch more to burn. The soft
sweet earthy wind crept in again to his room, bringing with it the scent of the damp woods, the heavy
scent of rottenness intermingled with the sweet fresh-
ness of the cool earth. The wind filled the cottage
and caressed Luke.

He started up in his chair. The soft wind had
drugged his senses for a moment, and now he seemed

to awake. All his former religion became one simple thing—Jenny Bunce. She was the manifestation in the flesh of God's goodness to man. Was it possible that such a sweet wonder could be made for him? No, it was more likely that he and the toads in Mr. Mumby's pond should make a wedding. He now broke out into so mighty a longing that he wept tears. She might be his. Jenny existed in the world, she was made and fashioned to be enjoyed, and he alone might enjoy her.

Luke suddenly turned to the candle. He had sat a long time, why was not the candle gone out? The candle was still burning. Luke buried his head in his hands; he dared not look up for fear the candle should be gone out.

When Luke Bird looked out from his cottage again, he saw that a Ford car was drawn up near to his gate, and that a stranger stood beside his door, who was evidently waiting for an invitation to enter.

To Luke Mr. Weston at once appeared like an old friend—nay, even more than that—he seemed like a friend that Luke had heard a great deal about all his life, but had never seen.

He did not know whom Mr. Weston was like. Mr. Weston had something about him like the squire of Dodder, and then Luke thought that he slightly resembled Sir James Hop.

But nowhere, not even at the inn, did Mr. Weston make himself more at home than at Luke Bird's. He sat down upon a small wooden stool, with as much pleasure as though the rough stool had been a kingly throne of white marble, and regarded Mr. Bird in the most fatherly and pleasing manner.

'You remind me very much,' said Luke, 'of our kind and good pastor, Mr. Grobe, who knows all Cowper's hymns by heart.'

'And I know them too,' said Mr. Weston.

'And you love Cowper as much as Mr. Grobe does?'

'I do,' said Mr. Weston, 'and I was always vastly sorry for him because he was so firm a believer in the Bible.'

'And was that wrong?' asked Luke.

'Certainly it was,' replied Mr. Weston, 'for no poet should ever believe the words of another, however true he may think his own. Poor Cowper never understood that. The best books have to end unhappily ; that is their only chance of success. I am a writer, Mr. Bird.'

Luke bowed.

'But it was not my fault that Cowper went mad, for I put as much, nay rather more, hope into my book, to its hurt I fear, than any one else. You must know that pessimism is the best and most enduring wear from cover to cover.

'But are you?' asked Mr. Weston pleasantly, 'interested in literature?'

'I read Law's *Serious Call*,' said Luke.

'Then,' exclaimed Mr. Weston gladly, 'you must know a little about my work too.'

Mr. Weston bent down very modestly and looked at the floor. He then raised his eyes to Luke's enquiringly.

'Though Michael and Mr. Grunter,' he said nervously, 'never wish to listen, would you object to my reciting a short chapter?'

' I should like nothing better,' said Luke Bird.

Mr. Weston stood up and repeated in a very fine manner the One hundred and fourth psalm.

' You are sure you don't think too poorly of that ? ' he asked Luke when he sat down again.

' No,' replied Luke ; ' I like it all very much indeed.'

' I only meant that one as a picture,' said Mr. Weston, ' but had I the proofs in my hands now I would certainly, when I think how much has been said against my writings, alter the last verse.'

' I know what you would say,' said Luke, smiling ; ' you would say, " Let the critics be consumed out of the earth ! " '

Mr. Weston nodded. He regarded Luke for a little in a most loving manner.

Luke was sure he could tell Mr. Weston everything about himself. He told him of his work at the brewery, for although he didn't now think that Mr. Weston was a partner or manager there, he knew that any wine merchant would naturally understand the difficulties that a young temperance reformer would meet in such a place.

Mr. Weston listened with kind attention.

Luke described his work as a clerk, and then he went on to tell of his first visit to Dodder, of his love affair there, and of his first attempt to convert the country people.

' But here,' sighed Luke, ' I have preached my last sermon, to Mr. Mumby's bull.'

' I am glad it was your last,' said Mr. Weston, ' for a bull is one of those beasts that might very well be sent mad by a lesson in divinity. But tell me, Mr.

Bird, wouldn't you like to do anything in my way ;
you know what I sell ? '

' Yes,' replied Luke Bird, ' I have seen your
advertisement in the sky, and I love Jenny Bunce.'

' How long have you loved her ? ' asked Mr.
Weston.

' I have loved her,' answered Luke, ' ever since the
day that I saw her flee away from Mr. Grunter and
hang from a little bough of the oak tree by her petti-
coat. I wished then to embrace all of her, and I believe that she alone of all womankind has a soul to
be saved.'

' I agree,' remarked Mr. Weston, ' for, as God
is love, the soul of a maid, when she is pretty, is
love too.'

Mr. Weston blushed then, as a tradesman will
sometimes do, when, in his efforts to please a customer and to make a new connection, he has unin-
tentionally let out a trade secret. He was, of course,
unable to recall his words or to alter them, for there
was never for him any shadow of turning from what
he had once said. But with the ready mind of a salesman, it was easy for him to put the matter again upon
a practical footing, even though he had been betrayed into chatting a little too freely.

' I think I ought to mention now,' said Mr.
Weston, ' before we deal, that, with the exception of
the beneficed clergy, squires, nobility, and members
of Parliament, who can always be made to pay when
we send a certain servant of ours to them, whose
name I will not mention—with the exception of these
gentlemen, the firm will only deliver its goods for
cash.'

Luke Bird went at once to the table. He handed all the money that he had saved to Mr. Weston.

'Now tell me,' Luke asked eagerly, 'how much wine this money will buy, for Mr. Bunce will not give me his daughter until my well is filled with wine.'

Mr. Weston leaned forward to Luke and spoke in a low and serious tone.

'What will you drink,' he enquired, 'if there be no water in your well, but only my good wine?'

'I had never thought of that,' said Luke, with a gasp.

'But what will you drink?' asked Mr. Weston again, even more seriously.

Luke was silent; he bent his head thoughtfully. He leaped from his chair and held out his hand to Mr. Weston.

'If your good wine, sir,' he cried, 'can give me such a bride as Jenny Bunce, whose soul is love, I shall drink your wine for ever.'

Mr. Weston rose from his stool and shook Luke warmly by the hand.

'You shall have her,' he said. 'Now go to your well and draw me a draught of water.'

A MARRIAGE IN FOLLY
DOWN

Luke Bird took up one of the large earthenware jugs and went out into the lane.

As he was going out of his garden gate he heard a soft sigh. Luke peered here and there into the darkness, but he could see no one—he fancied that the sigh had come from the Ford car. But it was so soft a sigh—as soft as a sleeping child might give who dreams a pleasant dream.

The sigh came again, more sleepy, more happy.

' What child or young girl,' thought Luke, ' would choose a Ford car to sleep in ? And did the sound come from there ? '

A little wind rustled the willow bushes—perhaps it was only the gentle trees that had sighed. The willows had always seemed to sigh and weep with him in all his troubles.

So tender had the little wood been to him that he had often longed—fearing that he could never have Jenny—to dig his own grave within it, and to die there, knowing that the trees would weep for him and sorrow for ever for his unrequited love.

' Yes,' he supposed, ' it was the willows that had sighed.'

The stars that had been out were dimmed again, and a clammy darkness was come. Luke Bird went into the darkness and walked into a man.

' I be Landlord Bunce,' exclaimed the apparition that Luke had stepped into, ' an' I be out of doors looking for Grunter. Once I thought I had him, for there be a man and a maid under oak tree, though 'tweren't to be seen which be which, but neither be Grunter.'

' I do not know, any more than you do, Mr. Bunce, where the clerk is,' said Luke, ' though I heard a little while ago Mrs. Grunter telling Mrs. Meek that her husband had gone mad.'

' Oh, they women will say anything but the truth,' observed Mr. Bunce, ' and 'tis I that have a question to ask of Grunter, and this it be—" 'Ave 'e or 'aven't 'e done what be wicked wi' any woon of they maids ?" '

' And suppose he isn't guilty, what then ? ' asked Luke.

' Then 'tis God who be,' shouted the landlord.

Luke hastily covered Mr. Bunce's mouth with his hand.

' You needn't shout,' he whispered, ' God isn't deaf.'

' Now, don't 'ee stifle I, though 'tis a strange night time,' gasped the landlord, ' for Squire Mumby be grown generous, which be queer and curious, for 'e have treated we all, and do say that the sight of wine merchant 'ave given 'e a thirst that no beer can quench.'

' You left the company happy, I hope ? ' said Luke, who wished to please.

' Yes, yes,' replied Mr. Bunce, ' I did leave they all a-singing the praises of Mr. Weston. Each did fancy that wine merchant can do best what they can do well. " Weston," Kiddle do say enviously, "would promise all they cows in Heaven "—(Mr. Kiddle's field was so named)—"to a poor man so as to put a sixpence in 's own pocket." Then 'twas Vosper who spoke. " 'Tis a pity," 'e did say, "that me wold 'oman don't know Mr. Weston's town, for then we should hear something of what be done in 'en." " Lord Bullman couldn't drink like him," Squire Mumby said. And poor Meek smiled.'

Landlord Bunce burst out a-laughing.

' We 've finished two barrels,' he shouted, ' and Kiddle 'ave drunk as much as bull calf 'e do talk of. But what be thee a-doing out in dark lane ? '

' I,' replied Luke Bird, ' am going to the well to draw some water for Mr. Weston.'

' 'E don't drink no water,' called out Mr. Bunce, ' an' if there be wine in well, thee may 'ave our Jenny to bed wi' 'ee this very night.'

' But will Jenny come to me ? ' asked Luke.

Mr. Bunce held up his hand in the darkness.

' Thee be a man, bain't 'ee ? ' he asked.

' Oh, yes,' replied Luke readily.

' And what be Jenny ? ' enquired Mr. Bunce.

' I have reason to think,' said Luke, in a very low tone, ' that Jenny is a young woman.'

Landlord Bunce laughed loudly.

Luke led him to the well. Luke slowly raised the cover. He reached down and filled the jug.

The jug had only touched the water when a wonderful odour of rare wine new-tapped, but of an old and ripe vintage, scented the damp evening air.

Mr. Bunce asked for the jug ; he raised it to his lips, and took a very long draught. Luke slipped the jug into the well again—the well was full of wine.

Luke Bird turned back to the cottage; he found Mr. Weston reading Law's *Serious Call*. As Luke entered, the wine merchant was reading a short passage aloud, in a rather critical tone :

' " Why does a day seem a trifle to us now ? It is because we have years to set against it. It is the duration of years that makes it appear as nothing."

' I don't agree with that theory,' said Mr. Weston, ' for I regard a day as quite as good as a thousand years. Now, in my book, I make every day in one week important.'

Mr. Weston shut up Law's *Call*.

' But he converted Dr. Johnson,' said Luke.

' So I have heard,' replied Mr. Weston dryly.

Luke placed the wine upon the table, and after doing so he went to Mr. Weston and kissed him. The wine merchant returned the embrace.

' A good tradesman loves a grateful customer,' he said.

He took Luke by the hand and led him to the Ford car.

' Look inside,' he said.

Instead of a pipe of red wine there was, behind the curtain of the van, Jenny Bunce, fast asleep. Luke didn't wait a moment; he raised her in his arms and carried her into the cottage, and laid her down upon his bed. As he laid her there, she partly awoke, and nestled against him most lovingly. She sat up, smiled at him, and began to undress.

Mr. Weston softly closed the cottage door—he had joined their hands in the parlour. He now stepped into the Ford car and drove away.

XXXVI

MARTIN MUMBY TELLS A SHORT STORY

THE two sons of Mr. Mumby, John and Martin, were smoking cigarettes in the dining-room at Oaktree Farm. They had not followed Jenny Bunce to Mrs. Vosper's cottage : after their attempt to ruin Jenny, which had failed owing to the sudden appearance of Mr. Weston's name in the sky, the young men had given up all chance of her for that evening, and had returned home to talk over their affairs.

Mrs. Mumby, whose only joy in life was collecting the eggs that her fowls laid, and was greatly distressed when they laid away amongst the nettles, had, with her mild look and white hair, attended her sons at supper and gone to her bed. The servants, elderly and respectable women, whom Mrs. Mumby had wisely chosen for their plainness, were also gone to the maids' bedrooms. Mr. Mumby still stayed at the Angel Inn. All the clocks in the house had stopped at seven.

The young men smoked, and we will watch and admire them. As the vast majority of farmers' sons in England are very like the Mumbys, we should, if we wish to be loyal to our king and country, be glad to hear what they say.

We take much pleasure in reminding our readers that Martin Mumby was a young man who would always enjoy himself so long as no money went out of his pocket into the hands of those who provided his enjoyment. Together with his accomplished brother he valued himself very highly, and each supposed that, if there was any paying to be done, a young and handsome gentleman was the last person in the world who could be expected to hand over.

The behaviour of these Folly Down brothers, under the kindly cloak of Mr. Grunter, was most natural and proper to their kind, and no unpleasant hint or comment could possibly be made about such lively young gentlemen, who had each in the past ridden a winner at the local steeplechase, and had also been asked by Lord Bullman himself to drive a car to the polls at an election.

Martin sat by the large dining-room table, tilting his chair and toying with an empty wineglass, which he would try to balance on the tip of his little finger. Unfortunately for them, these young gentlemen had nothing to go with their cigarettes in the way of drink, for the sherry decanter in the sideboard was empty, and their wise father, after the manner of My Lord Peter in *The Tale of a Tub*, always kept the cellar door locked, and carried the key, as Mr. Grunter did that of the church, in his trousers' pocket.

The young men sat in no very amiable mood. They could get to no drink. They also felt displeased, and very properly so, that a certain pastime, that has ever been the sole amusement of man, out of which all other joys are taken—the pit from which all merrymaking is dug—was, at that present moment, denied to them.

There were times, they knew, that of necessity must be given up to lesser enjoyment than the one vital matter of a young man's days. But now a black faceless thing might have been noticed, though the young men discerned it not, sitting beside each, that gave no other intimation of its presence than a feeling of ugly depression in each heart.

Never in their lives had John and Martin Mumby wished more greedily for a glass of wine than they did upon this evening in November.

When they were walking home from the oak tree, they thought that there was a strange and certainly, in such an out-of-the-way village as Folly Down, a very unexpected odour of wine in the air. Even at supper there had been nothing to drink, and the bullock's tongue that they devoured only increased their thirst, that they were too gloomy to quench with plain water.

When Bess, the parlourmaid, gathered the supper things together, though he did not know why, Mr. Martin rudely bid her leave the wineglasses.

Both the young men now drew their chairs to the fire. They began to talk of marriage, to make a mock of it, to express those pleasant and common views that have been long current in the country, and to which even John Bunyan refers, that it is cheaper to buy the milk than to keep a cow, and other similar and valuable sayings.

They spoke of summer banks as well as the oak-tree bed : they talked of the dead as well as of the living. They spoke of the pebbled shore, of the grassy side of a tumulus, where darker garments had entirely hidden, upon more than one Sunday afternoon, the pretty white of another kind.

There was indeed no barn or corner in the neighbourhood where the talk of the young men could not provide a picture of a modest ravishing.

The conversation turned to the Kiddles, and, not content with making fun of the girls' misfortunes, the Mumbys laughed at their mother too. Mrs. Kiddle had never left her house since her daughter, Ada, was drowned, and she amused the village inn now and again by making more than one attempt upon her own life, though unsuccessfully.

But sometimes, even amongst friends, the happiest subject of conversation takes an odd turning, and the pleasant shady banks, a captured and ruined maiden, are swept aside, and something ugly is seen. Sometimes the women, perhaps, may regard the honour done to them by such highly-placed young men as the Mumbys as a little too far-reaching in its results and make tearful complaints, and at other times another kind of girl, whose education has been sadly neglected, and who is by nature a kind of mawworm, may turn upon the pursuers.

Martin Mumby told his brother John how, when he had ridden his motor bicycle to Maidenbridge the very last Sunday, he had met a girl under the shadow of the town wall, who had had the extreme impertinence to demand a shilling fee for what happened there. The ostler of the Rod and Lion, she most meekly said, had given her two shillings for rendering the same service.

'Damnation,' swore the worthy Martin. ''Tis the first time I've been asked for anything.'

John Mumby concurred in expressing a very proper horror at such a dreadful exposure of female greed, and said, with a fierce oath, that he hoped his brother sent the little devil about her business with something to remember him by.

' Oh, I did that,' laughed Martin, ' for as soon as she named the shilling, I made quick work with her, and she 'll be turned out of the mayor's house—for that 's where she 's in service—and she 'll die like a drab in a ditch.'

' That 's the way to treat them,' laughed John.

' So it is, by God ! ' shouted Martin.

When the door of an old-fashioned farmhouse parlour is noticed to be slowly opening—a farmhouse, too, that has had the reputation for five hundred years of being haunted—it is natural that the occupants of the parlour in such a house, who have noticed the opening of the door, should look interestedly to see who will enter.

Had the dining-room door at Oak-tree Farm been opened by Mr. Mumby, a great deal of noise would have been made about it. For Squire Mumby, after spending so long a time at the inn, would have certainly made a pretty clattering with his feet, and have knocked over a chair or two in the hall, before he got to the parlour.

For a moment Martin's colour went. An odd fear that he had always so successfully conquered, rose again.

Had Ada chosen to visit him in her funeral frock and white stockings ?

But the door now opened completely, and a gentleman stepped into the room, with so little noise that, though their fear was gone, both Martin and John regarded him with considerable astonishment.

But their surprise soon left them, for the visitor

came forward and introduced himself as Mr. Weston, a traveller in the wine trade.

' I believe I know you, gentlemen,' Mr. Weston said blandly, ' for, if I mistake not, you are Squire Mumby's two sons. Your father has ordered a dozen of my wine, and I have hopes that you will buy a little apiece. . . .'

Here we think we should, as so many of his admirers have done before, offer an apology for a simple habit, in a business way, of Mr. Weston's. Mr. Weston had received no order from Mr. Mumby ; no one indeed who resided in Folly Down, with the exception of Mr. Bird, had offered any money for his good wine. But a trader's story, as so many newspaper advertisements show, need be no lie. And, in order to sell at all—(kindly consult in this matter any new business house)—it is necessary to get the public to believe that the goods are going.

In another way, too, we may view this matter. In some companies the most rare and wonderful truth one can well think of becomes a lie.

And lastly, Mr. Weston is a law to himself.

The Mumbys, who one can guess were not of the politest breed, did not take the trouble to offer Mr. Weston a chair, but he took one without being asked, though not with the same pleasure that he had seated himself upon Mr. Bird's stool.

' Please do not let me, gentlemen,' he began good-humouredly, ' interrupt your conversation. I believe, as I opened the door, you swore by Some One. I assure you I am, by no means, a person who is ever in any hurry. There will be ample time, for all the clocks in Folly Down appear to be a little slow this evening, to show you my good wine, and even to give you a taste if you will allow me, when you have finished the discussion that I fear I broke in upon. Please do not let my presence prevent your swearing again, Mr. Martin.'

Martin Mumby smiled. He was not surprised that Mr. Weston had heard what he said, for the traveller had most likely been listening at the door before he opened it.

John's fear of the stranger was gone as well as his brother's. Both had often been treated to drinks by commercial travellers at the Rod and Lion Inn at Maidenbridge, and they had always found that kind of gentleman the best of company and the most willing to tell all the droll tales they knew about the women.

'We were talking of nothing important,' said Martin, 'though I dare say we mentioned the girls.'

'Oh yes, the girls.' Mr. Weston smiled as he spoke. 'A pleasant subject, indeed, when none of them are present, and one, no doubt, that makes an honest man swear sometimes.'

'But how did you come in so suddenly?' asked John.

'I knocked at the door three times,' replied Mr. Weston, 'but as no one answered my knocking, I came right in. Ha! Ha!'—Mr. Weston seemed in a jovial mood.—'You know that few people dare to lock the house door against Mr. Weston's Good Wine.'

The same rare and rich odour that the Mumbys had noticed in the lanes of Folly Down now filled the dining-room at Oak-tree Farm.

Martin Mumby sniffed thirstily.

' Have you brought any of your wine with you to-night ? ' he asked of Mr. Weston.

' Yes,' answered the merchant, ' but, because I was not sure of your custom—for I believe another dealer visits you—I have left the quart bottle I carried in the churchyard for the time being.'

Martin Mumby looked a little glum, but Mr. Weston, who was a very practical salesman, knew exactly the proper way to introduce his goods to the young gentleman into whose company he had fallen.

' I have already called at the rectory,' he said, ' and Mr. Grobe finds my wine very much to his taste. Mr. Bird, too—although he is no gentleman—found in my van some of my best wine that his heart has long desired, and he is now wedded to the vintage. All the polite company at the inn, including your worthy father, are pleased that I have come to Folly Down.'

Mr. Weston watched the two young men keenly. He was not smiling now. He appeared to be anxious, and, perhaps, he wondered whether or no the Mumbys would agree to taste his wine, for no trades-man likes a kindness offered to be rudely refused.

' We may as well drink a glass,' said John Mumby carelessly, ' though we may not deal.'

' Come then,' said Mr. Weston, rising from his chair, ' for if the worms are thirsty, there will not be much left for us, you know.'

Though meanness and lust—lust that far exceeded the cravings of any brute beast after its kind—were the chief characteristics of Mr. Mumby's nice sons, yet they possessed a certain amount of inquisitiveness that showed itself in their wish both to see and to taste Mr. Weston's Good Wine.

And now a sound came into the room from somewhere outside the house—a sound that the Mumbys took no note of, for during a still night in the country many sounds reach the ears that cannot be exactly understood.

Mr. Weston heard the sound too, and he, being better acquainted with a certain matter on hand, knew what it meant—a curious digging with pick and shovel.

Mr. Weston held his hands to the fire to warm them. The fire, though it was died down to ashes, burned clear again, so that the wine merchant warmed his hands pleasantly, chatting genially at the same time, while about the room was diffused more surely than before the odour of the grape.

' Ha ! ' said Mr. Weston, holding one hand and then another near to the shining flame, as if he had a mind to thieve like Mr. Meek. ' It is not often that such a bottle of wine should be left in a churchyard where only a few broken ones are cast by the villagers. Ha ! the least drop from my wine-press is worth all the world. What, indeed, should it profit a man if he gain the whole world and lose my good wine ? '

Mr. Weston coloured, but the Mumbys had not heard him. They could only feel what a pleasant sensation it was to be athirst with so fine a bottle of wine so near. They jested merrily to one another going out of the door.

XXXVII

MR. GRUNTER FINDS HIS
LOST BOOT

OUTSIDE the door of the farm the sky was white with stars.

Mr. Weston himself opened the little gate that led into the churchyard from the squire's house. Neither of the Mumbys had offered to do this for their guest, because they considered that a plain wine dealer was not the sort of person to whom they chose to be a servant.

'The wine is beyond the yew tree,' said Mr. Weston softly.

The merry talk of the Mumbys when they came out into the night was all silence now. They were both a little gloomy. Perhaps they were beginning to fancy that this traveller in a very old line, who had come a little unexpectedly into their company, might like his jest now and again. Indeed, now that they looked at him a little more closely, he might have been One who more than once had had his laugh at the expense of others.

'You don't mean to make us pay for a drink of your wine?' asked John Mumby, 'for if you intend to make us pay anything, we prefer to look at the outside of the bottle.'

'No, no,' replied Mr. Weston, 'you shall drink freely this time.'

The Mumbys entered the gate, and Mr. Weston closed it behind them. John Mumby walked in front, but he had not gone many steps before he stopped.

' I shall go back,' he said, turning quickly. ' It 's so cold here, and the smell of the wine is changed.'

' I shall go back too,' said Martin, ' for death is here.'

' You are not cowards, I hope,' urged Mr. Weston. ' And it would never do for Lord Bullman to hear that you, who can ride a winner and course a meek hare, are afraid to drink a bottle of wine in a place where the dead are laid.'

' We had better go on,' whispered Martin to his brother, ' or he may talk about us at market.'

Mr. Weston hurried them on. They followed the path and came to the other side of the yew tree, where they nearly walked into a heap of earth, an open coffin, and Mr. Grunter.

The Mumbys, too stricken with terror to know what to do, looked at Mr. Grunter, who was carefully examining an old boot that he held in his hand.

Mr. Grunter looked at the boot very carefully by the light of his lantern. He was deciding whether anything could be done towards mending it by the local cobbler.

There is a strange power that often compels a man to look upon what he most wishes to avoid. This same power forced the Mumbys to see what was there.

What was there was Ada, but not the Ada whom they had known, but only the body corrupted, the soiled thing, the weeping clod.

Mr. Grunter smiled at his boot ; he believed that something might be done to it. He laid the boot carefully down and looked at Ada.

The coffin he had easily unearthed, for it was not his custom to bury any one deeper than must be, and the coffin lid, as he had expected, was all but rotted through.

'My good wine, gentlemen,' said Mr. Weston.

Though the worms had destroyed Ada's beauty, her shape was still there, and Mr. Grunter regarded her compassionately. He saw Ada as if she were a picture, which is the way that all wise countrymen regard the world or anything in it that seems a little curious or out of the common.

'When life bain't,' said Mr. Grunter slowly, 'death be.'

Mr. Grunter recalled to his mind that Ada Kiddle had once been a pretty living thing of blond flesh, and he looked thoughtfully at her.

A picture may move a man, and this picture affected Mr. Grunter.

Mr. Grunter stood back a pace or two and then addressed the company.

'I bain't going to be famous no more,' he said. 'I don't want no woon no more to mention I. I don't want to be noticed. I would rather bide about and be nothing.

'Ada,' he said, stepping to the coffin again, ''tain't I that have moulded 'ee, 'tain't I that have rotted thee's merry ways wi' wormy clay. I bain't to be talked of no more.'

Martin Mumby was less cowed now. Mr. Grunter's remarks had made him feel more like himself again, and Martin noticed, too, that Mr. Weston had covered his face with his hands, as if he wept.

'You are a liar and a cheat,' Martin shouted at the wine merchant. 'You promised us wine, and you show us the rotted corpse of a whore. Is this your wine?'

Mr. Weston said nothing.

XXXVIII

A WONDERFUL BULL

THE Mumbys strode away. They had seen no wine, and they had no wish to remain a moment longer near to death. They strode quickly out of the churchyard, meaning to visit Mrs. Vosper's cottage, in the hope of finding Jenny there, and of settling matters with her.

Outside the churchyard the Mumbys stood for a while, telling one another what fools they had been for ever having listened to such a madman as Mr. Weston. They could hardly believe themselves to have been so taken in. To be imposed upon by such a trick seemed to them a thing unheard of, when they considered what fine and clever fellows they both were, though they felt a little less hurt when they bethought them what a pretty penny Mr. Weston would have to pay to the gravedigger for that night's work.

Walking a little way up the lane a strange sound made them stop to listen. The sound was the thud thud of some heavy beast, footing the Folly Down mud.

'That's Kiddle's bull calf that has broken pasture,' said John.

They both laughed together.

Although the white stars were visible in the churchyard, in the low lanes of Folly Down there was nothing to be seen of them. The soft clammy mist mingled with the hedgerow trees, sank lower and became one with the mud of the road.

'Let us drive that lubberly calf into our barton,' said Martin Mumby. 'And we'll tie him to a post and geld him. Drunken Kiddle will never get his price for him then.'

'Ha! ha!' laughed John. 'That'll be a fine trick to play, and we'll say he got hurt in jumping the barbed wire fence.'

'Listen,' whispered Martin, 'only listen to the beast. I believe it's trotting round the oak tree.'

'Yes, I hear him,' replied John, 'and now I think it's running this way.'

'Its feet sound rather heavy for a calf,' muttered Martin, 'perhaps it's our large bull that's broken out.'

'If it's our bull,' said John, 'we had better hide in the ditch, for though our bull was quiet enough a while ago, it has begun its old pranks again, and if Vosper hadn't stepped in a hurry over the yard gate yesterday, he would have been a dead man.'

'He's coming near to us now,' said Martin.

'Oh,' whispered John. 'Oh, yes, I can hear its heavy tread in the mud, but what was that bellow? 'Twas more like a roar. No bull could ever make such a sound.'

'Hark!' said Martin. 'I believe it's a great cat that's coming. Do you hear how the thing swishes its tail? There's some horrid thing in the road, I'll be bound.' . . .

Mrs. Vosper still knitted in her cottage. When she had finished all the wool that she could find in her house, she unravelled a shawl and commenced

to knit another dress with the wool she had thus
obtained.

After Jenny left the cottage—Jenny had boldly
said that she wished to ask the wine merchant for a
taste of his wine—Ann and Phœbe Kiddle had settled
themselves upon the worn sofa and wished that they
had been bold enough to leave with Jenny.

Mrs. Vosper laid down her knitting. She looked
at the girls. She had amused herself with seeing
some of the fun, and now she began another amusement that rarely fails to give pleasure to those who
indulge in it. She began to accuse and torment the
fallen.

No one in Folly Down had a better or larger stock
of proper and virtuous remarks than Mrs. Vosper.
She could declaim against all sin and wickedness in
a manner highly commendable, and even her intimate knowledge of the rules of the game never prevented her from hitting below the belt.

Indeed, we may be sure that it was never to the
mind or reason of her victims that Mrs. Vosper
applied her blows, but entirely to the emotions,
and she would paint, in the most lurid colours, the
shame that would surely come.

Mrs. Vosper's intention now was to have done
with the Kiddles. There were younger and prettier
girls coming on in Folly Down, whom she hoped
to beguile to the oak-tree bed. There was Jenny
Bunce whom she might be sure of now. She saw all
she needed in Jenny. The Mumbys lusted hotly for
her, while she, by her coming to the cottage that
evening, showed a pleasant compliance to their
wishes.

There was even Miss Tamar. The painted figure upon the signboard might become Martin Mumby in a pair of blue trousers.

Mrs. Vosper watched the Kiddles, and her eyes blinked upon them with hatred.

'Thee be a nice, well-behaved maiden,' she said mockingly to Phœbe, ' to go so fast after the chaps. Bain't 'ee got woon bastard at home to pester mother wi' ? But none of 'ee don't go far from oak-tree bed when a man be about.'

Mrs. Vosper turned up her eyes to the ceiling.

'No maidens be modest now,' she murmured. 'It 's only we wold woons who do what be good. In time past folk did use to go to church to be wedded, and now, what be all maids, only harlots ? '

'Let us go, Phœbe,' sobbed Ann, ' and if it weren't for she we 'd both have been married and happy by now.'

'Married,' sneered Mrs. Vosper. ' 'Tis thik thee want, be 'en, though thee 've been married once too often by the look of 'ee.'

A village girl does not easily despair unless all her hopes are gone. The word 'marriage' had reminded Ann of something, and she dried her eyes.

'Can you remember,' she asked her sister, ' what the man said, who called here just now—the man who tried to get us to buy a bottle of his wine ? He spoke to us before Mrs. Vosper shut the door in his face.'

'And 'twas well done to shut 'en,' shouted Mrs. Vosper, ' for who do want to hearken to thik cheap-jack. Ofttimes I 've passed the wold liar in Maiden-bridge market, filling 'is bottle out of muddy ditch.

'Tis a wonder thik liar do show 'is ugly face at honest folk's doors. Most like 'tis to steal 'e do come.'

'But he spoke lovingly to us,' said Phœbe, whose eyes were shining more happily.

'Yes, he did indeed,' said Ann gladly. 'He told us we should need some wine before the month was out, for a wedding day.'

'They travelling folk be always talking,' growled Mrs. Vosper. 'But who be going to marry a maiden who bain't no maid?'

Mrs. Vosper shook her fist at the girls. She also spat upon them.

'Do 'ee both go out,' she shouted, 'and don't 'ee never come here no more.'

Phœbe knelt before Mrs. Vosper and clasped her hands.

'Let we stay,' she moaned, 'for 'tis still evening time, and when we do go home too soon our mother do begin to ask what be happened to Ada.'

'I can tell Mother Kiddle what be happened to Ada,' laughed Mrs. Vosper. 'She be well wormed and rotted in ground, and no woon bain't never to see she's face no more.'

'Let us stay a little longer,' begged Ann, 'for last night, when no woon didn't want we under oak tree, and we were home early, our mother did whisper to I asking where they black-handled knives were hid.'

Mrs. Vosper struck Ann with her fist.

Phœbe stood up resolutely.

'Ann,' she said, 'our mother be a poor weak woman, but three times she 've cut and blooded herself trying to die, and bain't we two brave enough to follow our Ada where she did go and drown?'

'Leastways I bain't afraid,' said Ann boldly, ' of they nasty snakes.'

Mrs. Vosper mocked them.

'Do thee walk into pond,' she said. 'They fine toads be nice to tickle a maiden, better than a man to lie with, be they pond beasts.'

Ann appeared to be listening.

'What noise is that ?' she asked. 'What is that out in the lane ?'

'I hear footsteps running,' said Phœbe.

Ann turned to the door, but before she could open it John and Martin Mumby burst into the room. John bolted the door, and Martin, staggering to the table, blew out the lamp. The firelight flickered but faintly.

No one moved in the room.

The heavy tramp of some great beast could be heard, trotting up and down in the lane. At times it would stop by the cottage door and make low grunts, and soon there came a terrible roar.

'It 's the lion,' whispered John Mumby, ' that 's escaped from Mr. Weston's car. He is no wine merchant but a showman, the keeper of that lion.'

'Yes, that 's true,' said Martin, ' for Kiddle was in Maidenbridge to-day, and a little boy ran by shouting that there was a big lion in a tradesman's van in the High Street.'

Ann lit the lamp.

'Phœbe and I care nothing for your lion,' she said. 'Since that man spoke to us of his wine, and we believed him, we have lost our fears, for he said, " If you drink my good wine, nothing shall hurt nor destroy you." '

'Yes,' said Ann, looking down at the cowering figures of the young men, 'they can be brave enough with a simple maiden, but when they meet a poor calf in the darkness they call it a lion. See how Martin shakes with fear, and how John cowers like a beaten dog.'

A strange sound came from Mrs. Vosper. She began to moan, she threw herself about in her chair, she struggled, she fought the air with her hands, as if she were trying to prevent a hideous beast from tearing out her heart.

'What is it?' asked Ann, leaving John Mumby, who had been whispering to her, and going to Mrs. Vosper, 'what is it that's hurting you?'

Mrs. Vosper groaned in agony.

'He's dragging me down,' she cried, 'he's dragging me deeper than the grave, he's dragging me to hell.'

Mrs. Vosper gasped, her throat rattled, she struggled for a moment and then lay still in her chair.

'Mrs. Vosper is dead,' said Phœbe.

XXXIX

MR. GRUNTER DECLINES
AN HONOUR

As soon as the Mumbys were gone from the churchyard—they had stepped proudly and held their heads
high—Mr. Weston and the clerk of Folly Down,
with their heads bent, lowered Ada once again into
the ground. But before doing this Mr. Weston
took off his overcoat and laid it tenderly upon the
soiled body of the dead girl, for the coffin lid was too
rotted to cover her.

' 'Twas me boot last time,' observed Mr. Grunter,
' that I did take off to ease me swollen foot, and now
'tis thee's Sunday coat that be going to be buried, for
woon thing be taken and woon be left.'

Mr. Weston looked down into the narrow pit.
He seemed pleased now that Ada slept so sound.

' Ha ! ' he said, ' when the first light of day broke
afire in my mind, little did I wot of the eternal sleep
that would come.   If I had never invented life, there
would have been no death.'

' And a good thing too, if there hadn't been no
death—at least for I,' said Mr. Grunter.

' Grunter,' said Mr. Weston solemnly, ' I long to
die.   I long to drink my own dark wine.'

' Thee bain't thirsty then,' said Mr. Grunter, who
had caught only Mr. Weston's last words, ' though
thee 've turned gravedigger.'

' I remember,' said Mr. Weston, ' the day when I

made death. It was the eighth day, and I saw a gathering of people in the plains, and, though all seemed to be happy, all were sad. I walked amongst the people and took a little child and laid her to sleep. And the people all gathered round that sleeping child and told me that she looked more lovely than anything else that I had created. But the child awoke and cried. And then I took a beautiful youth, whom I found sitting alone and sorrowful, and I laid my hand upon his head, meaning to comfort him, and he fell asleep, too, in my arms, until the colour of his face was changed and the people came about me and told me he was dead.

'And I buried him in the sand, but the people blamed me, for they said, " The young man will never rise, while time is, out of that sleep." '

'The people were right,' said Mr. Grunter, ' to blame 'ee for being a murderer.'

'I know it,' said Mr. Weston, ' though not a death happens in all the world but I wish it were mine own, and I would have every dying one to know that I long to die with him.'

'I bain't ambitious at no time at all,' said Mr. Grunter, ' for such an honour.'

'Ah, Grunter, perhaps you would prefer to notice another idea that I thought of, in answer to the prayers of mankind,' said Mr. Weston, smiling.

Mr. Grunter wiped his forehead and looked up into the sky.

'What be they shining white folk a-doing?' he asked of Mr. Weston.

'Only the stars,' replied Mr. Weston, 'only another of my ideas—only the white stars.'

'They white stars be dressed funny,' said Mr. Grunter, 'for they do bide about like angels, and thik shining woon '—the clerk pointed with his hand— 'be Ada Kiddle, and she be singing.'

Mr. Grunter gazed in another direction. He looked alarmed. An ugly grunt, followed by a loud roar, came from the village.

'What be thik noise?' asked Mr. Grunter, stepping near to Mr. Weston.

'Oh, only the old lion,' said Mr. Weston carelessly, 'that I turned out of the van before I took in Jenny Bunce, but now I must bind him for another thousand years.'

Mr. Weston took a chain from his pocket. This was a shining metal chain, and the wine merchant held it up for Mr. Grunter to admire.

'Where did 'ee buy thik?' enquired Mr. Grunter, who was always extremely anxious to know where anything came from, because he always hoped to discover a shop where a really good bargain could be found.

'At Mr. Meek's,' replied Mr. Weston.

'Thee mid lead a lamb by thik chain, but 'tain't nor good for a roaring lion,' was Grunter's comment.

Mr. Weston slipped a note for five pounds into Grunter's hand, and bid him a friendly good-night. He went down the path slowly, swinging the chain.

Mr. Grunter earthed up the grave. The evening was grown dim again. Soft drops of water fell upon Ada's grave from the yew. The tree wept at this second burying.

Mr. Grunter softly took up his boot. Ever since he was a boy he had suffered from sore and swollen feet, and he had often taken off one or other of his boots to ease them.

Mr. Grunter carried his boot home. He went into his cottage where his wife was.

' 'Tis a funny evening,' he said to her, ' for wine merchant, who do call 'imself by a name minister have no use for, be turned lion-tamer.'

' Maybe 'e be woon of they folk who do have two trades,' replied Mrs. Grunter. ' But what be 'en thee do carry so loving ? '

' Me boot,' said Mr. Grunter. He laid the boot upon the table, and, going to his wife, he kissed her.

Mrs. Grunter stepped back astonished.

' What be doing ? ' she asked, ' for I bain't no naughty woman under oak tree.'

' An' I bain't nor wicked wold man. I bain't nothing,' shouted Mr. Grunter in high glee, ' and if Mrs. Vosper do say another word about I, I 'll send she to hell.'

' She be gone there already,' observed Mrs. Grunter calmly, ' for she be dead.'

Some one knocked at the door.

' Mind out 'tain't no wild lion,' remarked the clerk anxiously, as his wife went to the door, ' for Mr. Weston mid never have held 'e firm wi' thik little chain.'

Phœbe Kiddle entered the cottage room ; she was happy and smiling.

' Sister Ann and John Mumby,' she said to the clerk, ' do wish their banns published next Sunday, and Martin Mumby 'ave asked for I, too, but I don't fancy 'e's funny ways who bain't no church-goer, so 'tis Miss Kiddle I 'll still be called at Christmas.'

Phœbe paid the fees. The clerk received the money very readily.

'What be happened,' enquired Mrs. Grunter of Phœbe, ' to roaring lion who be out-of-doors devouring people ? Poor Mrs. Meek be forced to shut she's door, for she don't fancy they doings.'

' Mr. Weston 'ave shut him up in his van,' replied Phœbe, ' and have driven 'is motor in front of rectory door.'

' The best place for 'en,' said Mr. Grunter, ' for the devil be safe there, even though 'e be only tied and bound by a sixpenny chain, for 'tain't no preaching 'e do want to listen to.'

When Phœbe Kiddle left the cottage the clerk went out too.

' Where be going ? ' asked Mrs. Grunter of her husband.

Mr. Grunter clinked the coins in his hand.

' Bunce do look at I,' he said, ' as if 'e do want 'is money. Bunce bain't so simple as God Almighty to believe all 'e do hear, and so 'tis best landlord be paid. Besides,' said the clerk, pausing, ' poor Vosper be up at inn, so Phœbe do say, and I did think to treat 'e to a pint now 'is wife be safe dead.'

' That 's all you think of we poor women,' called out Mrs. Grunter as her husband was departing. ' To curse at we when we be living, and to drink to we when we be dead,' and she shut the door.

XL

A DRINK OF DEADLY WINE

THE REVEREND NICHOLAS GROBE was drinking pleasantly. The evening had become, as near as any evening could, an everlasting one.

Mr. Grobe looked upon those things in his room that had ministered to his needs for so long. His eyes dwelt long upon his books, and he looked, too, at the picture of Alice, who used to display herself, in all her naughtiness, so merrily before him. He emptied his glass. He went to an old barometer that hung from the wall. Earlier in the evening he had noticed that the barometer was high, but now it was fallen very low.

Mr. Grobe turned to his chair again, intending to take another glass of wine, but he saw, to his surprise, that the flagon was gone, and in its place was the great Bible.

Mr. Grobe looked at his watch. The watch was still stopped at seven. He was yet in the eternity of a long evening, when the only act that need occupy a man was the act of drinking. But where was the wine? Had he been all the evening drinking out of that great book? Had that book been Mr. Weston's Good Wine?

Some one outside in the garden opened and shut the rectory gate. Mr. Grobe threw open the window and looked out.

' Who are you ? ' he called.

'I am Weston, the wine merchant,' came the answer.

'Enter then,' said Mr. Grobe. 'Enter, for you know the way.'

Mr. Weston lost no time in obeying this command, for he is a trader who has never failed to attend quickly to any customer who calls to him. He entered Mr. Grobe's study immediately. Mr. Grobe welcomed him with pleasure, though Mr. Weston noticed at once that the minister was very sad.

'You are sorrowful,' the merchant said compassionately. 'I fear you have not found my wine suitable to your taste.'

'It was certainly a good wine,' answered Mr. Grobe, 'and it gave my old beliefs back to me again, for I believe that my dead wife awaits me in paradise, where God is love.

'Listen, Mr. Weston,' he said, 'I have just read this out of a book—that Moses was rather for dying where he stood than go one step without his God. I feel so too.'

Mr. Grobe looked anxiously at his watch.

'I shall lose my belief in God, in heaven, and in my Alice, if time moves again,' he said very sadly. 'I know that nothing is sure here while time lasts. The beliefs that we cherish, our loves, our hopes, all pass away and are gone like the autumn leaves, and all we have left of them are hours of rank misery.

'"But his flesh upon him shall have pain, and his soul within him shall mourn."'

Mr. Grobe wept.

Perhaps a merchant might be more pleased to see a customer in tears than one too bright and happy, for the latter would be less likely to give heed to a bill. Mr. Weston may have thought thus, but he now took from his pocket a small flask, that was full of a very dark wine.

Mr. Weston did not care to see a good man weep, and so he turned away. He went to the weather glass and tapped it. He shook his head when he saw how low it was fallen.

Mr. Weston took a chair beside Mr. Grobe. He drew the cork from the flask.

He spoke to Mr. Grobe very lovingly, but in a very low tone, so that no one—no, not even if there had been others in the room—could have heard him.

' I have brought another wine with me,' he said, ' that you are welcome to drink. I only give this wine to those I love, but when you drink this wine you will sorrow no more.'

Mr. Grobe held out his hand to take the flask, but Mr. Weston restrained him for a moment.

' You have something to ask of me,' he whispered.

' My Alice,' said Mr. Grobe, ' shall I see her, shall I see her if I drink your black wine ? '

' She is a little goose,' said Mr. Weston, smiling, ' and she will flap her wings at you.'

Mr. Grobe poured out a glass of wine. He drank contentedly and seemed to fall into a deep sleep. But soon he sighed happily, and his breathing stopped.

Mr. Weston raised Mr. Grobe's head and placed the cushion more easily underneath it.

The wine merchant covered the face of the dead.

XLI

SOME ONE DO MIND THEY DEAD

On his way to the inn Mr. Grunter stopped beside the Folly Down green and looked at the dim shadowy presence of the great oak tree.

Above the oak there was pitch blackness, for a monster cloud hung there, thick and heavy—a cloud that might have held in its black womb all the tempests that had ever fallen upon Folly Down.

' I bain't nor boaster now,' said Mr. Grunter aloud, looking towards the tree, ' I be only the church clerk, and I have never known no other woman, only me own wife.'

Mr. Grunter looked at the tree and bethought him of Ada.

' I do miss thik maid,' he said. ' All hearts were glad to see she a-running upon they high hills. 'Tis a sad thing to see she laid so low.'

Mr. Grunter raised both his hands on high.

' By the bones of thik dead maid,' he exclaimed, ' who were ofttimes laid by wicked sinners in oak-tree bed, I do curse thik great tree.'

There was a low mutter in the heavens above the tree that became in a moment a dreadful roar of thunder. At the same instant the whole sky flared up, as if all the heavens were ablaze, and a forked flash of fire descended upon the oak tree. The huge tree was riven to the roots and crashed upon the green.

' Ah ! ' said Mr. Grunter, when his astonishment at what had happened allowed him to speak, ' some one do mind they dead buried maids, though we t'others mid forget.'

Even when time used to move Mr. Grunter was not the kind of man to be in a hurry. He now nodded at the sky and took a turn round the green before he approached the fallen tree.

But before he stepped upon the grass Martin and John Mumby came by. They walked stoopingly like dogs that had felt the lash. The Mumbys stopped ; they were glad to see Mr. Grunter.

' Where be going ? ' asked the clerk, in his usual slow heavy voice.

' To Kiddle's,' replied Martin, ' to Dealer Kiddle's.'

' Mind out thik lion don't kill 'ee,' said Mr. Grunter. ' It do all depend how thee do behave whether lion do have 'ee or no.'

Martin Mumby trembled with fear.

' The lion carried Mrs. Vosper to hell,' he said sullenly.

' Why, 'tis 'is work, bain't 'en ? ' remarked Mr. Grunter calmly. ' 'E do claw the wicked same as our cat do the wold 'oman's chair covers.'

' Do you know who Mr. Weston is ? ' asked John suddenly.

' Oh, yes, I do,' replied Mr. Grunter. ' 'E be me woldest friend.'

John drew near to the Folly Down clerk.

' Will you speak for us ? ' he said, ' will you ask him to save us from the devil ? '

' Perhaps I mid just name 'ee to him,' said Mr.

Grunter, ' though such high folk don't fancy being bothered wi' plain farmers' sons.'

' You shall work on our farm all your time,' said John.

' You shall have your house for nothing,' urged Martin.

' 'Tis best I have they words in writing,' replied Mr. Grunter, ' for me friend, Weston, did write 'is covenant in a book, and thee best do the same.'

' I hear no sound now,' observed Martin, ' so perhaps the lion is chained.'

' 'Twas a very thin chain,' remarked Mr. Grunter slyly.

The Mumbys hurried away. They wished to find shelter in a strong stone house. They hurried to Mr. Kiddle's.

Mr. Grunter stepped upon the green ; he wished to see all the harm that the lightning had done before he went to the inn.

Though the great tree had fallen, split in two halves by the lightning, the bed of moss still remained unspoilt. In this bridal bed lay Tamar alone. Upon her forehead there was a blue mark showing where the lightning had struck her. Mr. Grunter looked at her.

As he looked, Michael stepped upon the green. Michael raised Tamar in his arms as though she were a babe. The stars shone again in the heavens. Two shining stars fell upon the earth. These stars moved as winged beings to Michael and, taking Tamar from his arms, rose with her into the skies.

Mr. Grunter nodded approvingly.

XLII

TIME MOVES AGAIN

Mr. Grunter walked slowly to the Angel Inn. A woman, thin and crabbed, but with a look of surprise upon her face, entered the parlour. She came from the kitchen.

'I have pickled three bushels of onions,' she said, 'and there bain't room in kitchen for no more jars.'

'Then thee should be content,' said Mr. Vosper, in the proper and melancholy tone of a bereaved man.

'No, I bain't,' replied Mrs. Bunce, 'for all parlour shelf should be filled wi' pickle jars.'

'The longest evening is never long enough for a woman's wants,' observed Mr. Mumby, 'but if there be another drop of drink in barrel I could drink it.'

Mrs. Bunce went to the cellar.

The three barrels that had contained nearly thirty gallons of beer were empty, and not another drop could be drawn out of them by even the most careful tipping.

'They be all empty,' said Mrs. Bunce.

A bright light flashed upon the window, but when that was passed all was darkness. Even the lamp and fire were gone out. All the company went to the inn door.

A Ford car had passed swiftly, and its shining head-lights lit up the whole countryside. The car

climbed the hill, and the light appeared to vanish
into the sky.

Mr. Weston was gone.

And Mr. Meek was talking.

' Clock be going,' said Mr. Meek.   ' 'Tis striking ten.'

' And here be landlord,' exclaimed Mr. Kiddle.

Mr. Bunce was standing in the parlour.   He was
dripping wet.   He held up his hand to gain the
attention of the company.   As he usually did, Mr.
Bunce began to blame some one, but this time he
didn't blame God, he blamed Mr. Weston.

' Thik wold rascal,' he shouted, ' 'ave near
drowned I, and who have ever heard of well water,
after 'tis changed to wine, and a man be slipped in,
turning back into water again ? '

Mr. Bunce turned angrily to Mr. Grunter.

' Have 'ee done they things that be told of 'ee ? '
he asked.

Mr. Grunter shook his head.   He took two silver
coins from his pocket and handed them to Mr.
Bunce.   The landlord accepted them with pleasure.

' 'Tain't Grunter who have done no maid no
harm,' he said with assurance.

' Who be 'en then ? ' asked the clerk.

The landlord winked at the company, and said
that he believed that it was Mr. Weston who did all
the mischief.   Mr. Meek drew near to the door—
the company had stepped back into the parlour when
the landlord came in.

Mr. Meek spoke again.   There were no more
flames for him to steal that night, for the fire was out.

' As time be going, 'tis best for we to go,' he

remarked, ' for if Shelton policeman did come, 'e mightn't agree wi' we that time 'ave stopped in Folly Down.'

Mr. Bunce spoke to his wife.

' I did tell preacher Bird that 'e mid 'ave our Jenny, and she be gone to 'e,' he said.

' Be they married ? ' asked Mrs. Bunce.

' Most likely they be,' replied Mr. Bunce artfully.

Mr. Meek buttoned his coat. He stepped out into the darkness to go home. In that darkness he believed himself to be lost, and called out to Mr. Grunter for help, for Grunter, having performed more acts than drinking that evening, was the most sober man present.

Mr. Grunter led Mr. Meek away.

Mr. Meek walked nervously.

' Do 'ee please to mind,' he said, ' that I bain't no maiden.'

' And I,' said Mr. Grunter boldly, ' bain't no Mr. Weston.'

Mr. Vosper wandered home, a happy and contented man. He knew whom he had seen, and that evening he could eat his supper amongst the Christmas grandeur of his front room.

Dealer Kiddle invited Mr. Mumby to his house. He hoped that a little whisky might sell his bull calf.

In the dealer's parlour they found John Mumby sitting beside Ann. Phœbe was there, too, laying the supper, and Martin Mumby was crouched in a corner. Now and again he whined low, like a trapped wolf.

' 'Tis something 'e do see that don't please 'im,'

observed Phœbe lightly. ' 'Tis something that bain't no nice girl.'

Mrs. Kiddle was excited and happy. She informed her husband that a little while ago the church clerk had called, on his way to the inn, and had sworn by Mr. Weston's Good Wine, that he had seen Ada as a happy angel, singing in heaven.

' I be going to take John out of kindness,' said Ann to her father.

' A good girl,' laughed Squire Mumby, ' and 'tis the first time I 've ever bought a plump heifer from Kiddle for nothing ! '

' An' 'twill be the last time too,' remarked the honest dealer.

*

Mr. Weston's car had passed the inn in a moment, and as rapidly reached the summit of Folly Down hill.

Once there, however, a curious grating sound was heard in the bowels of the car ; the engine stopped, and the lights went out. Upon the hill there was complete darkness.

' The darkness pleases you, Michael,' said Mr. Weston in a gentle tone. ' I would that it pleased me too, but, alas ! as you know well enough, the darkness and the light are both alike to me. Michael, do not be unhappy. You delighted Tamar—and she died. . . .

' Ah ! ' said Mr. Weston, ' the new wine mourneth, the vine languisheth, all the merry-hearted do sigh. Remember, Michael, the writing upon the Indian loadstone that was as big as an

Egyptian bean, and was hung in the temple of the priestess Bacbuc—" All things tend to their end." '

Mr. Weston sighed. He turned towards Folly Down. The dawn was near. A lantern, a moving star, lit a carter's way from his cottage to Mr. Mumby's stable; a wakeful cock crew; the pleasant scent of wood smoke was in the air, and the clatter of a well-bucket was heard.

'We have forgotten Miss Nancy Gipps,' exclaimed Mr. Weston. 'She was the first, except for those rude children, who noticed us.'

'What made you remember her, sir?' asked Michael.

'I think I hear her voice,' replied Mr. Weston, ' praying to me.'

'Does she ask for wine?' enquired Michael.

'No, only for a husband,' Mr. Weston answered.

'She is a woman,' observed Michael.

'Yes,' said Mr. Weston, 'and it's time she were married, and she shall have the mayor.'

'There is still your old enemy to be thought of,' remarked Michael. 'Have you forgotten him as well as Miss Gipps?'

'I certainly had,' replied Mr. Weston, 'but don't you think he would like to be a serpent again—a small adder?'

'I fancy' said Michael, 'that he would prefer to disappear in his own element—fire.'

'And so he shall,' cried Mr. Weston. 'Will you be so kind, Michael, as to drop a burning match into the petrol tank?'

'And we?' asked Michael.

'Shall vanish in the smoke,' replied Mr. Weston.

' Very well,' said Michael sadly.

Michael did as he was told. In a moment a fierce tongue of flame leaped up from the car; a pillar of smoke rose above the flame and ascended into the heavens. The fire died down, smouldered, and went out.

Mr. Weston was gone.

THE HOGARTH PRESS

A New Life For A Great Name

This is a paperback list for today's readers – but it holds to a tradition of adventurous and original publishing set by Leonard and Virginia Woolf when they founded The Hogarth Press in 1917 and started their first paperback series in 1924.

Now, after many years of partnership, Chatto & Windus · The Hogarth Press are proud to launch this new series. Our choice of books will not echo that of the Woolfs in every way – times have changed – but our aims will be the same. Some sections of the list will be light-hearted, some serious: all will be rigorously chosen, excellently produced and energetically published, in the best Hogarth Press tradition. We hope that the new Hogarth Press paperback list will be as prized – and as avidly collected – as its illustrious forebear.

Some of our forthcoming titles follow. If you would like more information about Hogarth Press books, write to us for a catalogue:

40 William IV Street, London WC2N 4DF

Please send a large stamped addressed envelope

HOGARTH FICTION

The Revolution in Tanner's Lane by Mark Rutherford,
New Introduction by Claire Tomalin

Chance by Joseph Conrad,
New Introduction by Jane Miller

The Whirlpool by George Gissing,
New Introduction by Gillian Tindall

Mr Weston's Good Wine by T. F. Powys,
New Introduction by Ronald Blythe

HOGARTH HUMOUR

Mrs Ames by E. F. Benson,
New Introduction by Stephen Pile

Paying Guests by E. F. Benson,
New Introduction by Stephen Pile

The Amazing Test Match Crime by Adrian Alington,
New Introduction by Brian Johnston

HOGARTH CRIME

The Saltmarsh Murders by Gladys Mitchell

The Mysterious Mickey Finn by Elliot Paul

Death By Request by Romilly and Katherine John

The Hand In The Glove by Rex Stout

HOGARTH BIOGRAPHY AND AUTOBIOGRAPHY

The Journal of a Disappointed Man & A Last Diary by
W. N. P. Barbellion,
Original Introduction by H. G. Wells and New Introduction
by Deborah Singmaster

Pack My Bag by Henry Green,
New Introduction by Paul Bailey

Being Geniuses Together by Robert McAlmon and Kay
Boyle,
New Afterword by Kay Boyle

Samuel Johnson by Walter Jackson Bate

Flush by Virginia Woolf,
New Introduction by Trekkie Ritchie

HOGARTH TRAVEL

The Spanish Temper by V. S. Pritchett,
New Introduction by the Author

The Amateur Emigrant by Robert Louis Stevenson,
New Introduction by Jonathan Raban

HOGARTH LITERARY CRITICISM

The Common Reader, First Series by Virginia Woolf,
edited and introduced by Andrew McNeillie

The Common Reader, Second Series by Virginia Woolf,
edited and introduced by Andrew McNeillie

The English Novel from Dickens to Lawrence
by Raymond Williams

The Common Pursuit by F. R. Leavis

Seven Types of Ambiguity by William Empson

HOGARTH BELLES-LETTRES

Ivor Gurney: War Letters,
a selection edited by
R. K. R. Thornton

By Way of Sainte Beuve by Marcel Proust,
translated by Sylvia Townsend Warner,
New Introduction by Terence Kilmartin

HOGARTH POETRY

Collected Poems, C. P. Cavafy,
translated by Edmund Keeley and Philip Sherrard, edited by
George Savidis

Collected Poems, William Empson